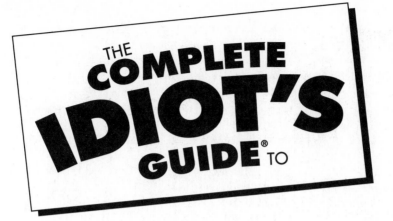

THE COMPLETE IDIOT'S GUIDE® TO

Faith

D0066818

*by Rev. Charles W. Moore, P.Min.,
and Robert Bittner*

ALPHA

A member of Penguin Group (USA) Inc.

ALPHA BOOKS

Published by the Penguin Group

Penguin Group (USA) Inc., 375 Hudson Street, New York, New York 10014, U.S.A.

Penguin Group (Canada), 10 Alcorn Avenue, Toronto, Ontario, Canada M4V 3B2 (a division of Pearson Penguin Canada Inc.)

Penguin Books Ltd, 80 Strand, London WC2R 0RL, England

Penguin Ireland, 25 St Stephen's Green, Dublin 2, Ireland (a division of Penguin Books Ltd)

Penguin Group (Australia), 250 Camberwell Road, Camberwell, Victoria 3124, Australia (a division of Pearson Australia Group Pty Ltd)

Penguin Books India Pvt Ltd, 11 Community Centre, Panchsheel Park, New Delhi—10 017, India

Penguin Group (NZ), cnr Airborne and Rosedale Roads, Albany, Auckland 1310, New Zealand (a division of Pearson New Zealand Ltd)

Penguin Books (South Africa) (Pty) Ltd, 24 Sturdee Avenue, Rosebank, Johannesburg 2196, South Africa

Penguin Books Ltd, Registered Offices: 80 Strand, London WC2R 0RL, England

International Standard Book Number: 1-59257-494-7
Library of Congress Catalog Card Number: 2005937488

08   07   06   8   7   6   5   4   3   2   1

Interpretation of the printing code: The rightmost number of the first series of numbers is the year of the book's printing; the rightmost number of the second series of numbers is the number of the book's printing. For example, a printing code of 06-1 shows that the first printing occurred in 2006.

Printed in the United States of America

Note: This publication contains the opinions and ideas of its authors. It is intended to provide helpful and informative material on the subject matter covered. It is sold with the understanding that the authors and publisher are not engaged in rendering professional services in the book. If the reader requires personal assistance or advice, a competent professional should be consulted.

The authors and publisher specifically disclaim any responsibility for any liability, loss, or risk, personal or otherwise, which is incurred as a consequence, directly or indirectly, of the use and application of any of the contents of this book.

Most Alpha books are available at special quantity discounts for bulk purchases for sales promotions, premiums, fund-raising, or educational use. Special books, or book excerpts, can also be created to fit specific needs.

For details, write: Special Markets, Alpha Books, 375 Hudson Street, New York, NY 10014.

Publisher: *Marie Butler-Knight*
Editorial Director: *Mike Sanders*
Senior Managing Editor: *Billy Fields*
Senior Acquisitions Editor: *Paul Dinas*
Development Editor: *Christy Wagner*
Senior Production Editor: *Janette Lynn*

Copy Editor: *Amy Borrelli*
Book Designer: *Trina Wurst*
Cover Designer: *Bill Thomas*
Indexer: *Tonya Heard*
Layout: *Brian Massey*
Proofreading: *John Etchison*

This book is dedicated to the ones who led me to faith—my parents, Herman and Blanche Moore, and my incredible wife, Marilyn, who has strengthened my faith.
—CM

To the memory of my father, Rev. Madison Bittner, whose example of faithful living will never leave me. —RB

Contents at a Glance

Contents

Introduction

Faith can be a wonderful thing. It gives us hope during the hard times, and it gives us a rope to cling to when it feels like we're drowning. Living life on a foundation of faith can be a very empowering way to live.

But faith isn't just meaningful for our dark days. It enriches those miraculous moments in life when we step back in awe, wondering at our good fortune. It adds meaning to our relationships, our work and school hours, the way we learn from the past, and the way we plan for the future.

Trusting in a power bigger than ourselves—trusting in a loving God—isn't always an easy choice. Everybody has doubts. Everybody wrestles with just how best to live faithfully in a world that can be, at times, faithless. And as we grow and change as people, the way we express and nurture our faith changes as well. That's exactly why I wrote this book.

The Complete Idiot's Guide to Faith helps you navigate the sometimes-frustrating path of faith—from the first step of choosing to believe to building a faith strong and resilient enough to last for the rest of your life. Drawing on the lessons in the Bible and my own experiences as a believer, pastor, and seminary president, I give you the tools you need to explore, express, and expand your faith.

Let me add one more thing right at the outset: I'm just as much a fellow traveler on the faith journey as you are. Sure, I have years of belief and experience under my belt. But I haven't yet "arrived." It's safe to say none of us has. As long as we have breath, our journey of faith isn't over yet. It isn't over for any of us until we exit this life for good. Until we reach that point, though, I look forward to sharing what I've learned while helping you find answers of your own.

We're going to have a great trip together.

How This Book Is Organized

This book is presented in four parts:

In **Part 1, "Exploring Faith,"** you discover just what faith is, why so many feel compelled to believe in and trust in God, and how to take your own first steps of faith.

In **Part 2, "Expressing Your Faith,"** you find practical information for nurturing your spiritual life. This part covers discussing faith with friends, family, and co-workers as well as plugging in to groups of fellow believers.

In **Part 3, "Living Faith,"** you get the inspiration and background you need to integrate your faith with every aspect of your life—from money and marriage to parenting and work. In addition, you get insight into how you can draw on faith to help you cope with life's darkest hours.

In **Part 4, "Expanding Your Faith,"** you explore some of the powerful "next steps" that can help your faith flourish. This part explores the value of listening to God, participating in a faith community, wrestling with the issue of doubt, reaching out in faith to those around you, and walking in faith for the rest of your life.

Special Faith Features

In the pages that follow, you'll see a variety of different sidebars. These boxes highlight interesting facts, important information, useful definitions, and warnings that can help you throughout your own journey of faith:

 Faith 101

These boxes offer information and practical tips for living a life of faith.

Behold!

Check these boxes for interesting facts about the Bible, faith, and faith-related topics.

def•i•ni•tion

These boxes hold useful definitions of faith- or Bible-related words that might be unfamiliar to you.

 Beware!

Warnings, myths, and common misunderstandings about faith are in these boxes.

Chapter and Verse

Unless otherwise noted, all the Bible verses quoted herein come from the New International Version (NIV). If you are looking for an easy-to-read yet highly authoritative Bible translation, the NIV is a great place to start.

Trademarks

All terms mentioned in this book that are known to be or are suspected of being trademarks or service marks have been appropriately capitalized. Alpha Books and Penguin Group (USA) Inc. cannot attest to the accuracy of this information. Use of a term in this book should not be regarded as affecting the validity of any trademark or service mark.

Part 1

Exploring Faith

Are you exploring the concept of faith, of believing in a spiritual power greater than yourself? Throughout the centuries, millions of people have chosen to put their trust in God. But that doesn't make it a done deal for anyone. Faith means putting your trust in God, and that can feel like an uncertain step.

In Part 1, you learn what it means to believe in God, where to turn for information about God and historical figures who followed him, and what practical steps you can take to explore the question of and value of faith for your own life.

What Does It Mean to Have Faith?

In This Chapter

- ◆ Defining faith
- ◆ Faith and belief
- ◆ The value of faith
- ◆ Living faithfully

Hope for the future, trust in others, wishful thinking—all these things come to mind when people talk about having faith. Faith in God, though, is something more. It can have a life-changing impact on all those who embrace it. Even though faith can't be seen or measured or proven in any scientific sense, we can look at what it means to have true faith and be faithful people.

What Is Faith?

In the classic 1947 Christmas movie *Miracle on 34th Street*, Natalie Wood plays Susan, a doubtful little girl who has been raised to be skeptical of fairy tales, make-believe, and anything that relies on imagination. Then she meets a lovable old man named Kris Kringle who claims to be Santa Claus. Everything about him seems to suggest that he's telling the truth about who he is. When Susan confesses to a family friend that Mr. Kringle couldn't possibly be Santa Claus because there is no Santa Claus, he calmly tells her that she simply needs to have faith.

> **Behold!**
>
> The word *faith* (as well as *faithful*, *faithfully*, and *faithfulness*) appears more than 400 times in the Old and New Testaments. To put that in perspective, the word *love* appears 550 times. Clearly, faith was a big deal to the authors of the Bible.

> **Behold!**
>
> The Bible was originally written in three languages: Hebrew, Aramaic, and Greek. The word translated into English as *faith* in the New Testament is the Greek word *pistis*. To first-century Greeks, *pistis* would have carried the ideas of assurance, strong conviction, fidelity, and, yep, even faith.

Not surprisingly, Susan isn't very big on faith, either. She frowns and says she's been told faith means "believing in things when common sense tells you not to."

Susan clearly thinks anything that goes against common sense is a big mistake. Yet her definition isn't a bad one. In fact, it isn't too far from what the New Testament writer to the Hebrew church said: "Now faith is being sure of what we hope for and certain of what we do not see." (Hebrews 11:1) Common sense tells us, "You can't see faith. You can't prove it scientifically. So faith must not be real. It's just 'good thoughts' or 'wishful thinking.' It's too risky to trust." Yet faith and common sense complement rather than contradict each other.

Many people who live their lives with common sense have no problem trusting in faith as well. The two aren't mutually exclusive. But they don't choose faith because it can be proved in a lab or a court of law—after all, it wouldn't exactly be "faith" then, right? No, they choose faith because they have experienced its impact in their daily lives. They are "sure" and "certain," to use the Bible's words, because they've lived it. They know in their hearts and minds that God can be trusted. He will do what the Bible says he will do. To them, faith isn't "blind" to reality or illogical. It's a reasonable, personal response to experiencing God firsthand.

Faith and God

Chances are that if you've ever stepped onto an airplane or a cruise ship, you might say you've had some faith. Faith that the plane or ship would carry you safely to where you want to go. Faith that those in charge knew what they were doing and could handle any problems that might arise. Faith that you'd enjoy yourself when you arrived at your destination. Faith that your suitcases wouldn't wind up in a forgotten-luggage bin in Madagascar.

It doesn't end there, though. Every time you get out of bed in the morning, you're taking the first steps toward a day filled with faith. You jump in the shower, having faith that the water heater is still working. You drive down the road, having faith that other drivers will keep their eyes and minds on the road. You order your Egg McMuffin, having faith that you won't wind up with food poisoning. Faith is essential to life.

Faith in God is both deeper and bigger than that "everyday" kind of faith. In fact, it's probably better to think of riding on a plane or ship in terms of trust or hope instead of faith. Faith in God is more than mere belief. Faith—at least faith as we're talking about it here—involves a relationship.

It's one thing to believe God exists, but it's another thing to have faith in God. In the New Testament book of James, the Apostle Paul wrote: "You believe that there is one God. Good! Even the demons believe that—and shudder." (James 2:19) Paul is saying that it's not enough simply to believe that there's a God; even demons know God exists, and that knowledge terrifies them. Faith goes further. It doesn't just acknowledge God's existence. It says God cares about his creation and cares about us as individuals, and that it's possible to choose to have a personal relationship with him.

Faith Isn't Just Feelings

Nearly 23 years ago, I told my soon-to-be-wife, Marilyn, "I will love you forever. I've never felt this way before about another human being. I am deeply, madly in love with you." But after I said "I do," I remember that those initial loving feelings lasted for about one whole week! I can still remember our first argument during the honeymoon. That's when

I discovered I was not married to a morning person. We were hidden away in a beautiful, romantic cabin in the mountains of West Virginia when Marilyn, having had enough of my attempt to wake her up, said, "Chuck, why don't you take a walk in the woods and go play with the bears?" Ah, yes. The honeymoon's over.

Feelings change. Emotions fluctuate. Passions vacillate. Yet Chuck is pleased to report that his and Marilyn's promise to be married continues to this day. In marriage, if we choose to follow our emotions and our feelings rather than trusting what we know in our minds and hearts and what we've learned from the past, we risk losing the benefits that relationship has to offer.

It's the same with faith. Faith isn't based on what we might be feeling at any given moment, because those feelings can wax and wane. Instead, faith is based on the unchanging promises of God. The Old Testament prophet Isaiah wrote: "'Though the mountains be shaken and the hills be removed, yet my unfailing love for you will not be shaken nor my covenant of peace be removed,' says the Lord, who has compassion on you." (Isaiah 54:10) In other words, no matter what happens, God will be there. He has made a *covenant*, or unbreakable promise, to be faithful toward those who put their trust in him.

def•i•ni•tion

In the Bible, a **covenant** is a formal, binding agreement made by God with his people.

Have you ever purchased something only to have it break after you got it home? You took it back to the store, expecting a full refund for the faulty merchandise. Then it happened. The sales clerk pointed to the small print in the warranty, explaining why you're not covered. You had your guarantee in hand, but it ended up being worthless.

God doesn't play that game. For God, a promise doesn't mean "I will … if I feel like it." It means "I will. Guaranteed!" When God promises, it always happens. It's a non-negotiable and nondebatable truth. Your world might be shaken. Your life might be moved. But God will remain faithful. And because we have that promise, we can have faith.

Tested and True

Timothy was a young convert who had become a Christian during the Apostle Paul's first missionary journey. Enthusiastic about his newfound faith, Timothy was close by Paul's side during the apostle's second and third missionary trips, learning as much as he could from his spiritual father.

Then Paul wound up imprisoned for his beliefs. He stayed in touch with the new churches and the growing ranks of Jesus' disciples by writing letters from his prison cell. Given their friendship, it isn't too surprising that he wrote to Timothy as well.

The New Testament contains two of Timothy's letters from Paul. And you don't have to read too far past "Dear Tim" to discover that Paul wasn't one of those "The weather's great! How's Aunt Cynthia's cat, Sparkles?" letter writers. Paul may have had a winning personality, but he wasn't exactly what you'd call chatty. He had some serious things on his mind.

The first-century Christians were being martyred and imprisoned for their beliefs. Paul knew it would be easy—lifesaving, perhaps—for a young believer such as Timothy to play it safe and turn away from his newfound beliefs. So Paul wrote to encourage Timothy to remain faithful. Paul, who defines his relationship with Timothy in 1 Timothy 1:2 by calling him "my true son in the faith," is concerned that his spiritual offspring stay the course and continue to grow in his relationship with God.

Why might Timothy have been tempted to quit? We can think of at least two reasons:

◆ Timothy is going through a time of personal separation from Paul. He has lost his mentor, teacher, and friend. Who's going to be around to encourage him, educate him, motivate him?

◆ Although we don't know exactly what was happening in Timothy's life at this time, the Bible leads us to believe that he was battling an intense amount of pain—maybe physical, maybe emotional. Paul had already endured many trials as a believer; he knew that pain, whatever the kind or cause, could lead Timothy to seek quick, easy relief and turn away from God altogether.

Let's shift our perspective from A.D. 67, the year in which 1 Timothy was written, to our own twenty-first century. In most parts of the world today, Christians aren't imprisoned or martyred for their faith (although it does occur). But that doesn't mean living a faithful life is easy these days. There's a menu of reasons why having faith is as much a challenge for modern believers as it was for Paul, Timothy, and anyone else in the past:

- Many of us live our lives immersed in a me-oriented culture frequently at odds with the servant-oriented character described in the Bible. As a result, people of faith often are swimming against the popular current.

- It's as easy as ever to be distracted from developing a relationship with God by an ever-increasing number of entertainment options, time commitments, family responsibilities, etc.

- Living a faithful life can be uncomfortable and, yes, even difficult. It's like being that twelfth juror who isn't so sure the defendant didn't commit the crime—and who chooses to speak up about it, even though it means she's going against the crowd and probably won't see her family for several more hours. It's tough being that stand-alone person.

- Faith looks risky. We live in a culture that wants the proof, the hard facts, the indisputable evidence. Why didn't more investors purchase shares of McDonald's and Wal-Mart when they were first offered? We love a sure thing. When it comes to what's really important in life, we don't want to play Texas Hold 'Em. Because faith involves giving our very lives, we want to be sure it will work.

All the influences that attempt to deter and distract us from faith nowadays are every bit as troublesome as the ones Timothy faced. Nevertheless, millions of people continue to have faith, living their lives with faith as their guiding light. Let's take a look at why so many believe faith is so worth the effort.

Choosing to Believe

Unlike a talent for singing or a tendency toward premature baldness, faith isn't something we can inherit. It also isn't something that can be given to or forced upon us. It's a choice each of us has to make for ourselves. Are we going to believe that God created the world and continues to care for his creation? Will we invest ourselves in living as if that belief matters? Are we willing to grow and change as a result of our faith, becoming better people in the process? These are the kinds of questions only we ourselves can ask and answer.

For the vast majority of faithful people, asking and answering those weighty questions is a daily event. Every day, life happens. Maybe a loved one becomes seriously ill or dies. Maybe a child adopts habits you believe are immoral or unhealthy. Maybe you meet the person of your dreams—or maybe you lose the person of your dreams. Relationships come and go. Jobs disappear. Disasters and disappointments take their toll.

But the truth is, the same sun that shines and the same rain that falls on the evil and the unjust also shines and falls on the faithful people of God. We can be overjoyed in the good times, believing we don't need help from God. We can turn away in the hard times, believing that a truly loving God could never have allowed such things to occur.

Whether we walk away or remain faithful isn't a once-and-for-all decision we never have to reconsider. It's an ongoing series of choices we each have to make every day as we face circumstances big and small. Here are just a few of the reasons why people decide to choose faith.

You've Got Questions? Faith's Got Answers

Why are we here? What's the meaning of life? Where can I find guidance for living on a daily basis? These are just a few of the Big Questions that confront most of us at some point in our lives. Faith offers equally Big Answers to help put our human existence into perspective.

When you're talking about universal questions about Life with a capital *L*, simple, pat answers just don't make sense. Faith provides a bigger framework for exploring those questions. Faith accepts that God created this world and put all of us here in it. We can discover who we truly were meant to be only when we choose to respond to God as Creator and Father. Guidance for making it through each day comes from having an active relationship with that Creator and Father.

Strength in the Hard Times

Christians accept by faith that Jesus Christ was the son of God, the bridge that made it possible for imperfect human beings to have a direct relationship with a holy and righteous God. So it's sometimes easy to think that Jesus never really struggled in his life here on Earth. After all, no one before or since has had such an intimate relationship with God. That must have made Jesus' experience perfect, right?

Well, no. Scripture says Jesus was tempted in every way everyone else is—including being tempted to give up on God when faced with terrible events. Being tempted and tried like this was the only way this perfect son of God could also experience true humanity.

Faith 101

If it seems unfair to look at the events in Jesus' life as realistic examples for faith today, consider Jesus' words in the New Testament: "I tell you the truth, anyone who has faith in me will do what I have been doing. He will do even greater things than these." (John 14:12)

One difficult moment in Jesus' life was the loss of his dear friend Lazarus (described in John 11). Jesus arrived in Lazarus's hometown of Bethany to find that his friend had passed away at least 4 days earlier. Lazarus's sisters, Martha and Mary, who knew of Jesus' healings throughout the region, were frustrated that he had not come in time to save their brother. "If you had been here," they told him through their tears, "our brother would not have died." Jesus was deeply moved by their grief—as well as their faith in his power—and he asked to see his friend's tomb. It's at the tomb that we learn just how much Jesus loved Lazarus, thanks to the Bible's shortest and perhaps most poignant verse:

Jesus wept. (John 11:35)

Yes, Jesus was God's son, but he was also a human being who experienced pain, sorrow, and loss. Yet even as he grieved, he held on to his faith in the father who had sent him to be at this place at this time. He knew God was still in charge.

"Take away the stone that's covering the entrance to the tomb," he told the sisters. That request probably didn't go over too well. Everyone—and by this time, a small crowd had gathered around the tomb—knew that after 4 days in the ground, Lazarus was, shall we say, a bit ripe.

But Jesus persisted. "I told you that if you believed, you'd see the glory of God," he reminded them. So they rolled away the stone. Then Jesus looked up and prayed a most unusual prayer: "Father, thank you for hearing me. I know you always do hear me, but I say this so that all of those listening to me now will believe that you sent me." Then Jesus shouted, "Lazarus, come out!" And the dead man walked out of the tomb and returned to life by Jesus' faith—a faith that remained strong and steadfast even though Jesus himself had experienced the weight of losing his friend to death.

Safe and Secure

Some people believe that having faith means having a pie-in-the-sky belief that, no matter what, everything is going to turn out fine. We don't necessarily object to pie in the sky, but let's be honest: how much real solace comes from trusting in a pie-in-the-sky hope that everything is going to turn out fine? Not much. Such wishful thinking might bring a modicum of relief, but it doesn't mean a lot in the long run. If that's how we perceive the world around us, it doesn't take long for reality to rear its ugly head and let us know that we've gotten it very wrong.

After all, not everything turns out fine. And why should it? It's not like the universe is going out of its way to be certain each of us has lives that are as happy and trouble free as they can be. A pie-in-the-sky kind of faith really isn't much of a faith at all.

People choose faith not because it promises better days ahead but because it brings meaning to today and provides the foundation for a much bigger view of life than simply what's happening in *my* world during *my* lifetime. Faith encourages us to see things from an eternal perspective. It's not like Little Orphan Annie singing hopefully that "the sun'll come out tomorrow." Faith isn't about believing that "tomorrow is another day" or trying to find the silver lining in the clouds that come our way. Faith means knowing that even if the sun doesn't come out tomorrow, God loves us and is still watching over us.

It's knowing that there's nothing in those clouds but thunderstorms, our lives are still in God's hands, and God is still in control. Faith is knowing that you are valued by God. Even when life doesn't make sense, he won't let you go.

Behold!

There's a story told about a young boy who, after falling over a cliff, grabbed a branch to stop his fall. (There are newsletters for preachers full of stories like this. Few of them have any real basis in actual events, but they can have some value as modern-day parables.) When some hikers saw him, they offered to help. Yet he refused to accept their reach, demanding instead that they get his father. When his father appeared, he lifted his son to safety. When asked why he would only accept the reach of his dad, the boy replied, "Because I know that he loves me and he wouldn't let me go."

Faithful people can feel safe and secure in any circumstance because they believe that flesh-and-blood life is not all there is. There is also soul. And there is an eternity ahead of us. When we can see the world in those terms, faith offers a sense of safety and security.

For these reasons and many more, millions of people through the ages have chosen faith—and experienced the life-changing benefits as a result.

Where do you begin? The best place is to start with the Christian's road map: the Bible. In the next chapter, we look at the Bible's role in Christian faith, as well as what relevance it has for today and how to begin reading and understanding the book Christians believe is truly the inspired Word of God.

The Least You Need to Know

- ◆ You don't need to throw out common sense to live a life of faith.
- ◆ Faith in God is based on having a personal relationship with him.
- ◆ Every day brings new challenges to your faith.
- ◆ People choose faith because it answers life's biggest questions and provides stability and strength.
- ◆ Faith enables you to view life from an eternal perspective.

Chapter 2

Beginning with the Bible

In This Chapter

- ◆ How the Bible came to be
- ◆ God's communication with his people
- ◆ Reading Scripture
- ◆ Getting the most from the Bible

For 2,000 years, the Bible—the Old and New Testaments—has shaped the beliefs and the lives of generations of faithful Christians. When it comes to understanding faith and its role in daily life, there's no better place to go than the Bible for inspiration. Still, many folks shy away from reading the Bible, daunted by its sheer size or frustrated by the assumption that they won't be able to understand it. But thanks to a large number of modern translations, it's never been easier to explore the book of Christian faith that has stood the test of time.

Why the Bible?

Christians believe the Bible is a unique book—inspired by God, written by men, and collected over the centuries to inform and inspire believers in every generation. Numerous books have been written that explore the Bible's historical accuracy, tracing original documents farther back in time than virtually any other ancient manuscript we believe to be true today.

But now is not the for a dull history lesson. It is, however, worth taking a closer look at the book in which so many believers put so much trust. So I'll offer a *little* history.

A Little Bible History

The collection of 66 books we have in the Bible today is called the *canon*. The entire Old Testament was considered Scripture—that is, divinely inspired—by the first Christians who began meeting together shortly after Jesus' death and resurrection in roughly the year A.D. 33. (They didn't divide years into B.C. or A.D. back then.) This was the Scripture every religious person in the ancient Middle East would have known; it was the stuff of their everyday life. But Christians saw it as something more: certainly, it was the story of how God had worked in people's lives in the past, but it was also a prophecy for the future that was fulfilled in the life, death, and resurrection of Jesus Christ. So they took the Old Testament and ran with it.

def•i•ni•tion

The **canon** refers to the 66 books of the Bible—39 in the Old Testament and 27 in the New Testament—that have been commonly agreed upon as being divinely inspired and authoritative for Christian faith.

And they didn't stop there. By the years A.D. 50 to 70, most of what we now know as the New Testament had already been written—primarily as letters to local groups of believers, known as churches—but it hadn't yet achieved canon status. That didn't happen until 350 to 400, when a series of synods, or church councils, firmly established the New Testament lineup we have today.

From the very beginning, the early church used a number of other writings for inspiration and instruction. Several of these writings endure. In fact, you can still walk into a bookstore and pick up a Bible that includes the *Apocrypha*, a collection of books that continues to provide meaning and insight for the lives of the faithful, even though these books aren't universally held in the same regard as the books of the canon.

def•i•ni•tion _____

The **Apocrypha** is a collection of books of pre-Christian and early Christian religious writings that were not deemed worthy of inclusion in the traditional Bible.

For more history about the formation of the Bible and the historical support for the Bible's accuracy, check out the resources in Appendix B.

Relevant for Today

My co-author, Bob, has always enjoyed writing to his favorite authors. It's even more fun for him when he gets a reply. He's proud to tell anyone who will listen that he has a signed postcard—pretty haphazardly typed—from Stephen King back in his *The Shining* days. Bob also has replies from children's author Katherine Paterson, essayist Annie Dillard, and science-fiction author Gene Wolfe.

No doubt, not a single one of these authors would remember writing these notes. They must have sent out hundreds over the course of their careers. But that doesn't make them any less meaningful to Bob, the recipient. For him, they're irreplaceable mementos that he keeps in a special place in his filing cabinet. You might feel the same way about a letter from the president of the United States, or a rock star, or a television personality.

If we value correspondence that comes from a dignitary or a celebrity, how much more should we value communication that comes from God? When we recognize that it really is God who is speaking, we won't dismiss Scripture or treat it casually. It'll hold a special place in our lives and our homes—and not just be a nice book that holds up our Nicholas Sparks collection. It will be relevant. And for the Bible to be relevant, we have to read it and reflect on it. And we need to be willing to let what we learn change us in some way.

Change can be tough. But I believe the Bible has earned the right to have that kind of influence on us. There really is no other book that has endured for so many centuries, that addresses so many diverse needs and concerns—including money issues, marital tensions, sexuality, coping with fear, and international conflicts—and that continues to have a dramatic, life-altering (and positive!) impact on those who follow its teachings. God has given us practical guidelines and standards for living. And although reading the Bible won't make your problems suddenly vanish and your questions suddenly cease, knowing God's standard and acquainting yourself with his guidelines are vital steps toward getting on with the business of finding a solution and exploring your own faith.

> **Behold!**
>
> A 2000 Gallup poll showed that 93 percent of Americans say they own a Bible. A 2002 poll revealed that 28 percent of those surveyed said they study the Bible to find direction for life.

How to Read the Bible

Maybe you've tried to read the Bible in the past and gotten frustrated. Maybe the words seemed too foreign and unfathomable: archaic ideas and ancient stories. I'd like to encourage you to try again.

When I was in college, I was required to read a text titled *The Heart of Old Testament Theology*. (I doubt it ever made the *New York Times* bestseller list.) For one full quarter, I endured the text, finding the whole book to be a reading ordeal. When I went to seminary, though, I met the book's author, who was working as a professor of the Old Testament. He was vibrant, provocative—even funny at points. *The Heart of Old Testament Theology* was required reading in one of his classes. I reluctantly opened it up, expecting to be bored—again. This time, though, I had an entirely different experience. The book challenged me, awakening a new understanding of the Old Testament. What had changed between the first reading and the second? I had met the author.

It's similar when it comes to reading the Bible. You can read it as history, as literature, as poetry, or even as an ancient document chronicling life in some long-gone era. But it won't truly come alive for you, it won't resonate with meaning inside you, unless you're willing to meet the author.

God's no bully. He won't beat you over the head with a message you don't want to hear. But if you come to the Bible open to discovering what God might be saying to you about your life today, your Bible reading will gain the power to change your life.

To make the going as relevant and meaningful as possible ...

♦ Choose a modern translation, such as the New International Version or the New English Standard Version. (Why wrestle with 400-year-old English if you don't have to?)

♦ Try to set aside a period of time each day dedicated only to reading the Bible.

♦ Begin by reading a chapter at each sitting and then adjust the length you read as necessary.

♦ Keep a notepad handy in case any questions come up as you read. (This is also good for noting unfamiliar words or concepts you'd like to look up later, or verses that are especially meaningful to you.)

Behold!

The letters, songs, biographies, and historical chronicles we now call the Bible were originally written in three different languages: Hebrew, Greek, and Aramaic. Although previous English-speaking generations swore by their King James Version Bibles—complete with "Thou shall" and "Verily, verily"—contemporary scholarship has led to modern English translations that are both more historically accurate *and* easier to understand for twenty-first-century readers.

It's easy to read the Bible through without letting it *get through* to us. Thanks to so many of the reference and research tools available today, it's also easy to get caught up in digging deep into the meanings of the original Hebrew or exploring the social context of first-century Rome—or just figuring out how to pronounce the name Nebuchadnezzar—and miss the point of all this effort.

The point is that the Bible is our best road map for exploring faith. With it, we have the power to learn and grow and change. Without it, we're left with just our opinions and our feelings.

How do you know if the Bible is becoming more relevant in your life? Ask yourself this simple question: *Am I growing for the better?* As the Bible becomes relevant to you, you naturally will act, think, and react in ways that demonstrate your growing faith. Imagine the difference that could make in your life and in our world.

Beginning with Bible Reading

With 66 different books that range from love poetry (Song of Solomon) to religious law (Deuteronomy), the Bible can be a diverse and daunting read. To help you get going on the right foot, I'd recommend starting with two sections that may have a ring of familiarity: Psalm 23 and the Gospel of Luke.

Behold!
Psalms means simply "songs about God."

Why am I recommending these passages out of the thousands of verses in the Bible? First, chances are good that they'll be at least slightly familiar, which should make them feel a bit more comfortable to you than some other less-well-known verses. Second, they provide a pretty simple yet solid foundation for what it means to be a person of faith—from trusting in God's providence, no matter what life might throw at you, to understanding the life, message, death, and resurrection of God's son, Jesus.

Getting Sheepish

If you've been to or seen a movie with a graveside service in it, chances are good you've heard at least a few verses from the King James Version of Psalm 23. Here it is in all its glory:

> The Lord is my shepherd; I shall not want. He maketh me to lie down in green pastures: he leadeth me beside the still waters. He restoreth my soul: he leadeth me in the paths of righteousness for his name's sake. Yea, though I walk through the valley of the shadow of death, I will fear no evil: for thou art with me; thy rod and thy staff they comfort me. Thou preparest a table before me in the presence of mine enemies: thou anointest my head with oil;

my cup runneth over. Surely goodness and mercy shall follow me all the days of my life: and I will dwell in the house of the Lord for ever.

It's no secret why this is a popular passage for those who are grieving the loss of a loved one. Yet it can also be a source of strength for any of us, at any point in our lives when we feel lost, anxious, or fearful. With poetic images and heartfelt language, this psalm reminds us that we have a Good Shepherd who is watching over us. No matter what happens, God is in control.

This is an especially poignant passage, because it—like many of the psalms (as near as we can tell)—was apparently written by King David, who endured much personal pain while serving as one of Israel's greatest monarchs (from 1010 to 970 B.C.). But no matter how close he got personally to the "valley of the shadow of death," he trusted in God as a sheep trusts in the shepherd to protect it from threats, to lead it to places of peace and rest, and to bring it safely home.

That's pretty much the textbook definition of what it means to have faith.

> **Behold!**
>
> I typically tend to favor more modern translations, but Psalm 23 is so ingrained in my psyche in the King James language, nothing else has quite the same feel to me. Of course, memorizing Scripture and carrying it with you wherever you go is a good thing!

Luke Here!

Unlike Psalm 23, I can't reprint the entire *Gospel* of Luke here. But I can tell you that my chosen text is one of four Gospels (literally "good news") in the New Testament that offer four different perspectives on the life of Jesus Christ. And it's a great place to start for an introduction to Jesus' life and teachings. (It's also well known for the way it tells the story of Christ's birth, familiar to anyone who has seen *A Charlie Brown Christmas* on TV.)

def•i•ni•tion

The word we translate as **gospel** simply meant "good news" in the original Greek. The four New Testament Gospels of Matthew, Mark, Luke, and John are, essentially, four men's stories of how God's "good news" for the world came to be.

The Gospel of Luke was written, not surprisingly, by a man named Luke, a well-educated physician by profession who is known to have traveled with the Apostle Paul during some of his missionary journeys. It was most likely written 30 to 50 years after Jesus' death and resurrection, using Luke's independent research on Jesus' life and work, as well as eyewitness reports and the apostles' preaching.

Essentials for the Reading Journey

These days, there's no shortage of tools to help folks get more from their Bible reading, including a wide variety of commentaries, Bible dictionaries and encyclopedias, and literally thousands of devotional books. I'm grateful for such tools available to help people in their Bible reading.

But tools aren't essential. You don't need a preacher's reference library or a seminary degree to read, understand, and apply what you find in the Bible's pages. What you do need are a willing heart, a willing spirit, and a little something I like to call "an ear for the music."

A Willing Heart

I'm a fairly typical man when it comes to not stopping to ask for directions while I'm traveling. But every once in a while I admit that I'm lost and ask someone for help. But imagine if I were to find a friendly face passing by on the sidewalk, pull over to the curb, ask for directions, and then ignore the person who was trying to help.

When you stop for directions, you don't ignore or debate with the person who's trying to point you down the right road. You trust them. You assume they're telling you the truth, and you're willing to hear what they have to say. When reading the Bible, it's best to approach what you read with a heart willing to hear what God has to tell you.

A Willing Spirit

How many young children assume their parents' rules and restrictions were created simply to stifle their independence and ruin their lives? (Okay, maybe that doesn't just apply to *young* children.) It's only when we get older that we realize the wisdom that usually lay behind those parental restrictions. Our parents wanted what was best for us. And sometimes that meant setting boundaries.

Faith brings some boundaries of its own. Living a faithful life means we choose to live life in some ways that people who don't share our faith would not choose and may not be able to understand. To them, these look like constrictions that limit us rather than boundaries that guard our relationship with God. And because it's simply easier to follow the crowd, it won't be surprising if we sometimes find ourselves wanting to break loose and rebel. But the only way God can really bring our faith to full flower is when we work to hang on to a spirit that's willing to follow wherever God is leading.

An Ear for the Music

I love music—all kinds of music. If you were to go on a car trip with me, you'd hear traditional and contemporary gospel, soft rock, classical recordings, and jazz.

I enjoy jazz so much because the instrumentalists don't merely play the notes, they interpret the notes. So much of the emotion of jazz is about what's happening when the notes *aren't* being played. It's what one artist has called playing *between* the notes.

When it comes to reading the Bible, a lot of people can recite "chapter and verse" if you ask them a theological question, but they haven't learned to read between the verses. That's what happens when God gets involved. It's what happens when your relationship with God is active and alive. It's what happens when you say, "I want to take the words, lift them off the page, and make them a part of my life."

Having an ear for the Bible's music means being open to being changed, transformed by the God you meet in Scripture. Ultimately, that's the real goal of the Bible. The Bible is not the destination. It's not the end. But it's the map that marks the path of your journey with God. It's the gift that enables you to know him, to get acquainted with him, to recognize him as the one who loves you and wants what is best for every aspect of your life.

The story is told—I can't say whether it's true or not—that author G. K. Chesterton was once asked, "If you were alone on a desert island, what one book would you like to have?" Now, Chesterton was a great Christian thinker and writer. The interviewer probably expected to hear about some serious theological or philosophical tome. But Chesterton was also a very practical man and had a great wit. His reply: "I'd like to have a copy of *Thomas' Guide to Practical Ship Building*."

Of course. When you're trapped and feeling alone, you want something that will help get you home. At that point, we don't want to be entertained or lectured to. We just want a book that will get us saved.

Faith 101

The odds are good that most of us have a copy of the Bible in our home. For some, it's just something that's always been on the shelf, looking appropriately serious and bookish. For others, it's a family heirloom, the place where births, marriages, and deaths are recorded for posterity. For still others, it's the book they plan on reading "someday." It's never too late to begin, to blow off the dust or brush off your apprehension and simply begin reading, discovering God's message for your life today.

We're looking for that book in life. The truth is we *are* marooned, trapped in a confusing world, and a lot of us are looking for a route to freedom, to real life. And that's where the Bible comes in.

The Least You Need to Know

- ◆ The Bible has been the believer's road map of faith for centuries.
- ◆ The Bible remains a relevant and vital handbook for Christian faith.
- ◆ Psalm 23 offers a good introduction to Old Testament Scripture.
- ◆ The Gospel of Luke provides a well-rounded introduction to the life of Jesus.
- ◆ If we are willing to be touched and changed by God, we can come to know him through the pages of Scripture.

Chapter 3

Wanting to Believe: The First Step Toward Faith

In This Chapter

- ◆ Filling our deepest longing
- ◆ God is real, not wish fulfillment
- ◆ Noah's example of faith in action
- ◆ Acting on faith

Christian musician Steve Taylor has sung, "It's harder to believe than not to." Yet belief is a challenge millions have taken up. Nothing else fills our deepest, soul-level human needs. Faith in God nourishes our spirits, even as it has the power to transform us into people of action who are striving to live out their God-given destiny.

Our Deepest Desire

I once was accompanying a group of 18 people from my church in Charlotte, Michigan, to Venezuela to participate in a missions experience—helping with building projects and things like that.

During the flight to South America, I had some time to peruse a catalog that comes with every seat on the plane: *SkyMall*. It's nearly 200 pages of stuff I can't believe anybody *really* needs: a tan-through bathing suit for the person who wants a complete body tan while they're out swimming; a floating putting green you can use in your pool; a lobster dinner complete with 6 lobsters, 36 clams, 6 ears of corn, 12 onions, and 36 baby potatoes (just add water!).

> **Behold!** °
>
> Seventeenth-century French mathematician Blaise Pascal (1623–1662) is credited with stating that "there is a God-shaped vacuum in the heart of every man which cannot be filled by any created thing, but only by God the Creator, made known through Jesus Christ."

Clearly, some people must want some of these items or *SkyMall* would have to close up shop. But these are all luxuries, frills for the person who already has everything they could possibly want. These kinds of superfluous gifts may look fun and fulfilling on the page, but they'll never satisfy the more fundamental hungers we all have—the deep longing we have for meaning and satisfaction in life. Just as you might get a stomachache when you're hungry for a meal, you can also experience a deep heartache or soul ache when you hunger for spiritual sustenance. Recognizing that ache for what it is, is the first step toward faith.

Searching for Satisfaction

I once counseled a college student who came to me and said, "I don't know what's wrong. I'm nearing the end of my academic career, and I've started to rethink the direction of my life. Four years back, I entered college on a fully paid academic scholarship. Academically, I did great. I'm near the top of my class, and I have several significant job offers. But the excitement, the fulfillment, the personal sense of satisfaction just isn't there. What's wrong with me?"

After talking some more with this student, I realized that academic accomplishment had been his number-one priority. He hadn't loved the subjects he studied as much as he loved proving he could master them. In the end, he'd demonstrated his brilliance, but he was hungering for some kind of passion in his work.

Many of us do the same thing. We chase the dreams, pursue the rainbows. We try to get more, become something different, or reach some new goal so we'll finally feel satisfied. Yet we wind up just as frustrated as a young, late-1960s Mick Jagger singing "(I Can't Get No) Satisfaction." No, no, no.

The Bible is full of men and women who started out singing that same song, although most of them didn't realize it at the time. For instance, consider Saul, a *Pharisee*, or teacher of the Law, who became one of the most outspoken opponents of the early church. His whole life was saturated by a sense of dissatisfaction in which he continually worked against everything God stood for. He wanted nothing more than to eradicate Christianity altogether. Then, on a trip to Damascus, Saul was unexpectedly confronted by God himself. The encounter was life-changing—so much so that Saul acquired a new name as a result. Ever after, he would be known as Paul, and he has become one of the primary heroes of the New Testament. His personal encounter with a loving and living Lord changed his life in a radical way.

def•i•ni•tion

The **Pharisees** were members of the largest, most influential religious/political Jewish sect in New Testament times. They were devoted to strict observance of the Law—and strongly opposed to pagan practices and anything suspected of diluting or corrupting the Law.

I believe that, like Paul, the secret to our satisfaction lies in having a life-changing encounter with Jesus Christ and living a life of faith in God. As one person has observed, "When I have Christ, I have enough. And when I don't have Christ, nothing else is ever enough."

Wanting and Wishing

There is a concept in psychology known as projection. It's the idea that we want to believe something so badly that we project our own desires on the world around us, interpreting everything we experience through a lens that distorts reality and tells us exactly what we want to hear.

Some people see faith in God as a form of projection, or wish fulfillment. The feeling is that we want to believe in God, so we make up a God to believe in. We then interpret all our experiences and feelings in life in such a way that we bring that God to life.

Faith 101

There is room for a wide variety of beliefs among Christians. But that doesn't mean *all* beliefs are truly godly beliefs. One way to discern belief in the one, true God—as opposed to a god of someone else's making—is to weigh just how closely that god fulfills human ideals. A god who doesn't care about sin, who doesn't call us to grow and mature, and who wants all our dreams—no matter what they are—to come true is not the God of the Bible.

If that were true, though, wouldn't you think we'd come up with a much more lovable, user-friendly God than the God of Scripture? Wouldn't most of us rather have a God who didn't care about sin? A God who wouldn't expect us to do anything that might make us uncomfortable? A God who would bring our every desire to pass, like a genie in a bottle?

That's not the God of the Bible, certainly. And it's not the very real, very personal God who has the power to transform lives, to heal broken souls, to empower us to reach out beyond ourselves and change the world.

Cementing Satisfaction

That point struck me during our church's mission trip to Venezuela. Why would a group of people take time to travel thousands of miles and live in near-primitive conditions for nearly 2 weeks? Why would they choose to live on a diet that would cause them to drop 10 or more pounds in 2 weeks? Why would they put up with fire ants, scorpions, lizards, and tarantulas? Why would they do any of it just for themselves?

I think the answer is clear: they wouldn't.

While we were there, we spent 2 weeks building a 400-square-yard basketball court for the neighborhood children. And we did it the hard way: we mixed the concrete, dumped it into a wheelbarrow, and rolled it 25 yards away, where we dropped it down a chute. There, it hit another wheelbarrow and traveled 25 to 70 more yards before it got dumped. And just when you thought you were making progress, it rained. How do you get rid of water on the cement when there are no wet vacs and not even any electricity? You cut up a mattress and use it to soak up the water. You wring it out and then you begin the process all over again.

At the end, we were exhausted. And when the final, cement-filled wheelbarrow was empty, we met together on that basketball court and prayed. Some of us even cried. Some were tears of relief, yes, but some were tears of joy as well—joy in knowing that even though we had given up a lot, we had gained so much. And inwardly, down deep, where it really counts the most, we felt satisfied.

Trust me, there are easier ways to get the warm, personal glow that comes from helping those in need. But we were drawing on something far stronger than our own charitable natures. We discovered that satisfaction comes when we reach out for our God-given purpose in life. Talk about satisfaction ….

Limping ... but Liking It

Have you ever heard someone dismiss faith as "just a crutch" that people cling to? They say it as if they have never needed help, as if it's best that people try to manage everything entirely on their own or that they have no spiritual needs whatsoever.

Such comments remind me of the well-known "Footprints" story. If you haven't heard it, here's the short version: a man had a dream in which he and God are walking side by side on a beach, talking about the man's life. The man looks back at their footprints in the sand, sometimes seeing two sets of footprints but sometimes seeing only one. "Thanks so much for walking beside me through so many difficult times, God," the man said. "But tell me about those times when there's only one set of footprints."

"Those were particularly difficult moments," God tells him. "Times when you were going through the deepest valleys you've ever experienced."

Behold!

Another problem with the "just-a-crutch" view of God: crutches are short-term helps. As soon as we're healed, we put the crutches in the closet. Faith, however, is an ever-present constant, not something we pick up and put down as our needs change. A faithful life is a 24/7 life of constant reliance on God.

"I remember. So why is there only one set of footprints?" the man demanded. "Where did you go? Why did you leave me all alone just when I needed you most?"

"I didn't," God said. "There is only set of footprints because that's when I was carrying you in my arms."

Call faith a crutch or anything else you like. But the fact remains that we simply cannot make it on our own without God. We cannot be the people God intended us to be if we are not building a relationship with him. We need his forgiveness, his compassion, his strength. There is no shame in turning to the only one who can help us. In fact, it's just the opposite: it's only by turning to God that we'll discover true joy.

On the Threshold of Faith

You've stayed with me this far, so either you've already decided to choose faith or you're at least open to discovering just what this thing called faith is all about. If you're still not 100 percent certain that you want to believe, that's fine. Faith can be life-changing. And even though the changes are for the better, they still represent a significant impact. It's okay to give faith some serious consideration.

At the risk of putting the cart before the horse, though, I'd encourage you to at least put one foot on the threshold of faith. One way to do that is to *act* as if you believe in and are willing to trust God, even though you have no idea what the future might bring or what faith might actually mean for your life.

I'm guessing that sounds pretty nebulous at this point. For an example of what I'm talking about, let's look at a Bible figure who will probably have some significant name recognition for you.

Noah's Way

Most people know the basic story of Noah and his family. Long, long ago, God told Noah that he was sending a big flood to cover the earth and that Noah should build an ark that would hold his family as well as two of every animal so people and animals would be able to survive the flood. So Noah built the big boat, herded up the animals, loaded up his family, and watched as the rains began to fall. Forty days and nights later, the rains stopped. And in their place, God put a rainbow in the sky to seal his promise that he would never again bring a flood to destroy the earth.

The Bible says that Noah "walked with God" (Genesis 6:9), but that's virtually all we know about their relationship before God delivered the instructions for building the ark. Thirteen verses later, the ark is done. "Noah did everything just as God commanded him." (Genesis 6:22)

It's easy to overlook some basic facts of the story here, like just how long it would have taken Noah to build an ark 450 feet long, 75 feet wide, and 45 feet high. Noah would have had to have spent literally *years*—decades, in all probability—building the ark, with no sign whatsoever of an impending flood.

Noah wasn't a perfect example of a faithful person. He made some mistakes. In other words, he was just like you and me. I think we can learn something valuable from his actions. Even though he had no certainty that God would do what he said he'd do, Noah continued to build his ark.

It probably didn't feel much like faith. Just him and a bunch of his friends (I'm assuming), working away on the world's biggest woodworking

> **Behold!**
>
> Incredible as it sounds to modern ears, the Bible tells us that Noah was 500 years old when he became the father of his 3 sons. By the time he and his family entered the ark, Noah was 600, and his sons all brought their wives along with them.

project ever. In truth, though, it was the most faithful act Noah could possibly undertake. In the words of James 2:26: "As the body without the spirit is dead, so faith without deeds is dead."

Faith and deeds (or "works") go hand in hand. Faith that isn't displayed through acts of some kind—whether that's building a giant boat or something as simple as counseling a friend at work—isn't worth much. Some people just talk about having faith; what's important is demonstrating evidence of faith in our daily lives. Our actions will tell people that we truly are believers in God.

Works and Faith

In the church, we typically talk about "faith and works" in that order, assuming that, obviously, faith comes first, followed by evidence of that faith. But that doesn't mean we have to wait until all doubts are erased or all questions are answered before we step out in faithful actions.

> **Beware!**
> The Bible doesn't allow any room for "faithful" people who demonstrate no evidence of their faith. In Matthew 7:19–20, Jesus makes it clear how God feels about such unproductive faith: "Every tree that does not bear good fruit is cut down and thrown into the fire."

Acts of faith can take a multitude of different forms. It isn't so much the act itself that makes it "faithful," it's the spirit in which that act is conducted. Noah probably wasn't the only guy building a boat in his day. But he was the only one building a boat out of obedience to God and faith that God would bring his will to pass in the world.

If you're on the threshold of faith—thinking that you might want to believe but not yet ready to commit yourself—consider performing any of the following "faith-starting" acts that mesh with your skills and interests:

- Serve at a local animal shelter.
- Deliver Meals On Wheels to shut-ins.
- Lead singing at a local rescue mission.
- Help at a church during its summer vacation Bible school.
- Work as a referee for a local Upward Basketball tournament.
- Offer to run the sound board during a church's Sunday morning services.

Some of these acts may not sound very "religious," but don't worry about that. After all, how "religious" does hammering together a giant ark sound? Not very. What's important is the fact that you're serving others—and that you're doing it from a spirit of seeking to discover God's reality in your life. That spirit colors everything you do, whether you're helping a child pick out a new puppy at the animal shelter or you're bringing a much-appreciated dinner to someone who isn't able to prepare his or her own meals.

The Least You Need to Know

◆ Humanity's deepest longings can only be met through a relationship with God.

◆ God empowers us to accomplish tasks we couldn't do on our own.

◆ A living faith is always accompanied by faithful actions.

◆ Even if you're not sure about faith yet, take the first step anyway. Your actions might help lead you to faith.

Chapter 4

Saying "Yes" to Faith: The Second Step Toward Faith

In This Chapter

- Mary's world-changing "yes" to faith
- Obeying God's call brings joy
- The changing power of "yes"
- Saying "yes" to God

It's one thing to acknowledge the desire for greater meaning and satisfaction in life. But it may feel like a much bigger deal to actually step out and decide to choose faith and say "yes" to God. In this chapter, I introduce several people who have taken that step of faith and discovered the rewards. We also look at just what it means to become a person of faith and how faith in God can change lives.

The Biggest "Yes" of All

The Bible is crowded with stories of individuals—and even entire nations—who decided to say "yes" to faith, "yes" to God.

For example, Moses came to his decision to follow God's call for his life, and lead the Israelites to their freedom, after a good bit of initial reluctance and some pretty creative excuses for why God should really pick someone else.

And then there's Jonah. After being told to go to the city of Nineveh, the would-be prophet at first offered God a big "no." As you may have heard, he ended up getting tossed off the boat he was riding in and being swallowed by a large fish, in whose stomach he sat for a couple days before getting vomited up on a beach. That was apparently all the coaxing Jonah needed. He decided to say "yes" to God after that and to proceed to Nineveh.

Hosea may be an unfamiliar name, but he deserves some respect for the way he said "yes." According to Hosea 1:2, God's very first request for the prophet was that he marry a prostitute who would bear his children while continuing to be unfaithful to him. I can't imagine how I would have responded to such a request. It would be a constant source of heartbreak. But Hosea understood that his marriage was to be a symbol of how God continued to love the people of Israel despite their own "adultery" of disobedience and idol worship. He said "yes" to God.

And surprisingly, Jesus' disciples immediately said "yes" when he asked them to drop their fishing nets, leave their families and businesses, and follow him without saying good-bye to their loved ones.

Behold!

One of the most well-known examples of modern faith in the last 10 years is Cassie Bernall, a student at Columbine High School in Littleton, Colorado. On April 20, 1999, two high school students went on a shooting rampage. After 46 minutes of terror, 12 other students and 1 teacher were dead—including Cassie. According to the survivors' reports, Cassie was in the school library when one of the gunmen held her at gunpoint and demanded to know if she believed in God. When Cassie said "Yes," she was shot point-blank.

But the biggest "yes" in the Bible—probably the biggest "yes" in the history of the world—was uttered by a mere teenage girl named Mary. The Lord's simple requests are often the stepping-stone to wonderful blessing. So it was for Mary. Her saying "yes" to God changed the whole world.

And it wasn't that God was asking something of Mary that was going to be easy for the young girl to give. God was asking this unmarried virgin girl to be the mother of his son. Not only would she risk serious societal penalties for her assumed illicit behavior. Not only would she risk being abandoned by Joseph, her fiancé. She would also hold the absolutely indescribable responsibility of bringing the son of God into the world.

Behold!

Being "betrothed" to Joseph, as Mary was, was a year-long, premarriage sacred state that could only be broken by divorce. Adultery during this period was punishable by death. The fact that Mary lived—and Joseph not only remained betrothed to her but went on to marry her—is a clear sign that Joseph said "yes" to faith as well, trusting that God truly was at work in Mary's life and that Mary had remained faithful.

Suppose Mary had said, "Hey, I've got a better idea: why not wait until I am married?" If she had, the world would have missed the greatest possible blessing. Mary and Joseph—after he spent a sleepless night wrestling with the message, following his own visit from an angel—ultimately were both obedient to what God showed them was his will. They said "yes" to God and took the grandest step of faith possible.

Blessings and Obedience

Obeying God in small matters is an essential step to God's greatest blessings. Think how many people were blessed by Mary's obedience and the support Joseph gave her.

But being obedient can sometimes require us to do things that seem unreasonable. Joseph could have thought having to support Mary in her condition was unreasonable. He was considering divorcing her until God asked him to be obedient. To Joseph's credit, he chose to obey.

As a result, he became an eyewitness to the divine coming into the world. When we obey God, we won't be disappointed. Joseph complied with God's simple request not to divorce Mary and within weeks found shepherds on their knees before the baby Jesus in his crib.

Faith 101

Mary and Joseph obeyed even when they had no idea what the future would hold. Some call this "blind faith" and dismiss it. "It's like stepping off the side of a cliff without any guarantee there's a net down below," they say. But the Bible looks at it a different way. "Which of you fathers, if your son asks for a fish, will give him a snake instead?" Jesus asks in Luke 11:11. In other words, a loving God keeps us in his care. That's a safety net like nothing Mary and Joseph could possibly imagine.

People hesitate to obey because they're afraid of the consequences, but consider Joseph's position. He may have suffered public humiliation. Obeying God might not have given him the outcome he wanted at the time, but he must have seen the blessings that flowed into the lives of so many people who came into contact with Jesus. Choosing to be obedient to God must have been ultimately more satisfying than the alternative.

By obeying God, both Mary and Joseph gained a deeper insight into God's personality. They were also able to see themselves in the context of a divine plan for the world. By saying "yes," they were able to see how God could use two average human beings to bring his will to fruition and demonstrate his holiness and sovereignty. God saw something in each of them they hadn't recognized in themselves. By saying "yes" to God, they had the opportunity to see their own unique gifts and abilities in a new light.

Options Aren't Optional

In life, the ability to choose is remarkable. If your major in school requires a math component, it's up to you whether you'll tackle advanced calculus or settle on "Algebra for Poets." You weigh your choices, choose the most appealing option, and say "no" to all the others.

Many things are forced upon us initially, though. None of us decides who will give birth to us, what city or town we'll grow up in, or what language we'll speak at home. But as we grow older, our world of options increases. As our options increase, so, too, does the impact our choices have on us and our loved ones.

Consider this: the most important decision you will ever make is what you will do with God.

If you're not so sure that's true, let's take it apart a bit. If God is who most people think he is—if God is who he says he is—then God is the most important being that exists. He is the Creator and Sustainer of the universe. He is the one being who has always existed and will always exist, eternal and *omniscient* and *omnipotent*.

Some decisions don't amount to a whole lot. If you decide to have onion rings instead of french fries, that's not really such a big deal. A plaid shirt instead of a red one? Doesn't matter, really. But choosing whether or not to say "yes" to God? That's as big a deal as deals come.

def•i•ni•tion

Omniscient means that God is all-knowing; he knows everything that possibly can be known. **Omnipotent** means that God is all-powerful; there is no greater being.

And that's exactly the situation we all find ourselves in at some point in our lives. For God has allowed us to say "I do" or "I don't" to him. We can say "yes" to faith or we can reject it. And saying, "Well, I'm going to decide that sometime down the road" is actually a decision in itself.

The Journey of "Yes!"

God stands ready and waiting to receive us, whenever we decide to finally come around to him. He is compassionate, and he is patient. He knocks on the door of our hearts and waits for an answer. He allows us to decide when and how we're going to respond.

What happens when we say "yes" to faith?

- ◆ Our hearts turn upward to focus on God.
- ◆ Our hearts look inward to examine ourselves.
- ◆ Our hearts look forward to the future God is preparing.

When God speaks to a heart that's open, he has an opportunity to lead, direct, guide, and support in the way he wants us to go.

Looking Upward

A heart that says "yes" to faith is a heart that is open. And an open heart is a heart that focuses on God. That's where the open heart always begins. It's not focused on self or on earthly concerns; instead, it looks heavenward.

I believe that when we meet God with open hearts, he will fill our hearts with his joy. Just listen to what Mary said when she was pregnant with Jesus: "My soul glorifies the Lord and my spirit rejoices in God my Savior, for he has been mindful of the humble state of his servant. From now on all generations will call me blessed, for the Mighty One has done great things for me—holy is his name." (Luke 1:46–49) That sure sounds like abundant joy to me.

Looking Inward

An open heart leads us to face the truth about ourselves.

During a powerful vision of God's glory, the Old Testament prophet Isaiah was suddenly confronted by something he didn't expect to see. He was awakened to the fact that he wasn't perfect. He still had to deal with this awkward human condition called sinfulness: "Woe is me!" he moaned. "I am ruined. For I am a man of unclean lips and I live among a people of unclean lips and my eyes have seen the King, the Lord Almighty." (Isaiah 6:5) In other words, "I'm not worthy!"

That's hard for most of us to say. I fall short everyday. I fail to meet God's design big time. I know that to be true with every fiber of my being. But that doesn't make it any easier to take a clear-eyed look at my life and honestly, openly say that I'm not worthy.

Most of us tend to want to accentuate our positives and downplay the negatives. We want to market ourselves so we look really good. We don't like to admit the struggles, the inconsistencies, the inadequacies—the "sin" stuff.

Yet the damaging truth of that practice is that when we fail to face the truth about ourselves, we fail to grow. With closed hearts, we don't change. Isaiah ended up growing and becoming more in the preceding story. In fact, he went on to experience the refreshing joy that accompanies the forgiveness of God. But he didn't get to the refreshment until he went through the repentance, saying, "Lord, change me. Work in me."

Behold!

Sometimes when I'm preaching, I'll look over the audience and notice the body postures of the worshippers. One of the body postures I tend to see involves a straight back and crossed arms. Do you know what that says? "I dare you to move me. I challenge you to say something that will stir my spirit." That's a closed heart. Open hearts say, "I'm not the person God calls me to be. I battle with imperfections all the time. I want God to do whatever he needs to do to make me into the person he wants me to become."

Looking Forward

Finally, open hearts look expectantly into the future that God has in store for us.

I can't imagine what kind of future Mary might have imagined for Joseph, Jesus, and herself. I feel certain that she trusted God to do something magnificent, something unprecedented, through his wholly unique son of God. But I also feel certain that she had no idea just how amazing and just how utterly heart-wrenching Jesus' life would be. Given what we know about Mary's life, though, I don't believe it mattered one bit. Her "yes" was for today, but it was also a "yes" for tomorrow ... and tomorrow ... and tomorrow. She was looking forward, wholly trusting God for every second.

My co-author, Bob, was visiting Mexico not long ago when he had the opportunity to ride a zip line. A zip line, if you're not familiar with the concept, is a long metal cable that's usually stretched anywhere from dozens of feet to more than a hundred feet above the ground between two high supports. Wearing a harness, zip-line riders clamp on to the cable at one end, jump off the support platform, and "zip" the length of the line to the other side. The whole trip might take 30 or 40 seconds, but the ride is exhilarating and, often, a bit frightening. Especially if, like Bob, you're afraid of heights. But how often does a guy get the chance to try a zip line in the Yucatan Peninsula? He had to do it.

Overlooking the hosts' casual approach to safety regulations, Bob put on the harness, climbed the tall tree, clipped onto the zip cable, and looked down—50 feet—to the jungle floor. He'd zipped before, but never at this height. And he was more than a little nervous before his turn came up.

That's when he discovered something unexpected.

The most experienced "zip-per" in the group didn't walk to the edge of the platform and look nervously down before he stepped off into the air. No, he ran off the platform and leaped out into the air, trusting completely that the zip harness and cable would hold him and speed him safely to the other side.

If Bob had allowed himself to stand on the edge of that platform and fret about the height, the safety of the harness, and the strength of the zip cable, he'd probably still be there. And the longer he stood there, the more worried he'd become. But Bob decided to trust completely. Following his predecessor's example, he took a running start on the platform and leaped out into the unknown.

Of course, he screamed like a little girl. But it was a scream of exhilaration and joy, not fear.

 Faith 101

> When facing your own personal "zip line into the unknown," try this: pray that God will lead and direct you through whatever you will face along the way. And then leap boldly. You can act with confidence, knowing that you are in God's hands and that God truly cares about what happens to you.

I think that's the way God would love to have us respond to his call to faith. Not a timid or hesitant "yes" that agrees to follow but never stops weighing the alternatives and second-guessing the choices. But an enthusiastic "Yes!" that, like Mary's, never looks back and only looks forward, trusting completely in God's power to pull us along into the future he has in store for us.

The Secret of Saying "Yes"

I have to confess: the "secret" of saying "yes" is that there is no secret. No magic words. No fancy footwork. Really. All you have to do if you want to say "yes" to faith is to tell God that you want to say "yes" to him and that you want to begin living a faithful life.

 Faith 101

If you want to say "yes" to faith but you're stuck for words, consider praying something like this:

> God, I still have lots of questions about this faith business. I don't know what it's all about. And I'm a little nervous about just how it's going to change my life. But I want to say "yes" to faith. I want to say "yes" to trusting you. So yes, God. Yes, show me how to become the person you want me to become. Yes, I want an open heart that's ready and willing to follow wherever you want to lead. Thank you for offering me the chance to say "yes" to all that you have in store.

How you tell him is entirely up to you. You can tell him silently, in your thoughts. Or you might find it more helpful to actually say the words aloud. I like the aloud approach, because actually hearing yourself saying the words can have an impact in itself, making the experience more tangible and real.

However you deliver your message, consider it the first statement in a lifelong conversation with God. What comes next? That's what we'll explore in the next few chapters.

The Least You Need to Know

- Mary said "yes" to God, and her choice led to Christ's entry into the world.

- ◆ Choosing faith leads to an eternal relationship with God and a deeper understanding of ourselves.

- ◆ Faith begins with telling God that you want to begin living a faithful life.

- ◆ Although none of us can know what the future holds, faith enables us to trust in the God who holds that future.

Chapter 5

Trusting and Yielding: The Third Step Toward Faith

In This Chapter

- ◆ Our ultimate example of faith
- ◆ Shifting from self to God
- ◆ God's leading voice
- ◆ Power in yielding to God

At this point, maybe you have acknowledged that faith is likely to provide the kind of deep satisfaction and meaning in life you desire. And maybe you've decided to cross the threshold into faith, saying that initial "yes" to God.

These are important, significant steps for anyone to take. They are the first two steps of a lifelong journey of faith. The next step is to trust in God and yield to his leadership. It isn't easy to turn trust away from self and focus it on God instead, striving to follow where he leads and become everything we were created to be. Let's look at the challenges ahead, as well as the personal responses that can help us grow as faithful people.

Self and Savior

Trusting and yielding apparently weren't too high on the list of priorities for the first-century church in Corinth. When Paul wrote to them in 1 Corinthians, he chided them for their self-centered attitude. Instead, he admonished them, they should turn to Jesus as their example. Then he said something very bold indeed: "Follow my example, as I follow the example of Christ." (1 Corinthians 11:1)

Note that Paul wasn't saying the Corinthians should follow his example because he was perfect or otherwise worthy of their emulation. No, he told them to follow his example as he followed Christ's example; Paul wasn't worthy on his own. Still, he was supremely confident in his devotion to living out everything that Jesus had taught. I don't know about you, but I don't know many—if any—people nowadays who would feel that confident in how they live out their faith.

Jesus lived a life of sacrifice, pouring all his personal and earthly interests in doing God's will. He completely yielded his will to God, putting his trust fully in his heavenly father. This is the call of faith, Paul says. And part of our success is measured by how completely we unseat the self at the center of our personal universe and give that throne over to God.

Quality Time

Like most families today, our family schedule is very hectic and extremely demanding. As a seminary president, I'm frequently traveling during the week, and I'm often speaking at churches all across the country come Sunday morning. When I am home, there's always something that needs to be fixed, telephone calls to return, and on and on. There simply doesn't seem to be enough time to sit down and to talk as a family, to enjoy the simple gift of each other.

I can remember when we reached a point as a family when we called a time-out from this kind of busyness. I decided that it was time to take control of my schedule. I'd read an advertisement in a newspaper about a hotel about an hour away that was offering a Friday night special: a hotel suite, an indoor pool, a whirlpool, and a full breakfast—all at the low price of $55. Marilyn and I decided to go.

It was a time of discovery for us. We stopped the train of life for a night and jumped off. It was great! We talked, we laughed, we teased, we joked, and we became reacquainted. And do you know what? The world didn't stop turning just because we'd decided to take a break. Nothing fell apart because we'd disappeared for a weekend together. There were no cataclysmic consequences. There was just welcome relief.

That weekend reaffirmed a basic truth I believe: if we want to build strong family relationships, we have to spend time together. The same thing is true in our relationship with our heavenly Father.

> **Faith 101**
>
> If we want a relationship with God that is growing, active, vibrant, and alive, we have to be willing to call a time-out to living for ourselves and turn our attention to God.

Of course, that can be frightening. What if God ends up leading us someplace we don't think we want to go? What if we feel like he's asking us to change something about ourselves, to bring us more in line with his will for our lives? Or worse—what if we choose to trust in God and yield ourselves to him … and then we have no idea what he really wants us to do?

Hearing God's Voice

Several years ago, I was counseling a young woman who was filled with regret. She said that in looking back over the last few years of her life, she realized she had made a tragic mistake. When I asked her what had happened, she informed me that she had married the wrong man. At 19, she had fallen for an older man who was not a Christian. She decided to marry him. Now, just 2 years later, she was searching for a way to escape. As she put it, "I knew that what I was doing was wrong. But I found a way to make it feel right. I wish I would have listened to what I think God was trying to tell me. I can't bear the thought of divorce. But I can't bear thinking that this is it, that this is all I'm ever going to know in life."

Behold!

In extraordinary circumstances, God has chosen to speak audibly to faithful people. Moses heard his voice in a burning bush. A boy named Samuel, who would grow up to be an Old Testament prophet, was awakened by God's audible call in the night. There are other examples as well. However, the faithful today are far more likely to hear God's voice in more subtle ways such as through the movement of their conscience and the counsel of godly friends.

It's not easy to yield to God's voice—especially when our own voices can be so much more forceful and convincing. But as we work on our relationship with God, his voice will take on greater clarity.

On Monday, October 31, 1988, I had the privilege of seeing President George H. W. Bush just before he was officially elected. (I'm never going to forget that date!) That morning, as I was driving to the office at my church in Mansfield, Ohio, a news bulletin came on the radio, announcing that he would be flying into the Mansfield airport within the next few minutes. His last-minute visit had been hurriedly arranged to provide a boost to Ohio's Republican returns.

I couldn't help myself. I knew the office could wait. And how often does a person have a chance to see someone who could be the next president of the United States?

When the aircraft touched down, Bush walked out of the plane, down the ramp, and stood 10 feet in front of me, where he made a speech before departing in a waiting limousine.

It was great to be a part of history in the making. However, simply because I saw George Bush and listened to George Bush and stood near George Bush does not mean I now know George Bush. (Oddly, I've never received a Christmas card from him. Hmm.) He hadn't called before his visit to say, "Hey, Chuck, I'm gonna be in town. Whaddaya say we do lunch?" Of course not. He didn't know me. And he still doesn't.

The same is true when it comes to listening to the Spirit of God. The Spirit only speaks to those with whom a relationship exists. He can only break through to those who are inclined to trust and yield in God.

How God Leads Us

What is God's Spirit saying to you? What he's saying to me may be something completely different from what he's saying to you. What he's saying to the person beside you on the morning train or in front of you in the supermarket checkout lane is different from what he's saying to you.

God might be saying ...

- *To the person without a job:* "Don't worry. I have it all under control."

- *To the person who is grieving:* "I am the resurrection and the life."

- *For the one wrestling with faith:* "Right now. *This* is your day."

- *For the person struggling with a major decision:* "I will guide you every step of the way."

- *For the tempted:* "Lean on me. Let me be your power."

One thing is for sure: if you're seeking to trust God and yield to his will, he will do some serious talking.

Of course, the Really Big Question is: "*How* will the Spirit speak to me?" God speaks directly to people in two common ways.

> **Beware!**
>
> Some people like to use the Bible as if it were a Magic 8-Ball. They ask God a question, randomly open a Bible, and plop their finger down on a verse to arrive at God's "answer." Not surprisingly, that was never God's intention for Scripture.

The Voice Inside

First, the Spirit will speak to you on the inside. Through your conscience, in your mind, he will talk to you. He will gently whisper.

This is how many of us get the sense that, "Well, I feel like I should be doing *this* now" or "This decision just isn't sitting right with me."

The Voices of Others

God sometimes speaks to you through other people—friends, church leaders, counselors and mentors, etc.

We really do need each other. You and I aren't called to make it all alone. We are invited instead to live in community—to be with each other, to pray for each other, to support each other, to love each other. It is in our involvement with other people that the Spirit often makes its message known.

That's one reason why I am so committed to the small-group experience. (I discuss this more in future chapters.) I have discovered that when I'm open and vulnerable with people who are just like myself, the Spirit often breaks through and talks to me.

In one of my former ministries, I participated in just such a group. In addition to myself, it consisted of a physician, a pharmacist, and a contractor. Twice a month we met at 6:30 in the morning for coffee and fellowship. We shared our struggles and our fears. We talked about our insecurities and our apprehensions. Whether it was a decision to buy a new car or to make a move, we discussed it. Taking the risk to become vulnerable with one another often allowed God's Spirit to say something significant to each one of us.

> **Faith 101**
>
> When questioning God's call for your life, weigh your conscience, seek the counsel of others, and then ask God to give you discernment as you make your decisions.

Giving It Up

Russian novelist Fyodor Dostoyevsky once wrote, "As long as man remains free, he will strive for nothing so incessantly and so painfully as to find something or someone to worship." (This echoes Pascal's "God-shaped hole" we so desperately want to fill.) Dostoyevsky, who wrestled throughout his life with God's call, may have intended his statement to be taken cynically. Yet it calls to mind a very positive image for me: like a seed under the soil, our souls only come to life and grow when something is over us.

I have often thought that this is one of the soul's most astounding and, in some cases, most difficult admissions to make—the confession that we need to yield, that we come into our own as human beings only when we are eclipsed by something far grander than ourselves.

Some folks yield their lives to astrological charts. Others prefer the pith of a good fortune-cookie message. Still others—and I won't name names—are convinced that man-made systems, such as Scientology, are the thing worth yielding to. Eastern religions, paganism, druidism, Earth worship, and the darker belief systems of cults and the occult all have adherents who believe they have found the perfect thing to trust.

Faith 101

Yielding isn't easy. Just as a seed has to die to itself to be reborn as a full-fledged plant, yielding to God's call may sometimes be uncomfortable, even painful. But once we acquire the desire to follow God, yielding will be the small "pain" that results in tremendous—and perhaps unanticipated—"gain."

Even though we may not worship the sun or even check our horoscopes in the morning paper, it's easy to find ourselves yielding to things that, frankly, aren't worthy of our supreme devotion. I'm thinking of things like our careers, our possessions, our hobbies, and our finances. In themselves, these can be perfectly good things. But they aren't worth yielding to. Looking and searching for something bigger than we are, we give ourselves to them without even questioning.

I've had the rare privilege of standing at the bedsides of more than a dozen people at the moment when they pass from this life into the next, and I've never once seen a stock portfolio come to the rescue. Never once have I seen a professional career give confidence or faith at that crucial hour. Never once have I seen a person look death squarely in the eyes and say, "I'm glad I was consumed by that hobby, that task, that position, that possession. Now I can face death head-on."

Contrast that with just two of the Bible's descriptions of God himself:

> No one is like you, O Lord; you are great, and your name is mighty in power. Who should not revere you, O King of the nations? This is your due. Among all the wise men of the nations and in all their kingdoms, there is no one like you. (Jeremiah 10:6–7)

> But the Lord is the true God; he is the living God, the eternal King. (Jeremiah 10:10)

What Yielding Yields

Yielding to God typically results in two benefits (though they may not immediately sound like benefits): direction and correction.

Direction

When God becomes the Lord of our lives, we no longer dictate the direction of our lives. We surrender control of our existence to the one who brought us into existence. He calls the shots. He dictates the rules. And he does it in love, looking out for our behalf.

And why shouldn't he? Here's my take on it: he knows my life and this world better than anyone. He made the earth by his power, he founded the world by his wisdom, and he stretched out the heavens by his understanding. Why shouldn't he direct me through it?

Correction

Correction, for many, doesn't sound like the kind of thing we typically relish or welcome. We want to be free. We don't wish to be restrained or controlled. And yet how did the writer of the book of Hebrews put it? "God disciplines us for our good that we may share in his holiness. No discipline seems pleasant at the time, but painful. Later on, however, it produces a harvest of righteousness and peace for those who have been trained." (Hebrews 12:8–10)

Yielded ... and Free

Yielding to God might sound like it requires you to give up your God-given freedom. (There's a paradox for you.) Yielding doesn't sound very free, does it? In fact, it probably sounds a bit constraining.

Being a pastor, that leads me to think of a story: when I was in college, I worked in a lumberyard. One afternoon, I was in the basement of the store, splitting some 2×4s on a table saw. It was the first time I'd done that, but I thought I knew what I was doing. No worries.

Then my boss appeared. Stepping in front of me, he shut down the machine. "Ever run a power saw before?" he asked me.

"No," I said.

"Trying to kill yourself?"

I didn't think I was.

"Why?" I asked.

"You're forcing the lumber through. You're pushing too hard. Here," he said, "let me show you what happens to a piece of lumber when you try to force it through a saw. Stand back, out of the way." Standing off to the side, he inched a small piece of wood into the saw's blade by pushing it with another piece of lumber. Then it happened—the saw kicked back. Like a missile, the little piece of wood shot backward— right where I'd been standing when I was splitting my 2×4s.

> *Direction:* Do it like this.

> *Correction:* Don't do it like this.

Staying You

No matter how adult we may be, how responsible and mature we may be, we need someone who will master us in love, directing and correcting us. We need someone who stands above us and over us, looking out for us; caring for us; calling for our worship, devotion, and affection.

A woman once confessed to me that she was afraid of what would happen if she became a Christian. "I'm afraid that if I became a Christian,

I would disappear. I would be nonexistent." She dreaded losing who she was as a person. She was afraid that making Christ her master meant she would have to conform to some cookie-cutter mold. She was wrong.

Yielding to God doesn't mean you relinquish who you are. You don't have to dismantle your personality, your passions, and your unique bent on life. Yielding merely means that you allow God to direct and correct you in ways that are for your good and God's glory.

In fact, when God is your master and you lose yourself in him, you actually find yourself in him. In the next chapter, we consider just what that kind of faithful life can look like.

Faith 101

Some folks say they'll consider faith after they get their "fun" out of the way. To them, God is some kind of a cosmic killjoy. As most believers readily admit, though, faith can turn mere "fun" into deep, real joy. It's the kind of joy that can come only when we find the power to become all we were meant to be—power that comes through faith.

The Least You Need to Know

- ◆ The faithful life is characterized by trusting in God and yielding to his leading.

- ◆ The closer we grow to God, the better we can follow his leading.

- ◆ God leads us through our conscience and the counsel of others.

- ◆ God is worthy of our trust.

- ◆ Yielding to God empowers us for true freedom.

Chapter 6

Living a Faithful Life: The Fourth Step Toward Faith

In This Chapter

- ◆ Faith and holiness
- ◆ Faith's challenges and rewards
- ◆ God's plan for his people
- ◆ Steps to developing trust

So far you've considered your desire for deeper meaning and satisfaction, choosing to say "yes" to faith, and taking the step of trusting in God for your future and yielding to his leading your life. Now, let's bring the pieces together and look at what's involved in living a life of faith—from understanding what it means to be holy to allowing yourself to be changed for good by God.

The Key to a Vital Faith

Think of some synonyms for *faithful*. Words such as *steadfast, true,* and *trusting* might come to mind. But there's another important facet to faithfulness: holiness.

If just seeing the word *holiness* makes you think we're moving away from practical, real-world faith and heading toward something "religious" or something you just don't want to be, give me a chance to explain. *Holiness* is one of the most misused and misunderstood words around when it comes to faith. And yet, it's an absolutely essential concept when you're talking about what it means to live a faithful life.

I wouldn't be shocked if *holiness* brings to your mind images of people who might be a little bit peculiar or odd, people who are so out of touch with contemporary culture that they don't even seem to belong. From that perspective, I could understand if you said, "Well, who wants to be holy?"

I'd like to offer a different perspective, though. In 1 Peter 1:13–15, Peter writes, "He who called you is holy, so be holy in all that you do. For it is written, 'Be holy, because I am holy.'"

To put it another way, holiness is an essential element of the Christian life.

What does it mean to be holy? The Greek word for holy simply means to be uniquely different. No, not in a weird or out-of-touch sense. But special, set apart. People who choose faith—who choose to put their trust in God—are set apart by God for a special purpose. They have opened themselves up to being used by God to make a real difference in the world. They are on the path of holiness.

Beware! _____

Holiness is not about following a long list of spiritual do's and don'ts. Even though some of the do's and don'ts might be good to keep in mind, making any of them our focus can cause us to become more concerned with following the letter of the law than with following God. We also have to remember that holiness isn't something we attain on our own just by doing A, B, and C. Holiness comes from choosing to let God work through us.

Let me put it this way: holiness is what happens when we connect with God in such a way that his character makes an imprint on our lives.

Holy Impossibility?

Living a faithful, holy life can sound impossible. After all, maybe you're thinking, *Hey, I'm only human. I get angry. Sometimes I swear. I think about a lot of things I probably shouldn't. I don't exactly walk on water.*

Yeah, me neither.

When God calls you and me to be holy, he doesn't expect overnight miracles. That would be like a professional carpenter who builds a house and then turns to his 7-year-old daughter and says, "Okay, now *you* build one." No, holiness for the Christian is both an event and a process. It's something we achieve once we come to God, but it's also something that occurs over the rest of our lives.

Imagine a college student graduating and signing a contract to work for an engineering firm. She takes the necessary tests. She passes the exams. Is she an engineer? Yes! And yet … even though she has the credentials to be called an engineer, she's just beginning the process. She needs experience. She has a long career ahead of her.

In a sense, that's the way it works with this business of holiness. The moment we say "yes" to God, we become holy. Yet authentic, deep-rooted holiness is still a process.

Preachers love to talk about things in sets of three. So here are three things involved in the process of moving toward holiness.

The Renewed You

First, we must have our minds renewed. And notice I didn't say *we must renew our minds*. Why? Because the ultimate transformation that needs to take place in our values and our thinking is not the sort of thing we can accomplish on our own. God's got to do it.

That's not to say we just sit back and wait for it to happen. We open the door to God's renewing power by encountering him through the Bible and through prayer. As the writer of Proverbs 2:4 put it, "We are to look for the truth of God's word as though we are looking for silver and searching for a hidden treasure." That's how engaged God wants us to be when it comes to his Word. That's the kind of spiritual hunger that grows holiness.

You read the Word, your mind is affected, your actions are changed, and—*voilà!*—you are moving to holiness.

Guarded for God

We often think of temptation in terms of things such as lust, but temptation can come in many different forms. More subtle kinds of temptation can distract us from being holy. The urge to always have the latest thing, the compulsion to always win in all our relationships, the pull to misuse our positions—these are oftentimes the temptations in our world that can sneak up and catch us unaware.

How do we beat them back? Jesus gives us some simple insight in Matthew 26:41: "Watch and pray that you do not fall into temptation," he says.

Now, that sounds easy enough. But it actually involves some real work on our part. *Watch* suggests that we know where we're vulnerable, so we can keep our guard up when those weak points are exposed. (Do you know your areas of vulnerability yet?) And praying for strength in times of temptation puts us in touch with the one who can empower us to say "no" and walk away.

Faithfully Following

Every day, you and I face thousands of choices. But whatever the choices, the options, God says, "Obey."

Some words are going to come up a lot as we talk about being people of faith. *Obey* is one of them. In the everyday business of holiness, obedience is critical. When we separate ourselves from sin, when we cleave to and obey our God, we are growing in holiness.

The Bible offers some pointers to what obedience might look like in a person growing in holiness:

- ◆ Lay aside falsehood, and speak only the truth.

- ◆ Do not let the sun go down on your anger.

- Let him who steals steal no more.

- Let no unwholesome word come out of your mouth.

- Get rid of all bitterness and wrath and malice.

- Be kind to one another, forgiving each other.

- Walk in love.

- Do not practice idolatry in any form.

- Abstain from immorality in your physical relations.

> **Faith 101**
>
> As Mother Teresa put it, "Our progress in holiness depends on two people: God and ourselves—on God's grace and on our decision to obey and to will what is right."

These are just some of the qualities that typify obedience and a desire to grow in faith and in holiness.

It Don't Come Easy

I will always remember one of the most powerful experiences I have ever had: witnessing the birth of my children in the hospital. There's something incredibly amazing about witnessing the greatest miracle in God's world. But I have to tell you that when I first became a parent, like most fathers, I was a little bit naïve. I actually thought I had parenting figured out. I thought to myself, *How tough can this be? I'm in charge. I'm the adult.* But even now, with three grown children, I still look back and wonder, *Will I ever get it right? Will it ever get easier?*

Living a faithful life is something like that. The rewards are incredible. But there will definitely be challenges along the way. If you decide to live a life of faith, to say "yes" to your mission for God, your experience may end up being a lot like learning to play a musical instrument, understanding a new piece of software, losing weight, or quitting smoking. It might get harder before it gets easier.

In Luke 10:3, Jesus is getting ready to send 72 of his followers out into the world to spread the gospel. Look at what he says: "Go! I am sending you out like sheep among wolves." In other words, don't expect to feel the love simply because you show up and announce "I'm on a mission from God."

Expect challenges as you grow in holiness. But keep in mind that you won't face such challenges on our own. When God gives us a plan, he also gives us the means to carry out that plan.

> ### Faith 101
>
> Here's a story I like that sums this up: for many years, the Mississuki Indians inhabited the Florida Everglades. The Mississuki Indians are, among other things, great alligator wrestlers. One day a tourist was talking to one of these Indians and commented on a necklace he was wearing. She wanted to know what it was made of. "Alligator teeth," he replied. "Ah," the woman said, smiling, "is that kind of like wearing a necklace of pearls?" "Well ... not really," he told her. "Anyone can open an oyster. How many people do you know who can take on an alligator?" At times, the faithful life will feel more like wrestling alligators than opening oysters.

God's Grand Plan

How do we nurture holiness and strive, every day, to live faithful lives? It's worth taking a quick look at the life of one who constantly struggled to be faithful and yet went on to be one of the great examples for believers today.

In Exodus 3:7, Moses first hears God's plan for the people of Israel: "I've seen the misery of my people in Egypt," God says. "I've heard them crying out in their slavery, and I'm concerned about their suffering. So I'm going to rescue them from the hand of the Egyptians and lead them into a land flowing with milk and honey."

Moses probably thought, *Great, God! It's about time you woke up and did something about that mess.*

Moses probably wasn't anticipating God's message in verse 10, though: "I am sending you to Pharaoh to bring my people, the Israelites, out of Egypt." As if that weren't bad enough, in something like the next breath, God also mentions that Pharaoh's heart will harden against him, making the mission nearly impossible.

I talk about some specific, everyday challenges to living faithfully—and their solutions—in upcoming chapters. I don't want to ignore the hurdles every faithful person is going to face. At the same time, we can't forget that God has a plan. God's message to Moses was that, yes, there are going to be challenges, but never forget that I am God. Things may look impossible, but again, I am God.

Training for Trust

Training means arranging your life around certain practices that will enable you to reach a goal. Sometimes willpower alone isn't enough. The mere fact that you *want* something just isn't sufficient. Sometimes you need to reprioritize, recommit, reevaluate, and reorganize.

That's a spiritual truth that can revitalize your life. If you are ever going to get to the life you've always wanted, you're going to have to organize your life in such a way that you do the things necessary to reach your goals. You're going to have to train for trust in God.

Faith 101

I once met a man who had decided to go back to school, even though he was in his 40s. I asked, "What changes did you have to make to make this happen?" First, he had to change jobs, finding one that would accommodate his new schedule. Next, he had to downsize his lifestyle, moving to a cheaper apartment and saying good-bye to his premium cable channels. He also had to get out of debt so he wouldn't be adding his college loans to his credit card bills. To put it simply, he was reorganizing his life so he could reach his goal.

When it comes to faith, our goal is to build a trusting relationship with God that reflects the character of Jesus Christ. But how do you do that? Some of us *try*. We start out the day saying, "Today, I'm going to reflect Jesus in all I do." But what happens? Sooner or later, something goes wrong. It doesn't even have to be something big. Another driver cuts us off on the way to work. We lose the contract. The bank tells us we're overdrawn. The school tells us our child is having a serious problem. And suddenly the goal becomes a fantasy. Jesus isn't evident in our lives; in fact, it might look like he's checked out altogether. The problem? We're *trying* to be faithful, not *training* to trust.

Three Ways to Train

Training for trust doesn't have to be complicated. It's really just about going back to the simple practices of the Christian life, things I'll continue to focus on throughout this book:

◆ Reading the Bible

◆ Telling others about your faith

◆ Helping others to grow in their faith

These training tips come from Paul, writing to Timothy in 1 Timothy 4:13. Paul says, "Devote yourself to the public reading of Scripture, to preaching, and to teaching." Bible reading is something I've already talked about, but "preaching" and "teaching" might sound a little scary right about now. Let's take them one at a time.

Paul believed that one of the best ways to strengthen your spiritual muscles and to follow good training was through what he calls "preaching." That doesn't necessarily mean you need a church or you have to stand behind a pulpit. (It also doesn't mean you have to stand on a box in the middle of Times Square on a Saturday night.) But in your ordinary everyday relationships, you can connect others with God by telling them about your own faith journey. Don't think of "preaching" in terms of telling others what to do; that's "preachy," which nobody likes. Think of it simply as telling someone else about what led you to your current decisions about faith and about what you see God doing in your life.

Faith 101

Nobody likes to be preached at. But the best preachers—and the most influential believers in general—simply approach "preaching" from the perspective of someone saying, "Hey, this is what I've discovered. I think you'll discover something similar, and you'll really benefit from it." Teaching is the natural next step, the response to the questions of "Well, how do I find faith like what you've found?" or "What does it really mean to believe?" or "How can I learn more?"

"Teaching" is sort of in the same boat: you don't need a classroom or a degree. You just need to build personal relationships in which you can encourage someone else to discover God's place in their lives.

Impacting the life of a person who is just in the process of discovering God will do for you spiritually what working out on a treadmill can do for you physically.

A Powerful Spirit

There's one more vital ingredient in training to trust: allowing God's *Holy Spirit* to work in your life.

So far, I've talked a bit about God and about Jesus Christ. The Holy Spirit is the third "person" Christians talk about when they talk about the holy Trinity, or the three persons of God.

The power and the presence of God's Spirit is the most important tool you can use in the training process. Why is it so vital? Because the Spirit can do in our training what our willpower cannot.

Reading the Bible, sharing your faith story with others, and helping others make progress in their own faith can all be tough things to put into practice. Like the marathon runner who struggles at times, there are points at which those approaches don't come easy. That's where the Spirit's power comes in.

def•i•ni•tion

Whereas Jesus was the human embodiment of God, someone who lived in a specific time and place in history, the **Holy Spirit** is the indwelling embodiment of God, the one that fills the hearts and souls of believers.

In the children's book *Frog and Toad Together* by Arnold Lobel, Frog and Toad are baking cookies—and having a hard time not eating them. "We really must stop," Toad says. To which Frog responds, "We need more willpower."

"What's willpower?" Toad asks.

"Willpower is trying very hard not to do something you want to do very much," Frog tells him.

We've all been there. We've all encountered moments when will alone just won't do. When the power and the presence of the Spirit starts working, though, you'll be amazed at your ability to put the other techniques into practice.

Beware!

If we're not careful, spiritual training techniques could become nothing more than religious obligations in themselves. They could become merely another list of spiritual have-to's. Spiritual training isn't about keeping a list and checking it twice to prove you've been spiritually nice. It's about change, progress, and growth.

Changed by the Spirit

A couple years back, my congregation at First Baptist Church in Charlotte, Michigan, participated in a year-long "read through the Bible" campaign. We had nearly 100 individuals read through the Bible. We also had some drop-outs. And I was one of them.

One morning, I was trying to make my way through that great, inspiring Old Testament book of Leviticus. (Picking up on my subtle sarcasm?) I was reading through all that technical material associated with the ritualistic laws. Then it hit me: I was reading the words, but nothing was sinking in. At that point, I felt a question rise up inside: *Chuck, why are you doing this?*

"Because I'm the pastor," I admitted. "A lot of people in the church are reading through the Bible this year. I need to model success for them if I'm going to be a leader."

I was missing the point. The goal of that particular training technique was not to complete my reading of the Bible in a year, as though to suggest that if I did that, I would somehow be a better Christian. The goal was to read in such a way that God's Spirit could continue the work of transforming my life.

Our primary task in practicing training techniques is never to calculate how many verses we've read, or how many people we've talked to about our faith, or how many personal connections we've made with people we might mentor. Our primary task is to expose ourselves to God's Spirit and to let him get on with the business of changing our lives.

Making the Choice

This life of spiritual training—of putting yourself in a position to be changed by God—doesn't happen accidentally or by coincidence. You don't just drift into it. You *decide* that this is for you.

Have you ever seen a television infomercial in which an amazingly fit person is selling a piece of exercise equipment? They show us what the body can become through repetitive, disciplined action. They've invested time, energy, and, sometimes, more than a little bit of cash to reach their goals.

Most of us want results *now*. But the bodybuilders of America remind us that it takes time, effort, and commitment. But most important, it takes an initial decision to begin.

Consider 1 Timothy 4:15: "Be diligent in these matters; give yourself wholly to them so that everyone can see your progress." If we *really* want the life we've always wanted, a life of meaning and faithfulness, we need to get off the "maybe" and jump into "yes." We'll never achieve our fullest potential as human beings created in God's image until we make up our mind to pursue lives of faith. We need to move from "maybe" to full acceptance, to a life-changing relationship with God.

The Least You Need to Know

- When we say "yes" to faith in God, we say "yes" to growing in holiness.

- Holiness is a process that involves renewal, victory over temptation, and obedience to God.

- Living a life of faith comes with real challenges.

- God empowers us to grow in our faith despite the challenges.

Chapter 7

Making Room for God

In This Chapter

- ◆ Growing a relationship with God
- ◆ Time to meet God
- ◆ Challenges and rewards of a quiet time

Several of the home-and-garden cable channels on television now feature reality shows in which homeowners and apartment dwellers bring in a team of experts to help them sort through their accumulated clutter, discard what isn't needed, and make room for a better life. Just like the rooms in our house, our personal lives can get cluttered with things we think we need to cling to but that just take up space and keep us from living the life we were born to live. As you explore the role of faith in your own life, it can be helpful to take stock of what might be filling up your personal world—and make room for faith to grow.

Building a Relationship

During my nearly 25 years of marriage, I've discovered that if my relationship with my wife, Marilyn, is going to stay alive, I have to be willing to work at it. I have to be willing to give the time it takes to nurture it. Relationships don't just happen. If we're not careful, our busy schedules can quickly rob us of the time we need for the level of interaction necessary for intimacy. We have our jobs, our responsibilities at the house, our personal interests and hobbies, our social engagements. And if we're not careful, we could end up passing one another in the hallway or driveway without ever stopping to seriously interact.

That's why we're committed to taking a two-night getaway every few months. That's also why we occasionally turn down other social invitations so we can go out to dinner together and just talk. I don't want a marriage absent of romance or feelings. I don't want to merely go through the motions. I don't want to end up with the sort of relationship where, 20 years down the line, all we do is sit in the living room rocking chairs, staring at the television or hiding behind the newspaper while we thumb through the classifieds and ignore one another. I want our marriage to be alive.

If you have said "yes" to faith, you have a relationship with God. It may just be in its beginning stages, but it's a relationship nonetheless. And because you've said "yes," you can have an active, vital, and alive relationship with God. God can be a personal friend with whom you deeply connect—closer than your best friend, closer than a spouse.

But it doesn't just happen on its own, without any effort. You have to be willing to make the time to spend with God. A vital relationship with Jesus Christ, a relationship in which you feel deeply connected to God, takes time. And not leftover, throwaway, occasional tidbits of time, either, but quality time used for conversation, listening, solitude, and reflection.

Faith 101

Good intentions are good to have, but they aren't enough if we fail to follow through and establish a regular, daily quiet time with God. It takes a strong desire to arrange (or rearrange) schedules to ensure we give God the space he needs in our lives to truly move and make a difference.

As we explore the many ways we can express and expand our faith in upcoming sections, I get into some of these areas in much more detail. But at this stage in your journey of faith, it can be beneficial to focus on one specific way to make room for faith in your life: establishing a regular time to read the Bible, pray, and reflect on what God wants you to do and how you can best do it.

Your Appointment with God

Many Christians talk about "having devotions" or setting aside a "quiet time." No matter what you call it, it's a regular appointment with God marked by reading and studying Scripture, praying for your needs and the needs of loved ones, asking God for guidance, and listening for his response. Unfortunately, it's quite possible that more Christians talk about having a quiet time than actually follow through. It's something many of us believe is important to our spiritual growth, but it's also something that all too often ends up getting pushed aside in favor of the more pressing concerns of daily life.

Do you know what? I believe that if most of us could see the benefits of keeping a daily appointment with God, we would become more interested in doing it.

In Psalm 1, David understood full well that he was going to receive a payoff because he had an appointment with God on a daily basis. All throughout the psalm, David celebrates the benefits, applicable to your life as well:

 ◆ We will be happier people. The psalm begins with the phrase, "Blessed is the man …"

 ◆ We reach our true spiritual potential. "He is like a tree planted by streams of water, which yields its fruit in season and whose leaf does not wither." (Psalm 1:3)

 ◆ We live at peace. "For the Lord watches over the way of the righteous, but the way of the wicked will perish." (Psalm 1:6)

And it all happens because of what David says in verse 2: this person's "delight is in the law of the Lord, and on his law he meditates day and night." There is an incredible, delightful, and surprising payoff reserved for the person who says, "I'm going to keep a daily appointment with God on an ongoing basis."

Pulling Up Stakes

When I was in Russia a number of years ago, I attended the Moscow circus. As I sat in the stands looking down on the circus arena, something caught my eye. I noticed that the elephants were tied to some very tiny stakes. I wondered, *What keeps the biggest animals in the circus from pulling up the stakes?* Later, I learned the answer to my question.

When the elephant is a baby, it is tethered to a small stake, but one that is strong enough and well enough sunk into the ground that the elephant can't pull it up. Day after day, the elephant may pull and tug, but it can't get free. Finally, it resigns itself to the situation and gives up. And no matter how strong it becomes, it never again will try to pull out a stake.

Many Christians feel frustrated, guilty, and angry because in their lives they have unmet goals, unfulfilled expectations, and unaddressed temptations that end up being like those little elephant stakes and keep them from growing in their faith and connecting with God. These little things don't need to have power over people. In fact, the believers should have defeated them a long time ago. But they didn't. And I think one basic reason why is because they are missing out on this daily appointment with God.

Getting Quiet

Okay, so how do you do it? How do you carve out time for you and God to get together despite everything else happening in your life?

On a poll taken among people who don't attend church very often, one of the questions asked was, "What really bothers you when you do go to church?" One of the answers was, "It really bugs me when the preacher tells us what we need to do but then he doesn't tell us how to do it." That's not a sin I want to be guilty of in this chapter. (Or any chapter, for that matter!) So here are five things to consider.

Just Do It

At some point in life, a lot of us make the decision to start eating right and exercising daily just for the sake of our health. And so we begin.

We set the alarm clock for 6 A.M. so we can jump out of bed and do our aerobic exercise before driving to work. But what happens? A couple days into the experience, our legs get sore or maybe our back begins to hurt, and we find ourselves beginning to make excuses so we won't have to follow through.

Why does this happen? We're still debating. We're still playing this mental game of ping-pong in which we volley thoughts about whether or not we really want to do what's required to stay in shape.

Sometimes we do the same thing with our daily appointment with God. We start off with a bang, but then the schedule gets busy, the other appointments appear more critical, the to-do list gets longer, and we begin to come up with a list of reasons why it can't be done.

Nothing will change if we don't first stop the debate within ourselves. Make the decision that a quiet time with God is important and that it's something you are going to do.

Let me let you in on a secret: that struggle will probably take place for the first 21 days you are trying to keep your appointment with God. Psychologists tell us that's just the way the human mind operates. When making a lifestyle change or practicing a new habit, a minimum of 21 days usually is necessary before the internal conflict stops and you decide to really follow through with your decision.

> **Faith 101**
>
> If it feels like you're spending your quiet time reading the Bible but nothing seems to be sinking in, try reading the Word aloud. The very act of speaking Scripture aloud can direct your thoughts better than silent reading and help you discover nuances you might otherwise overlook.

During that 21-day span, walk away from the debate. Quit arguing with yourself. When the conflict threatens to emerge, stop and remind yourself that there is a payoff waiting for you.

Set Realistic Goals

After you stop the debate, set realistic goals. Don't sabotage yourself by establishing unrealistic expectations at the outset.

Let's run through the scenario: you decide to have a daily appointment with God, so you set your alarm for 5 A.M. because you're going to get

Faith 101

When a third grader goes to a piano teacher, the teacher doesn't place Mozart's "Symphony in E Flat" or Beethoven's "Moonlight Sonata" on the music stand and say, "Here, play this." The piano teacher starts by saying, "This key is called middle C." Where's middle C for you?

up and read 10 chapters of the Bible, spend 2 hours in prayer, then write in a journal for a while.

Like exercising, it's important that we set small goals at the start. We need to be comfortable walking short distances before we move on to bigger challenges. It's important that we don't force ourselves to take on something we're not yet ready to handle.

Maybe that means making a commitment to spend 5 minutes a day with God 4 days a week. Then take it up to 10 minutes a day. Then move it up to 5 days a week. Small steps. Start off slowly. Give yourself room to grow.

Stay Flexible

Two of the greatest reasons people drop their daily appointment with God is because of staleness and sameness. The time either becomes dried up and tasteless or boring and predictable. A person who stays at it is a person who has an arsenal filled with flexibility.

Here are some tips for adding variety to your daily appointment with God:

Change locations. Having a particular place where you can read and pray in peace may be helpful to you, but a simple change in scenery or surroundings could go a long way.

Use music. If you like contemporary Christian music, listening to artists like Steven Curtis Chapman, DC Talk, Rebecca St. James, Mercy Me, or Relient K can help. Or maybe you find classical music or easy-listening instrumental music more conducive to faithful reflection. Whatever your personal preferences and tastes may be, music can be a great vehicle through which God's Spirit can speak.

Try journaling. I have a colleague in the ministry who said his daily appointment with God was virtually nil until he started writing down his thoughts and faith experiences in a journal.

For those of you who have never tried this experience of writing down thoughts concerning your spiritual life, the whole thing may sound a little bit strange. But why not consider the option, even for a brief period of time? Writing can be a method of recording, reflecting on, and remembering key points in your walk of faith.

Faith 101

To get started journaling, purchase a notebook, carry it with you, and just write. (Tough, huh?) Or if you can't bear the thought of doing something so nineteenth century as actually *writing*, journal on your computer. The medium isn't as important as the message. Write your reflections about God, your concerns, and your prayers. And when you believe God has answered one of your prayers, write that down, too. Your understanding of faith is bound to grow as you chronicle the way God is at work in your life and in the world around you.

Consider this: Israel's King David was a journaler. His spiritual life—from the highest mountain peaks to the deepest valleys—was recorded in the Book of Psalms. He wrote his questions about God, his arguments with God, and his praise to God. He didn't hide anything or hold anything back. That's a great approach to take with our own journals.

Use the Bible

It's worth noting that in Psalm 1, the man who is considered blessed didn't settle for just thinking about God or just hearing others talk (or sing) about God. He spent significant time in God's Word.

I'm thankful for Christian musicians we have today and the wide range of music they offer. There has never been such a diversity of Christian music on store shelves—and not just on *Christian* store shelves. Today, we're blessed with everything from alternative rock to praise-and-worship, from rap to reggae. I'm also grateful for the devotional tools we have nowadays: pamphlets featuring

Behold!

Psalm 1:2 describes a man whose "delight is in the law of the Lord." In King David's day, that would have meant the first five books of what we now call the Old Testament, then called the Pentateuch.

inspirational stories that bring Scripture to life, Bibles that explain real-life applications for the verses, etc. I'm also thankful for the influence of Christian radio and television.

However, if we rely on all these wonderful tools to the extent that they become crutches for our faith, we may be robbing ourselves of one of the joys of our daily appointment of God: allowing God to speak to us, to touch us, in a personal way.

If you are new to this daily appointment journey, let me share an additional point before we move on: it feels only logical to start reading the Bible at the beginning, with Genesis 1:1, but you may quickly get bogged down in some of the Old Testament's hard-to-pronounce names, obscure places, and—when you hit Deuteronomy and Leviticus—long passages related to laws and religious observances. Instead, you may want to start with something simple, something more readily accessible. Consider the Old Testament Book of Psalms or the New Testament Gospels of Mark and Luke as good starting places. (Matthew and John are fine, too, although John takes a somewhat different approach to telling the story of Jesus' life.)

Anticipate the Impact

It may not happen instantaneously. You may have to be patient and give yourself some time. But you can expect your daily appointment with God to make a difference in you.

I know that when I'm connected to God, it makes a difference in me. I know it when I'm teaching and God's Spirit does something through me that I couldn't do on my own. I know it when I come home from a day at the office and suddenly I'm more sensitive to my wife's needs. I know it when things get a little hectic at the house and I'm more patient with my children. I know it when I'm encountering conflict or resistance and God keeps me steady. I know it when I go out on a limb as a leader and say, "This is what we need to do," and inside I'm feeling half-scared.

If you haven't started, make the commitment today to make room in your life for a daily appointment with God. If you're struggling with that, don't get discouraged. Don't quit. A vast vault of riches is waiting for you in your day-by-day discoveries.

The Least You Need to Know

◆ Building a deeper relationship with God requires us to make time in our lives to read Scripture and pray.

◆ It takes effort to make a daily appointment with God a priority in our life.

◆ A variety of steps can help you make the most of your quiet time with God.

◆ Keeping a regular quiet time will yield spiritual riches.

Chapter 8

Making the Most of Mentors

In This Chapter

- ◆ Defining mentoring
- ◆ Growing through mentoring
- ◆ Aspects of the mentoring relationship
- ◆ How mentors help

Given enough time and stick-to-itiveness, it's possible to learn a variety of things entirely on our own or with only minimal help from books or manuals. But there's a good reason why so many professionals have apprentices: it's far easier to acquire knowledge and new skills when you have a trusted, experienced person to mentor you. The same holds true when it comes to spiritual matters like faith. In this chapter, we look at finding a spiritual mentor and working effectively with another believer.

What Is a Spiritual Mentor?

Professional trades from guitar makers to electricians have apprentice-ships. Medical professions require internships. And of course, even Donald Trump and Martha Stewart recognize the value of their business-oriented apprentices. Why do these relationships exist? Because personal attention from experienced practitioners helps people master essential skills, attitudes, and knowledge.

The mentor/mentee or mentor/disciple relationship carries over to the world of faith as well. Moses had Joshua. Naomi had Ruth. Paul had Timothy. And Jesus had his 12 disciples.

What's the value of having a spiritual mentor? A spiritual mentor can provide another set of eyes for your situation, offer advice and encour-agement based on his experience, and hold you accountable. Basically, a spiritual mentor can help you reach a level of spiritual maturity you might not be able to reach on your own without a great deal of effort.

When my co-author, Bob, lost weight through the Jenny Craig fran-chise, he was assigned a mentor who would weigh him in every week, keep a chart of his progress, ask about specific challenges or tempta-tions, and be sure he stayed focused on his diet. As a result of his own commitment and the mentor's support, Bob ended up losing 108 pounds. Mentors can obviously help.

When it comes to questions of faith, mentors can help us discover God's will for our situation, pray with us, offer counsel, and encourage us to avoid temptations, keep our daily appointments with God, and so on. It can be empowering to have a flesh-and-blood relationship that helps us nurture our spiritual progress.

Becoming a Disciple

Having a mentor when you're exploring faith can be incredibly valu-able. As believers, you and I are called to become mature. We are invited to enter the joy-filled experience of growing up in our faith. And although you may be a newcomer to faith right now, soon you'll want to move beyond the basics. You'll be ready to move beyond milk and start chewing on some real spiritual meat. Mentors can be a catalyst for our growth.

Maturity doesn't mean we become perfect. It doesn't mean we have all the answers to all the weighty theological issues of our day. Spiritual maturity simply refers to our ability to keep on going with God, to get closer to God, to know God better. It means moving beyond the ABCs of our faith and into a deeper faith relationship.

At first, that may sound like strenuous work. But with the guidance of a trusted mentor, you can discover a powerful payoff.

Growing in Discernment

First, you will achieve a spirit of *discernment.* Hebrews 5:14 tells us, "Solid food is for the mature, who by constant use have trained themselves to distinguish good from evil."

That word *train* the author of Hebrews uses suggests that spiritual discernment takes time and effort, just as a physical workout takes time and effort to replace fat with fat-burning muscle. You can't commit your life to God and expect to miraculously draw the distinction between right and wrong overnight.

def•i•ni•tion

In spiritual terms, **discernment** is the God-given wisdom to recognize God's will and to choose wisely between good and evil—or even good and not-so-good choices.

It's a process that takes time. As you commit yourself to growing closer to God, however, that capacity to label right right and wrong wrong becomes a little clearer. The guidance of a mentor can help.

Growing in Self-Awareness

There is also the benefit of increased self-awareness. Mentees gain increased sensitivity to what were formerly considered their blind spots. They have another human being listening to their experiences and their concerns; they have another set of eyes examining their life.

Granted, that can be a pretty scary thing to consider. None of us likes to look weak or vulnerable. But if a mentoring relationship is really going to be beneficial for us, we need to be transparent with our mentors. We need to open up and let them see our weaknesses so we can address them.

Growing in God's Blessings

Hebrews 6:7 contains a very vivid image: "Land that drinks in the rain often falling on it and that produces a crop useful to those for whom it is farmed receives the blessing of God."

When you grow in faith, your life is like rich farmland that takes in every drop of water, water that manages to find its way into the hidden crevices of your soul. What happens then? The crop of God's blessings are produced!

The gifts we can savor are almost too numerous to even mention: we exchange our critical spirits to become more loving, we swap our blandness for joy, we replace our anxiety with peace, we replace mere tolerance with godly patience—suddenly, our lives become more beautiful.

That's growth. And while it's possible to grow on our own, our progress will be much improved if we reach out to a mentor.

The Mentoring Relationship

The Carreys were planning to start a new life serving as missionaries in Belgium. But even as they were making preparations for their trip and their new experience, the couple found themselves asking each other, "Do you really think this is what we should be doing?"

The Jeffersons lived in the same city as the Carreys, and they, too, were trying to make sense of God's will for their lives. They were back in the States after having spent their entire working lives serving as missionaries in the city of Brussels. Now retired, the Jeffersons were wrestling with the question of "What's next?"

Faith 101

A mentor can only be as strong as his depth of spiritual experience and maturity. When looking for a mentor, seek an adviser who has at least spent several years learning and growing in the faith.

God brought these couples together, and it was a perfect match. The Carreys were able to talk with an experienced, seasoned couple who had been where they were going and done what they were preparing to do. They could ask questions about everything from cultural attitudes to the best shops to buy chocolate. In the process, the Carreys felt that their call to Belgium really was what God wanted them to do. And the Jeffersons discovered a new role as mentors.

Mentoring might sound like a give-and-take kind of relationship—where the mentor constantly gives and the mentee constantly takes—but that doesn't have to be the case at all, as illustrated by the example of the Jeffersons and the Carreys. There can be numerous benefits for people who are willing to mentor someone else.

Mentors (even pastors) gain a real sense of significance. Sometimes, many of us wonder if what we're doing in life is really making a difference, if anyone else notices or even cares. In a mentoring relationship, though, mentors work with people who are hungry to grow and eager to learn. There is a much more visible "return on the investment" of time and energy.

Plus there's personal growth. When a mentor discusses character issues with a mentee, both are forced to look at their own character issues. After all, it's hard to look at someone else's life without also taking a close look at your own. And when you're being held up as a mentor for someone else, you need to be sure you're someone whose example should be followed.

Faith 101

It isn't always easy to find a mentor who will be in tune with your specific needs or situation. An obvious first stop is a member of the clergy with whom you've already begun to establish a relationship. If you are involved with a Bible study group or other small group, you might ask other members to serve as mentors or to recommend people to you.

What Mentors Do

The actual work a mentor does varies with the mentor, with your available time and your needs, and with the kind of relationship you both want to develop together.

If you plan to mentor someone else at some point, the following aspects of the mentoring relationship provide some good points to keep in mind as you move forward. And if you're evaluating someone as a possible spiritual adviser for yourself, consider the following points as positive traits to seek out.

A Mentor Builds Trust

It's up to the mentor to create an environment in which trust blossoms. Trust can grow as you each share your personal stories of faith—how you came to be where you are today. This can help open doors and generate discussion. Sharing your struggles with each other can also help take the relationship to a deeper level.

Some mentees become like another member of the mentor's family. They spend time at their home, playing with their kids and eating meals. Other times a mentor simply meets with a mentee at the office, over coffee, or over lunch.

Part of building trust involves being clear about what the mentoring relationship can and can't do. Mentors do not want mentees to expect too much or too little. Both problems can be avoided if expectations are discussed openly. Everything from "Is there homework?" to "Okay, who pays for the Starbucks run?" should be talked about early on so each person understands what the boundaries are. Unrealistic or unexplored expectations can come back to haunt you later.

> **Faith 101**
>
> Whether you're mentoring yourself or being mentored, take time early in the relationship to discuss some of those boring, nonspiritual things like how often you'll meet together; when, where, and how long your meetings will last; and what you both want to accomplish.

A mentee may expect you to be empathetic and offer a shoulder to cry on whenever she feels the need. The mentor may expect something the mentee is simply unwilling or unable to give. In the beginning, both should be willing to say, "This is what I think I can give. These are my gifts. This is my range of experience."

A Mentor Maintains Trust

When the mentoring relationship gets rolling, it's important that the mentor works to maintain the trust established earlier. This means being honest, open, and transparent throughout the process. It also means following through with any promised commitments and maintaining confidentiality.

A Mentor Learns

The best mentors are not the people who come across like they already have all the answers. The best mentors are open to learning and growing in their own faith as much as they possibly can. But they can't learn much if they do all the talking; to learn, mentors should be engaged listeners.

A Mentor Offers Perspective

By virtue of their age (perhaps) and their experience (hopefully), mentors have something mentees do not. A mentor should, therefore, be able to offer mentees the gift of their perspective.

For newcomers to faith, a range of new experiences, new things to read, and even a new vocabulary can get overwhelming. Mentors can help you step back, take a breath, and see the big picture without getting swept away by the details. Mentors help keep us focused on why we're doing what we do and who we're doing it for

A Mentor Asks

One of the most important duties of a good mentor is to ask the right questions. A mentor is not The Answer Person, but rather, the one who gets the mentee to figure out the answers for himself.

Sometimes questions help identify a deeper issue. A colleague once mentioned that a student he was mentoring wanted some help meeting his need for exercise. But as the mentor asked questions, it became clear that exercise wasn't the student's main issue; the deeper issue had to do with time management. And that was something affecting not only the student's ability to exercise sufficiently, but also his quiet time with God as well as the efficiency of his time spent studying.

Beware! _____

Don't assume that your mentoring experience will be like an episode of *The Apprentice,* where you're "fired" as soon as you find yourselves hitting a rough spot. Find a good mentor, and you may make a trusted friend who will remain at your side for many, many years.

Other times, questions lead to issues that need to be confronted. Maybe a mentee mentions that a co-worker had asked her some questions about her faith and she was at a loss about how to respond. A series of questions might uncover that the mentee doesn't feel sufficiently confident yet in her new faith, needs help gaining familiarity with the Bible, or just needs to practice this kind of conversation with someone she can trust.

A Mentor Pushes—in Love

Mentors often nudge mentees in directions that at first feel uncomfortable. One of the lifelong lessons in the Christian life is learning to depend on God. Taking risks and working outside of our previous experience can help promote growth and trust in God. But many of us would never choose to take too many risks on our own; we need that mentor's nudge.

A Mentor Confronts

A final skill mentors should demonstrate is the skill of correcting. Mentors are like mirrors helping mentees see what's preventing them from being all God wants them to be. They aren't there to attack the mentees or demean them in any way. Instead, as one mentor said, "I just want to hold up the mirror and say, 'Do you see this?'"

If a mentor has taken the time to build a relationship of trust, the mentee is naturally going to be more inclined to accept whatever correction the mentor offers. He'll understand that his mentor truly cares about him and wants to help him.

All Christians are called to follow Christ with integrity. But in a mentoring relationship, there is an even greater platform for accountability. If a mentee's actions or statements are inconsistent with her stated goals and commitment, the mentor needs to mention it. This is a living example of the Bible's observation that "as iron sharpens iron, so one man sharpens another." (Proverbs 27:17)

Time Is on Our Side

Building and sustaining an effective mentoring relationship takes time. It's not for the impatient or for folks who want a quick fix. It's one of the most effective means of developing effective people of faith, but it can also be pretty time-consuming.

Nevertheless, mentoring fulfills a very real need. All of us need to grow in character and competency when it comes to living a faithful life. All of us need people who will hold us accountable to do what we say we're going to do and to live how we claim we want to live. Mentors can fulfill that role in our walk of faith.

The Least You Need to Know

- ◆ Mentors can be an aid to growing in faith and spiritual maturity.
- ◆ The mentoring relationship yields benefits for mentors and mentees alike.
- ◆ Mentors offer fresh perspective, counsel, and correction.
- ◆ A strong mentoring relationship can be a lifelong source of strength and encouragement.

Part 2

Expressing Your Faith

There are any number of ways people of faith can express their beliefs in a meaningful way.

In Part 2, you are introduced to four main avenues for spiritual expression, including two public forms (talking about and demonstrating faith to others as well as participating in a church with a community of other believers) and two more private forms (prayer and a selection of spiritual disciplines), that focus on the expression of faith between people and God. Whether you are new to faith or still testing the waters, you get a fuller picture of just what it means to be a person of faith, day in and day out, in the real world.

Chapter 9

Talking and Living Your Faith

In This Chapter

- ◆ Every believer ministers
- ◆ Faithful for the long haul
- ◆ Sharing our faith story
- ◆ Planting seeds of faith

Spiritual concerns and spiritual activities are frequently at the forefront of modern culture. Even so, it can still feel awkward and daunting to express our faith to others and share what God has been doing in our lives. Yet this is one of the most rewarding experiences we can have as believers: giving our friends, co-workers, and loved ones the opportunity to choose for themselves the life of faith we have discovered.

Everyone a Minister

On the evening before I left home to attend seminary, my father took me into his study to give me a gift, something very special. As we walked into his study, he pointed to his desk.

"Your grandmother bought me that desk when I entered college," he said. "She thought I was going to become a minister. Now that you're going to be the minister in the family, I'd like you to have it." In deep gratitude for a gift that represented so much, I took it. And throughout my seminary years, every time I sat down at that desk to write a paper, study for an exam, or craft a sermon, my mind went back to that conversation with my father.

While there may be something genuinely touching about that story, there is also something that's very sad. I have relived that conversation many times over, and every time I replay it, I feel a sense of discomfort. I finally discovered the cause of my discomfort. It was in my dad's statement: "Your grandmother thought I would become a minister."

My father diligently served God for more than 70 years. He has served in the church as a Sunday school teacher, as an elder, as a church council chairman, as the treasurer, and as the Sunday school superintendent. As a public-school teacher, there was never any question of his commitment to God. It wasn't unusual, for example, for my father to give the invocation at school banquets. One year he was the keynote speaker at the National Honor Society's induction ceremony, where he spoke openly about living a life of purity and integrity. He served God in the family; he was a wonderful provider and an ongoing encourager.

> **Beware!**
>
> Even lifelong churchgoers can get caught up in the idea that "ministry" is the job of the church's paid staff. Visiting the sick, holding the hand of someone during a difficult time, talking about the struggles and joys of faith—these are the duties of *all* believers.

Instead of saying, "Your grandmother thought I was going to be a minister," he really should have said, "I *was* a full-time minister. In my daily life, on an ongoing basis, I served God. No, I didn't have the seminary degree. No, I didn't stand in the pulpit every Sunday morning. But make no mistake about it. I was and still am a minister of the gospel."

Ministry is for everyone. It isn't something we're qualified to do only after going to school and studying Greek, Hebrew, systematic theology, and the like. Ministry is something we are enabled and empowered to do because of our relationship with God.

When we minister to the world around us, when we talk about our faith and live out our faith, we are expressing our faith in very real ways the whole world can see—even when we don't always see it ourselves.

The Ministry of Serving God

When I was pastoring the First Baptist Church in Charlotte, Michigan, we went through a church-wide experience called The 50-Day Adventure. Nearly 200 participants read selected passages of Scripture daily and pondered such questions as, "What is the significance of Christ in my life?" "How will my life be different if I will realize that Jesus is with me and in me every moment of every day?" "How might my life change if I become more deeply aware of the presence of my Lord?"

One thing I took away from this experience was that when we become more aware of the presence of God, we strive to serve him, whether in the workplace, in the home, in the church, in the backyard, or in the school. As a result, we become ministers.

As you consider how you can talk about and live out your faith—how you can be a true minister right where you are now—keep the following three points in mind.

Many Ministers, Many Ministries

Not everyone has the same ministry. Not everyone is called to serve God in the same way. Instead, each believer should go through a period of introspection in which, guided by the Holy Spirit, our ministries are affirmed in us.

That's the whole point of Paul's image in Romans 12:4: "We have many parts in the one body, and all these parts have different functions." To put it in an even more explainable way, every part of the body is crucial to its success. Yet that obviously doesn't mean each part is to have the same function. The eyes, the hands, the feet, the ears, all the way down to your tiniest toe—every part of the body has its own function. That's the way we as God's people also minister in the body of Christ.

You may minister by sending someone a note of encouragement. Someone else may minister through visiting a shut-in. Someone may minister by taking meals to a family that's going through tough times. Someone may minister by giving a financial gift to a family facing a crisis. Someone else may minister through in-depth prayer. It doesn't matter. The point is that each of us must be willing to go through a series of questions in which we ask God to illuminate the means of ministry he has designed for us. Ask yourself questions such as ...

- What sorts of things come naturally to me?

- Is there someone God has allowed to enter my life who needs some help?

- What can I do to alleviate a need?

Frankly, I think if we would allow ourselves the freedom to go through this sort of an introspective process, the hurting, the oppressed, the damaged, and the disenfranchised among us would be touched. In addition, many of us would be free from the guilt trips that often accompany the overwhelming feeling that we must do it all. One of the freeing experiences Christians sometimes have when they look into their lives and ask, "God, what have you called me to do?" is to come to the realization that God doesn't call us to do everything—just *something*— for him.

Faith 101

Expressing your faith to others can be easier than you might imagine. In many casual conversations, questions and comments about faith, meaning, God, etc., often arise. Take these opportunities to mention how God is at work in your own life. You're not trying to "save" anyone; you're simply sharing something happening in your life in a nonthreatening, nonpreachy way.

A Long Engagement

When we express our faith by reaching out to others, our ministries will demand ongoing participation.

I realize that you probably couldn't care less about New Testament Greek verb tenses, so I'll keep this brief: the tense of the verbs Paul uses in Romans 12:6–8 indicate that Paul expected the ministries he mentioned to be ongoing and long term. He wasn't talking about something that could be done for a short time and then laid aside. In Paul's eyes, ministry was an eternal calling that began on the day people said "yes" to faith and continued ... well, forever.

In verses 7 and 8, Paul writes, "If it is serving, let him serve; if it is teaching, let him teach; if it is encouraging, let him encourage; if it is contributing to the needs of others, let him give generously; if it is leadership, let him govern diligently; if it is showing mercy, let him do it cheerfully." In other words, "Keep on doing the good works of ministry that you've been doing." We can't minister as though our ministries were old automobiles: sometimes they run, sometimes they don't.

Faith 101 _____

How can you be certain your ministry is ongoing? Begin every week with this prayer:

> Lord, bring into my life one person to whom I can minister. Bring into my life one person who needs a lift, a boost, an uplifting compliment, a helping hand.

You can't help everyone in need. But you can be certain your ministry is ongoing if you ask God to direct and guide you.

A few years ago, I deliberately prayed that God would bring someone in need to whom I could minister. I was concerned that I had not had adequate opportunity to share my faith in Jesus Christ, and I was concerned that most of the people I knew were already Christians. So I prayed, "Lord, expand my ministry beyond the Christian community. Bring individuals into my life who need to know you. Open the doors so that I don't clumsily and awkwardly break them down." Do you know what happened? Over the next 12 months, no less than 3 individuals were brought into my life who needed to hear about the God who loves them.

No Force Required

When it comes to ministry for God, you can't force the action. You can't push yourself through artificial means. You can't psyche yourself into moving. The motivation must be deeper.

First, there is the motivation of love. In Romans 12:9–10, Paul reminds us that without the exemplary quality of love, our ministries will fail. Sincere love that looks out for the needs of other people must be something we continually practice. That sort of love is powerful. It's the one power that is capable of overcoming the evil that sometimes invades Christ's church. That's why Paul wrote, "Let love be sincere. Abhor that which is evil." He knew loving deeds and evil acts could not coexist. Where loving acts of ministry are taking place, evil will flee.

Second, our ministry needs to be motivated by the realization that when we minister, we are not serving people, we are serving Jesus Christ. In Matthew 25:40, Jesus said, "I tell you the truth that whatever you did for one of the least of these my brothers, you did it for me." That's motivating, to think that the real recipient of our ministry is no less than Jesus himself.

Behold!

D. L. Moody, a great evangelist of the nineteenth century, once said:

A great many people have a false idea about the church. They have the idea that the church is a place to rest in, to get into a nicely cushioned pew, and contribute to the charities, to listen to the minister and to do their share in keeping the church out of bankruptcy. The idea that ministry is for them has never entered their mind.

Becoming sensitive to the presence of Jesus will motivate us to serve him with enthusiasm. It will motivate us to roll up our sleeves and jump into the action. It will cause us to be genuinely concerned about each other, to involve ourselves in people's lives, to bear one another's burdens.

Talking About Faith

I have a pastor friend who tells a humorous story about his own pre-ministry attempts to share his faith with others. During one of his college summers, he was employed in a factory. As a young man preparing for the ministry, he spent a great deal of time talking to other people about Jesus. In fact, before the summer was over, he had individually invited every employee to make a commitment to Christ. So open was he that they called him "Preacher." In his enthusiasm to share his witness for Christ, however, he allowed some of his work to lapse—so much so that his boss actually called him "the creeping Jesus."

The next summer he found another job. This time, he worked on a construction crew. When he accepted the job, he decided he wasn't going to make the same mistake again. Remembering that his lackadaisical work habits may have actually hurt his witness with his former boss, he determined that this time he would work hard. In fact, he worked harder than anyone else. He seldom took breaks. He seldom conversed. He was going to impress everyone with his work ethic. Finally, at the end of the summer, one of his co-workers approached him and said, "I understand that you're planning on becoming a minister."

"Yes, I am," he eagerly responded.

His co-worker replied, "You'll never make it. You don't talk about religion enough!"

Sometimes you just can't win.

Make no mistake about it. Talking honestly about your faith can be a difficult task. And sometimes—no matter what you do, how you act, or what you say—you find yourself wondering, *Have I done it correctly? Have I done enough?*

We've Got a Job to Do

In Romans 10, Paul has a heavy heart. He's wondering if he's done enough in terms of reaching out to his own people, the land of Israel. Paul had met the Messiah, Jesus Christ. He had a dramatic, experiential encounter with God on the road to Damascus. And nothing concerned him any more than the realization that his very own people had chosen to reject Jesus as the Messiah. In Romans 9 and 10, Paul goes to great lengths to remind his readers that God has not abandoned his people. There is still the opportunity for them to come to know God.

My guess is that everyone reading this book could probably provide their own lengthy list of individuals about whom they are equally concerned: co-workers, friends, neighbors, relatives—people who share your hunger for meaning and satisfaction in life but who have not yet said "yes" to faith in God. Like Paul, we are genuinely concerned for those whom we love the most.

Paul makes four points we can keep in mind as we endeavor to express our faith to those around us.

Tell the Story

Paul says reaching our world happens when we're willing to tell the story. In Romans 10:14, he asks a rhetorical question for which the answer is quite clear: "How can they believe in the one of whom they have not heard? And how can they hear without someone preaching to them?"

I almost wish we could translate that term *preaching* another way. In most of our minds, when we hear that word, our minds fill with some rather negative images. We think of the child who says to the parent— or the student who says to the teacher—"Quit preaching to me." It brings to mind images of a person standing in a position of power, hovering over us, maybe even shouting at us to get his or her point across. But *preaching* here is a word missing those negative connotations. Simply put, it means "to tell" or "to announce the good news."

To be honest, I don't think it's possible to be an effective witness for our faith without telling the story of Jesus.

I once met a man in my first church who insisted that the best way to tell others about faith was simply to model good behavior. It's a nice idea. But as important as good behavior may be, it's not enough. Millions of nice people on this planet don't know God. A lot of honest people on this planet know nothing about what it means to be a person of faith who has a living relationship with God. At some point or another, we must move beyond the modeling of nice behavior and tell the story of God's love.

No, that doesn't mean we have to corner individuals, pin them down, and tell the story in all sorts of rude, obnoxious, or disrespectful ways. But in our own way, when the time is right, and the Spirit is moving us, we must be willing to let the story pass through our lips.

It might be a relief for you to hear what I've discovered: many people are eagerly waiting for us to tell them the story. As I look back and think of three personal friends I led to Christ, in each case, when the opportunity came for me to tell them the story, the response was virtually the same: "I thought you were never going to tell me."

Share and Share Alike

Paul reminds his readers that it's every believer's responsibility to share the story of their faith.

Paul is writing to a Gentile audience about Jewish people who do not know Jesus Christ. You can well imagine that many of them would have assumed the primary responsibility for delivering this particular message sat completely on Paul's broad shoulders. After all, he was the one with the Jewish background. These were his people. He could relate to their culture. He could understand their history. But Paul is careful to remind his readers that he does not stand alone in this adventure. Everyone shares in the task.

Behold!

Paul must have knocked people out of their first-century sandals when he wrote about the importance of ministry. Just a few years earlier, he had been so vehemently opposed to Christianity that he was personally overseeing the killing of Christians. Now, he was truly a new man, encouraging all believers to reach out in love to others—regardless of past experiences, economic differences, or cultural differences. Paul did a complete 180-degree turn in his life, becoming a living testimony to the transforming power of faith.

I've often thought about some of the songs we Christians sing about reaching our world. And I've thought that if we rewrote the songs with an added touch of honesty, they could be quite different. Because despite some of the songs we sing, many of us are very, very reluctant to step out and publicly talk about our personal faith—even if the "public" is just a couple of our closest friends.

For example, in the churches I've been in, we sing one hymn that says, "I love to tell the story of Jesus and his love …" But if we're really being honest, we might add "… just so I'm doing it in the cozy and comfortable environment of the church where there are others who think like I do." Or what about this one: "Go tell it on the mountain … because no one lives up there anyway, and it's a safe place to go."

Let me say this as delicately and lovingly and yet as honestly as I possibly can: don't expect any professional minister to do the job of ministry without you. It won't always be easy or comfortable to talk about something as personal as faith. But there's at least one aspect of sharing our faith we don't have to worry about: none of us has to convince anyone of anything. That part of the equation is in God's hands.

In God's Hands

You may be the most winning speaker to ever utter the word *faith*. Or you may feel so self-conscious about discussing your beliefs that you stutter and stammer your way through the simplest discussion of faith. But the fact is that, no matter how gifted we may or may not be when it comes to expressing our faith, people have to come to their own conclusions about what we have to say. Some will believe. Some won't. Some will seriously consider what we've said. Some will blow us off.

I've discovered that the possibility that our message will be rejected is enough to dampen the fervor for many believers. But you are not responsible for the decisions anyone else will make. You cannot force people to open their lives up to God. (Besides, imagine how you'd have responded if someone had tried that with you.) You are only responsible for giving them the choice. For the process to have any real credibility and value, listeners must always be able to choose between saying "yes" to faith and saying "no."

Faith 101

The Bible tells us that when we plant seeds of faith in others' lives, we will have no idea how or when those seeds might actually take root and flourish. Your conversation today could lead to someone else's conversation tomorrow or next year.

I have had many individuals say "no" to me. It's discouraging and frustrating, there's no doubt about it. But I have also had many individuals say "yes." How will we know which response we'll get if we don't even give folks the chance?

Closing the Deal

Let me leave you with one more thought. Imagine walking into an automobile dealership and looking over a new car. After a few minutes, a salesman walks up and offers to demonstrate the car's many great features. He opens the doors, explains everything on the instrument panel, and describes the luxurious interior. He pops open the hood and goes into detail about the intricacies of the engine, the fuel efficiency, and the brand's outstanding repair record.

You're convinced. You need this car. (Well, you at least *want* this car.) And just as those very words are about to roll off your lips, the salesman smiles, says, "Thanks for stopping by," and walks away without ever asking the most important question of all: "Would you like to *buy* this car?"

Sadly enough, that's sometimes how we act when it comes to expressing our faith. We exemplify Christian behavior. We arouse a person's interest. We even pass on some information. But we never allow others the luxury of making the choice between the possibilities. Expressing our faith and reaching our world means giving people the opportunity to accept or reject, to say "yes" or "no." We must not make the choice for them by robbing them of the privilege.

The Least You Need to Know

- Every person of faith is a minister on God's behalf.
- Each of us has unique gifts that we bring to our personal ministries.
- Talking about faith may not always be comfortable, yet it is something each believer should be prepared to do.
- Ultimately, the responses of others to our stories of faith are in God's hands.

Chapter 10

Why Prayer Matters

In This Chapter

- ◆ The ingredients of effective prayers
- ◆ What prayer can accomplish
- ◆ Jesus' model for powerful praying

So far, I've talked a bit about how prayer and the Bible go hand in hand in our private times. But I haven't touched on just how prayer helps us express our faith.

Prayer is a privilege, the opportunity to bring our every thought and feeling before God and know he will hear and respond. Prayer can also be an incredible source of strength and spiritual power. Yet prayer can also feel daunting, overwhelming: *What do I tell God? How do I say it? And how do I know he's really listening to me?* In this chapter, we consider those questions as well as the valuable role prayer can play in the life of faithful people.

What Prayer Is ... and Isn't

James 5:16 says that "the prayer of a righteous man is powerful and effective." Sounds good, huh? But what is prayer? Does it really work? And if it does, *how* does it work? And what role does prayer play in a faithful life?

First things first: prayer is a conversation with God. That's it. It doesn't require that you talk to God with a deep, James Earl Jones voice. It doesn't have to sound pious or be filled with long, religious-sounding words or include "thees" and "thous." In fact, it doesn't have to be spoken aloud at all. It just has to be an honest and intimate expression of ourselves toward God. That takes care of our side of the conversation.

We also need to be willing to listen for God's response. Chances are, God won't speak to us from a burning bush or a bolt of lightning. Those kinds of "telegrams from God" are for extraordinary conversations. The stuff of everyday prayer is more subtle, more personal. In Bible terms, this kind of prayer requires listening for God's "still, small voice."

This is the kind of voice God used when he first called out to a boy named Samuel, described in 1 Samuel 3. It was night, and Samuel was trying to sleep. But he kept being awakened by the distant sound of someone calling his name. Each time, Samuel got out of bed and ran to Eli, the priest who was watching over him. But each time, Eli told him, "I didn't call you." After it happened three times, Eli realized that God must be calling the boy. So the priest told him, "Go and lie down, and if he calls you, say, 'Speak, Lord, for your servant is listening.'" (1 Samuel 3:9)

Call it "prayerful listening," if you like.

Up Close and Personal

An effective prayer is characterized by closeness. When Jesus prayed, he called God his father. And the Aramaic word Jesus used for "father" was *abba*, which could be translated "daddy" in contemporary English. ("1970s Swedish pop group" is not an accurate translation.) *Abba* is one of the first words a first-century child would have learned, a word full of affection and intimacy.

Even though Jesus truly was God's son—in a way no one else can ever be—he isn't the only one who can approach God on such intimate terms. In Romans 8:15, Paul makes an interesting observation concerning *abba*: "You received a Spirit of sonship," he writes to the early church. "And by him we cry, 'Abba, Father.'" Paul is saying that when you commit yourself to a life of faith, you are adopted by God. You become a part of his family, spiritual sons and daughters. Because of that new relationship, we truly can call God "Dad!"

Does it feel odd to think this way about the Creator of the universe? Here's an illustration that might help put it into perspective: one of the most popular photographs of President John F. Kennedy shows him seated at his desk in the Oval Office, surrounded by government officials. But on the president's face is a look of amusement. Why? His young son, John Jr., is playing under his desk. At the time, Kennedy was one of the most important and powerful men in the world. But the closeness he shared with his son allowed John-John to interrupt his dad in the middle of national business.

That's the same sort of relationship we can have with God. He's never too busy. He's never preoccupied. He wants his children close to him.

Faith 101

Many people set aside time for prayer just before they go to bed at night. To encourage yourself to wake up in an attitude of prayer, avoid ending your nightly prayer with the traditional "Amen" closing. You might be surprised to discover that you'll wake up in the morning with the sense that your prayer was left unfinished, and you'll start the day concluding the prayer you began the night before.

Great Expectations

It's one thing to have an intellectual assent to the power of God. But when that belief is allowed to move from our minds and into our hearts, when we approach God with the expectation that he really does hear our prayers and that he really does want to respond, prayer then has the power to enrich and enlarge our faith. It can have a tremendous impact:

- It frees us from the need to try to control every situation.

- It frees us from worry, enabling us to leave matters in God's hands.

- It fills us with confidence, knowing that if God chooses, he can intervene or interrupt the situation.

Prayer anticipates God's active involvement in our lives. Faithful prayers expect that their prayers really can change things.

Bold Is Beautiful

Faith in the power of prayer is naturally going to affect what we say to God and how we say it. The author of Hebrews wrote, "Let us then approach the throne of grace with confidence, so that we may receive mercy and find grace to help us in our time of need." (Hebrews 4:16)

Confidence here is sometimes translated *boldness.* It was the same word used to refer to the freedom of speech citizens enjoyed in ancient Greece. It was the right to speak up without fear, to be honest without repercussion. Citizens could say exactly what was on their minds.

We should feel similarly emboldened when we approach God in prayer. Such confidence isn't arrogance or cockiness. It's openness and honesty with God.

Acceptance Speech

Whether we start praying as children or adults, our first attempts at prayer often end up being a list of requests—sometimes very serious requests, but requests nonetheless:

♦ "Dear God, please bless Mommy and Daddy and please let Santa know I *really* want that blue-sparkle drum set for Christmas."

♦ "God, please help me find the person I can spend the rest of my life with."

♦ "God. I can't believe I just got fired. Please help me find a job that will keep a roof over our heads. And soon. Please."

I don't want in any way to minimize the very real needs that often lead us to approach God in prayer. After all, it's only natural. We're most inclined to turn to God when we're feeling helpless and needy on our own.

Yet while our effective prayers carry with them an attitude of expectation or anticipation, they also have an attitude of acceptance. In other words, we approach God saying, "This is what I want and what I think I need, God. I'm asking you to provide it. But if it isn't what's best in the long run, help me accept whatever comes."

Faith 101

I once was driving through Columbus, Ohio, when I decided to stop for the night at a Red Roof Inn. The front-desk clerk said they were full, but she could arrange a room for me at the local Hilton for the same price. Sounded good to me, so I drove to the Hilton. There, I learned that all the Hilton's standard rooms were full. "But," the clerk added, "I could give you a suite—at the Red Roof price, of course." That's the way an accepting prayer works.

Sometimes God responds to our prayers with, "Absolutely! You're ready for this now." Sometimes God says, "The time isn't quite right yet." And even if God says no, there's always something better. God only acts in your best interest. And even if he allows circumstances to occur that could be painful, I believe that, in the end, we will come out better for it.

Powerful Praying

Prayer can do many things in our lives. I'd like to highlight three basic things you should expect prayer to accomplish:

- First, prayer deepens our awareness of our need for God. It leads us to the conclusion that we cannot make it without God. On our own, we are limited, often inadequate and flawed human beings. We need God's help.

- Second, prayer nurtures knowledge. Prayer enables us to know God in a more personal way. Like a conversation with a friend over a cup of coffee, you become better acquainted with one another. You become absorbed in a rewarding and mutual friendship.

- Third, prayer produces power. An effective prayer may not necessarily alter some of the chaotic circumstances in your life, but at the very least it will produce the power necessary for you to cope.

> **Beware!**
>
> Prayers aren't magic words or secret codes that somehow get God to give us goodies. The impact of prayer on the pray-er's life can't be judged solely by the immediate material or emotional "payoff" we might receive. Faithful prayer deepens our relationship with God, regardless of the results that may or may not be immediately obvious.

Lessons from the Lord's Prayer

When my co-author Bob and his wife, Sylvia, moved into their current home, they loved the fact that it came with several very well-tended gardens that included a mix of herbs, perennial flowers, flowering vines, and butterfly-friendly bushes. But neither Bob nor Sylvia knows much about plants. It was just a matter of time before all the lovely garden plots began to get overrun with a dazzling variety of weeds and wild-flowers. Bob can't tell a future flower from a current weed, so he picked up the phone and started looking for a gardening professional.

> **Faith 101**
>
> If you've never tried praying before, consider using the ACT model:
> - **A**cknowledge that God *is* God—and that he can meet your needs.
> - **C**onfess past mistakes, clearing the way for God to work in your life today.
> - **T**hank God for being present in your life and hearing your prayer.
>
> Many people still find it useful to keep this model in mind, even after years—*many* years—of praying.

That's the way many of us operate. We look to an expert—someone who knows what they're doing, someone with a track record of success.

Evidently, that's the same way Jesus' disciples felt. During the 3 years of Jesus' public ministry, his disciples saw how his prayers revitalized and refreshed him. So they asked him for a crash course in how they should pray. Jesus helped them out with a model prayer they could follow. In slightly different forms, it's commonly known as the Lord's Prayer and it is still being prayed today:

> Father, hallowed be your name, your kingdom come. Give us each day our daily bread. Forgive us our sins, for we also forgive everyone who sins against us. And lead us not into temptation. (Luke 11:2–4)

This is kind of like the Gettysburg Address of prayers: short, simple, and to the point. It won't win any awards for outstanding oratory or grand theological thought, but that's not why we pray anyway. And short and sweet as they were, these four sentences held the seeds of everything profound and meaningful that could come later, as the disciples' faith deepened, their relationship with God developed, and their prayer skills improved.

Let's take a closer look.

Behold!
Some church traditions use the word *debts* or *trespasses* instead of *sins* when reciting the Lord's Prayer. There is no right word choice here, although *trespasses* and *sins* are probably clearer and more to the point than *debts*.

A Loving Embrace

Jesus begins his prayer by calling God "Father," using the word *Abba*— "Daddy"—I talked about earlier. God is not some distant unknowable. *Abba* describes a father who is tender, gentle, affirming, understanding, and kind.

I realize that, sadly, not everyone can relate personally to this image of a loving father. Many people have had broken or abusive relationships with their earthly fathers, making the idea of a heavenly father a bit hard to grasp. Yet despite our own experiences, it's likely that we still know what *should* have happened at home, what kind of relationship we *should* have had with our fathers. God is a father who fits the ideal.

Acknowledge God's Character

When it comes to understanding the nature of God, you can think of one of two extremes. One is to see God as CEO of some distant megacorporation. He's important, in charge, and unapproachable. The other extreme is to bring God so far down to Earth that there's little difference between the Creator of the universe and the guy behind the counter at the gas station who jokes with you every time you come in. God's our buddy. We hang together.

Jesus recognized some solid middle ground between these two extremes. While he could call God "Daddy," he could also call him "hallowed"—holy and separate from his creation.

No matter how close we grow to God as we explore faith, we can't forget that God is still *God*. Why is that so important? Because if God is not both holy and wholly different from us, what in the world are we putting our faith in? There's no *God* left to trust—just someone who is more like an invisible friend.

Our perception of a person's character has a direct impact on how we respond to them—even if that individual is God. Thinking about God's hallowedness when we pray can help us get off on the right spiritual foot.

Ask for What You Need

According to a 2004 report from the Population Division of the Department of Economic and Social Affairs of the United Nations, there are more than 6.5 billion people in our world. By the year 2050, that number is expected to rise to 9.1 billion.

That's a lot of people. And yet the most astonishing, amazing, surprising, and perhaps even shocking piece of good news is that God is aware of each person's needs. And he's not only aware; he's also concerned.

Beware!

Because God knows our needs and our circumstances, some believers assume they never need to voice their desires to him. But our relationship with God grows, our reliance on him deepens, when we actually communicate with him about the things in life that are important to us. God wants to hear from you.

He cares about the car that won't start. The course you can't pass. The marriage that's dying. The checking account that's overdrawn. The deadline at the office. The diagnosis we can't bear to hear. Concerns both trivial and traumatizing.

It's said that when Raphael, one of the great artists of the Renaissance, worked on a new painting, he placed a candle at the top of his canvas to keep the shadows at bay. He didn't want any dark spots to appear on the canvas. He wanted the picture to be brilliant and bright all the time.

If your prayers seem dark and dreary, shadowed by the thought *God doesn't care*, it's time to light a candle of your own. Give yourself a daily reminder that God does care—and he is able to meet our desire for daily bread, as well as all our other needs. As Jesus pointed out in Matthew 6:25–34: God takes care of the flowers in the field. He looks out for the sparrows in the field. Dare to ask for what you need. Then have faith that God will take care of you.

Admit Your Mistakes

This is tough. No one likes to admit their mistakes—especially when "mistakes" become "sins," those missteps that actually raise a wall between us and God. But sin is real. And if it's left unaddressed, it has the capacity to shut God out of our lives.

What is it about sin that keeps us from God? Remember God's hallowed nature. God is holy. Sin runs in direct contradiction to who God is.

That's why it can be so beneficial to come to prayer with a humble spirit and a willingness to look hard at our lives and admit where we've fallen short. Once we've cleared the boards of our past mistakes, we can come to God without any barriers standing in the way.

Forgive Others

Communication with God may be personal, but it's never private. It carries with it the relationships in which we're involved every day of our lives. As a result, a broken or damaged relationship is going to throw a stumbling block into the path of our faith.

Jesus recognized this interrelationship, which is perhaps why he was quick to include in his prayer, "Forgive us our sins, for we also forgive those who sin against us." The dagger has to be put down. The sharply spoken word has to stop. The unjust accusation must be faced. A relationship that's not healed can be a wall between us and God.

Faith 101

The fact that God forgives us our sins can be a powerful aid to us forgiving others. If we're honest with ourselves, we'll admit we've probably done some things that might be pretty hard to forgive in God's eyes. Yet he does forgive us. With the love and understanding he provides, we, too, can forgive those who have done hard-to-forgive things to us.

Seek God's Strength

Jesus concludes the model prayer in verse 4: "Lead us not into temptation." Jesus' words mean, "Don't let me be tempted beyond my capacity to cope. Through your grace, God, get me through it."

For some of us, that is the struggle. So many different things can tempt us in so many ways. And it isn't hard to come up with any number of justifications to explain or excuse our behavior. Yet where temptation is concerned, consistent compromising chips away at our faith and negatively affects our prayer lives.

Maybe it all comes down to facing up to the options. What can we do? Well, we can be embarrassed or ashamed about our temptations and do nothing. Or wanting to deepen our prayer life and grow in our faith, we can work on the problems. The first option, remaining embarrassed or ashamed, accomplishes nothing in our lives. In fact, it becomes a hindrance to our growing at all. But the second response can lead to the refreshment and revitalization that come with living a life of faith.

The Least You Need to Know

- ◆ Prayer is a conversation with a loving God.

- ◆ Praying encourages us to turn control of our situations and our lives over to God.

◆ Accepting prayers ask God to meet our needs while also seeking his help in accepting whatever the future might bring.

◆ Praying deepens our dependence on God, brings us closer to him, and produces power in the world.

◆ Jesus gave us the Lord's Prayer as an example of what an effective prayer should be.

Chapter 11

Exploring Spiritual Disciplines

In This Chapter

- ◆ Exercising a new set of spiritual muscles
- ◆ Praying with power
- ◆ Faithful fasting
- ◆ Serving God by serving others

Discipline doesn't typically sound like it's going to be much fun. And although it wouldn't be 100 percent accurate to call spiritual disciplines "fun," they can be enriching elements in our walk of faith. In fact, these more reflective, more quiet ways of expressing our faith can actually be highly visible and powerful reflections of God's work in our lives.

Growing What We Plant

The story is told that, once upon a time, a group of men from a large Midwestern metropolis left their jobs in high-rise office buildings, moved to the prairie, and bought some farmland.

"We're farmers!" they congratulated each other. And all summer long they went out to their fields to watch their crops grow. But when September rolled around, their fields were filled with goldenrod and all kinds of wildflowers and weeds.

"Huh," said one of the men, perplexed. "Where's my corn?"

"Corn?" his companion muttered. "Why aren't there any beans in my field?"

"Beans?" said a third man, who was equally baffled. "I was hoping for potatoes. I'll be darned if I can find a single spud out there."

And each of them wondered what they could have possibly done wrong.

I'm afraid that a lot of believers in churches today have much in common with these city-slickers. Like those men, they purchase the land, but they do nothing to cultivate a field in which growth could take place. And in the end, they're left wondering, *Where's my spiritual growth? Where's my deepening sense of joy?*

Just because someone calls himself a farmer doesn't mean corn will magically appear. He must cultivate the ground, plant the seed, water the plants, and allow nature to take its course. With care, the harvest will come. This is the way it is with spiritual growth as well. Spiritual disciplines can help us become more mature believers, with a deep and abiding connection to God.

I won't cover them all here, but spiritual disciplines include such things as *intercessory prayer*, fasting, contemplation, and solitude. They go beyond the basics of prayer and Bible reading to deepen our faith, introduce us to new aspects of God, and prepare our hearts to be further transformed by the power of God. They don't create transformation in and of themselves. Instead, they bring us to a place of openness before God that allows change to happen.

def•i•ni•tion

Intercessory prayer is prayer prayed for the benefit of others, asking God to intervene on another's behalf to help or to heal.

Walking With God

I've often wondered why the Bible uses the word *walk* to describe our experience of faith in God. I think the conclusions I've discovered have a lot to do with the important role spiritual disciplines can play in our life.

Here's what I've concluded: a walk indicates you're going someplace. You are not standing still, you are not idle or complacent. There is an activity unfolding.

In your relationship with God, standing still leads to stagnation. In your relationship with God, disciples are called to be on the move, going where God is taking them, following and responding.

Walk also indicates a sense of peace-fulness while on the move. Contrast a walking pace with running feet. When we run, exhaustion can set in. But in our walk with God, as we are moving to the place he wants to take us, there's a sense of inner peace and tranquility. There's the realization that the one who has called us and is leading us is also with us. Far from having to hurry the pace along, we rely on his timing.

> **Behold!**
>
> Everybody thinks of changing humanity and nobody thinks of changing himself.
>
> —Leo Tolstoy

Finally, *walk* carries the idea of a daily experience. It is something we do every day. What happens when we don't walk every day? We risk coming to the point at which we don't walk at all. Our limbs become fragile. Our muscles lose their firmness. The slightest physical exertion becomes too much to handle. And so ... we stop. In a similar way, our encounter with God needs to be a daily affair.

I discussed in Chapter 7 the value of making room in our lives and our schedules for quiet time with God, so I won't labor the point here. I'll just say that if you're struggling with that aspect of your spiritual life, try thinking of it as an opportunity rather than an obligation.

When Marilyn and I dated during our 4 years of college, I can never remember getting ready for a date and thinking to myself, *Gee, I have to do this. I have to take Marilyn out to dinner tonight,* or, *I have to escort her to a movie*, or, *We have to go to that game together.* There was no "have to" about it. Instead, there was a sense of excitement and anticipation. I loved her, and I enjoyed being in her presence.

Behold!

Want to get away to explore some more serious spiritual disciplines? Consider a brief stay at a Christian retreat. Nearly every state has a number of Christian retreat centers and monasteries where the faithful can escape the bustle of the world to turn their attention completely to God for an extended time. (Not surprisingly, the Internet can be a great tool for finding such retreat opportunities. Start by searching for the phrase "Christian retreats.")

Experiencing God works in a similar way. The walk with him that is so critical to knowing and doing his will grows as we spend time with God, listening to him and getting to know him.

The idea of walking is key to the following spiritual disciplines. They require slow effort, thoughtfulness, and intentionality. They should not be hurried or you'll sacrifice the benefits that come from seriously slowing down, closing out the world around you, and turning your full attention quietly toward God.

Intercessory Prayer

Intercession might be defined as love on its knees in prayer for others. It is pleading to God on behalf of the needs of someone else.

Intercession can be one of the most exciting, creative, and rewarding experiences in the Christian life. No matter where you are, no matter what's going on around you, you can pray for people and concerns around the world. You can be a vital, integral part of a worldwide ministry though the power of intercessory prayer, creating a powerful foundation that allows God to work in mighty ways.

Praying from the Bible

Reading a psalm or any passage of Scripture might spur thoughts and concerns for others—people you know as well as people you don't know. Read the Word slowly, meditating on it verse by verse, and it will provide you with a number of prayer opportunities.

For example, Psalm 37:34 begins, "Wait for the Lord and keep his way." It's a simple verse that might lead you to pray for patience for yourself as well as patience and faith for those who have trouble "waiting for the Lord" and obeying his commands.

The Bible also is full of blessings and prayers of blessings, and we can use these to pray for others. For example, consider this passage as a prayer: "I pray also that the eyes of your heart may be enlightened in order that you may know the hope to which he has called you, the riches of his glorious inheritance in the saints, and his incomparably great power for us who believe." (Ephesians 1:18–19)

And when you don't know what to pray, remember this verse from Romans 8:26: "The Spirit helps us in our weakness. We do not know what we ought to pray for, but the Spirit himself intercedes for us with groans that words cannot express." When our words run dry, when the needs are too overwhelming to even mention, we can trust that God nonetheless hears the deepest prayers of our hearts.

Faith 101

When you pray, consider having a Bible, a pen, and a notebook on hand. Find a quiet place to pray. Try praying aloud. But also don't be bothered by periods of silence, pauses when you're not sure what or how to pray next. (Praying aloud can also help keep your mind from wandering to work or family issues or what you're going to pull out of the freezer for dinner.) If there is a pressing need of your own on your mind, offer it to God in prayer, too.

Praying for Healing and Acceptance

There is no harm whatsoever in asking God for what you want. In fact, that should be a regular part of our prayer life. If he has a different plan in store, he will tell you. But he wants his people to come to him and lay their desires before him. That's what happens when we pray.

If a loved one is ill in body or spirit, feel free to pray for healing. Intercede on their behalf when they cannot or will not pray for themselves. But also pray that God will allow you to accept his answer—no matter what that answer may be.

Faith 101

Service doesn't have to occur with grand gestures. I know a woman who purchases dolls at rummage sales, cleans them up, sews new clothes for them, dresses them, and sends them off to a hospital in Haiti. There, the dolls are given away to the children who come in for treatment. A simple, small gesture ... with an immediate result.

Praying for Change

How many of us know someone who is, apparently, making mistake after mistake in life? Through the power of intercessory prayer, we can ask God to change their hearts and minds, bringing them to the point where the light will dawn and they will say "yes" to faith.

Fasting for God

What is fasting? Typically, fasting means abstaining from food and drink to focus on a period of spiritual growth. We deny something of the flesh to glorify God, enhance our spirit, and go deeper in our prayer life. Fasting isn't commanded by Christ or required by Scripture; however, the book of Acts records believers fasting before they made important decisions. Fasting and prayer are often linked together in the Bible.

Too often, the focus of fasting is on the lack of food. (It's never easier to get hung up on the mental image of a hamburger than when you're specifically trying to do without.) Of course, food doesn't have to be the thing we're giving up. The purpose of fasting is to take our eyes off the things of this world and instead focus on God. Fasting is a way to demonstrate to God and to ourselves that we are serious about our relationship with him.

Anything you can temporarily give up to better focus on God can be considered a fast. (This is the whole point of the Lenten ritual of giving up something for the 40 days prior to Easter.) Fasting should be limited to a set time, especially when the fasting is from food; obviously, extended periods of time without eating can be harmful to the body. Fasting is not intended to punish our flesh, but to turn our hearts and minds toward God.

How does giving up food—or anything else, for that matter—help us focus more on God? It's pretty simple, really. If we're abstaining from food for a day or 2, every time we think about food during that time period—and we'll certainly be thinking about food—we will be reminded of why we're not eating. We can choose to say a prayer at that point, making our communication with God ongoing throughout the fast, or we can simply use our thoughts and hunger pangs as little reminders of our desire to grow in faith and to grow closer to the God we serve.

> **Beware!**
>
> Fasting can be a powerful and beneficial spiritual discipline. But it was never intended to be a biblical approach to weight loss. We shouldn't fast to lose weight, but rather to gain deeper fellowship with God.

Everyone can temporarily give up something to focus on God. Even unplugging the television for a period of time can be an effective fast.

Service to Others

As with most, if not all, of the spiritual disciplines, service and submission go very much against the grain of our culture. However, when we make them a part of our life, we find incredible freedom from a life of manipulation, arrogance, and resentment.

Jesus taught that the way up is to go down. He taught his first disciples that the secret to becoming great is to become the servant of all. What does a servant look like? Consider this description of Jesus' servanthood in Philippians 2:7–11: Jesus "made himself nothing, taking the very nature of a servant, being made in human likeness. And being found in appearance as a man, he humbled himself and became obedient to death—even death on a cross!"

That's far from the kind of glamorous acts that get recognition and public attention these days. And yet, in God's eyes, servanthood is rewarded like nothing else: "Therefore God exalted him to the highest place," Philippians continues, "and gave him the name that is above every name, that at the name of Jesus every knee should bow, in heaven and on earth and under the earth, and every tongue confess that Jesus Christ is Lord, to the glory of God the Father."

Service for Jesus wasn't just a series of acts or the willingness to do a few miracles here and there. It was his guiding orientation for all of life.

One of my co-author Bob's favorite movies is the, in his words, "shamefully underappreciated" remake of *The Razor's Edge*, starring Bill Murray in his first dramatic role. (The movie might be overdue for a comeback, thanks to Murray's more recent dramatic roles.) In the film, Murray has discovered the value of orienting his life around servanthood. And even though his character becomes a follower of Eastern religions, his approach to life is similar to that of a follower of Jesus.

In one scene, Murray is sitting on a boat in a busy Asian harbor, trying to understand what it means to approach every activity, no matter how menial, with a servant's heart. His mentor has him washing the morning dishes in the river. His mentor asks him something along the lines of, "Are you finding this spiritually fulfilling?"

Murray laughs good-naturedly. "Oh, sure," he says with a wry grin. "I think I'm feeling it." At this point in the story, he's open to the possibility, but he's not yet entirely convinced.

The fact is that the mentor's guidance is also in line with something Paul wrote to the Colossians: "Whatever you do, whether in word or in deed, do it all in the name of the Lord Jesus, giving thanks to God the Father through him." (Colossians 3:17) Our significance isn't in our great achievements or our renown; it's found in our approach to some of life's smallest or most menial tasks. Our servanthood isn't measured so much by what we do as by what our attitude is when we do it.

In our work situations—maybe even in our homes—we may sometimes feel like telling those around us, "You're not the boss of me." But when we choose to follow Christ in service, we take the opposite approach, telling people, "You *are* the boss of me." We choose to make ourselves available and, often, vulnerable. (Sometimes, we might even be taken advantage of.)

Tips for Service

As you practice the discipline of service, consider these suggestions:

- Ask yourself if you are doing this service to please God or to please yourself or others.

- Don't make a point of highlighting what you're doing. At the same time, don't be upset if someone finds out about it.

- Keep tabs on your natural desire for recognition or appreciation.

- Be open to serve anyone you meet.

Servanthood and Submission

Submission is almost as unpopular a word these days as *servanthood*. But the two go hand in hand. An attitude of submission—toward others and toward God—provides a solid foundation for subsequent acts of servanthood.

If submission sounds a little uncomfortable, a little too demeaning, consider these positive examples of submission: a piano student submits herself to the direction of her instructor. She doesn't say, "I think I'll begin with this piece of music because it's my favorite." She follows her teacher's direction and learns her scales and chord progressions. Likewise, a basketball player submits himself to the direction of his coach. He doesn't say, "I can't make free throws, so I'll just practice my around-the-back-reverse-layup." He asks the coach how to improve his form and rhythm in shooting his free throws.

So it is in the spiritual life. We submit ourselves to each other in confession, in openness to correction, in service, and in obedience "out of reverence for Christ." (Ephesians 5:21) In submission, we reject the idea that we are above anyone. We acknowledge that we are all under the authority of the King of kings.

The Least You Need to Know

◆ Practicing spiritual disciplines can develop spiritual muscles and bring new depth to a relationship with God.

◆ Intercessory prayers give the faithful the ability to minister around the world through their quiet time with God.

◆ Fasting turns our hearts and minds to God with renewed attention.

◆ In serving others with an attitude of submission, believers model the character of Jesus Christ.

Chapter 12

Choosing Church

In This Chapter

- ◆ Identifying your perfect church
- ◆ Finding strength in church
- ◆ Attributes of a godly church

We all have a better chance of remaining faithful and growing in our faith if we join with a community of other believers—in other words, if we plug in to a church. But for some people, *church* brings to mind images of dullness or old rituals that just don't mesh with the kind of vibrant, living faith they've encountered in Jesus Christ. There's no doubt about it: churches aren't perfect. Yet their value for our spiritual development far outweighs any drawbacks.

In this chapter, we take a look at how to find a church where you can fit in and what to expect when you get there.

Your Perfect Church

What would the perfect church look like to you? For the moment, forget architecture, the size of the congregation, even the style of worship. What would the *atmosphere* of the church be like? What would it feel like to enter the doors as a stranger? What would draw you back, week after week, when golf games, exercise classes, kids' soccer practice, shopping trips, work responsibilities, friends, and the rest of life could so easily pull you away? How would the people act toward one another? How would they respond to you, a newcomer?

Just for the sake of discussion, imagine this: as you walk from your car to the front door, somebody you don't know says hello. As you enter the church, people smile, shake your hand, direct you to the information desk, and tell you they're glad you could make it today.

They don't clump together in tight little groups that shut out everyone else. If they happen to be wearing suits and dresses when you felt like jeans and gym shoes, they don't care. If the shade of your skin makes you stand out from the crowd, they don't care about that, either, and they don't stare. Instead, they go out of their way to make you feel as if you belong, no matter how different you might look on the outside or feel on the inside.

Faith 101

Unless you have an unusually negative experience, it's very hard to judge whether or not a particular church is right for you after just a single visit. If possible, give a potential church at least two or three tries before deciding whether or not it's a good fit for you.

In a perfect church, everyone's unique gifts and talents are identified and put to use. The members make personal commitments and stand by them. Honesty, sincerity, and trust are the hallmarks for every gathering, whether it's the Tuesday night book discussion group or the annual all-church business meeting. The church has strong spiritual goals every member can describe and support with enthusiasm.

Sound like a fairy tale? Or do you have even greater expectations for your perfect church? Would it take these traits—and even more—to get you to walk through the doors of a church again?

The Problem with "Perfect"

The problem with our idea of the perfect church is that it must, by necessity, contain pews or chairs full of imperfect people. There's no way around it. None of us on this earth has attained the elusive state of "sinless perfection."

Even if a flock of perfect churchgoers existed, their church would still face hurdles simply because our individual ideas about what makes a church perfect differ significantly. While some members thrive on hymns from the 1920s, others yearn for songs from the 1960s, while another generation is bored by anything less than cutting-edge multimedia. Even if we were all somehow perfect, our different educational backgrounds, family experiences, and personal tastes pretty much guarantee that "perfect" doesn't necessarily mean "compatible."

New believers of any age who have not had previous church experience often attend their first service expecting a lot more than they get. Maybe they've been forewarned that the choir won't always sing on key. Maybe they've heard that the

> **Behold!**
>
> There are well over a dozen major denominational groups in the United States, which can be further broken down into literally hundreds of varieties of different churches throughout the country— enough styles and settings to appeal to virtually every believer.

preacher isn't as entertaining as some others. Even so, they arrive at the doors expecting that the *attitude* will be ideal, that this church will be a place where everyone openly loves, trusts, and accepts, just like the Bible says.

Maybe your own church experience has been something less than perfect. That's okay. So has mine. But I couldn't let you leave a book on faith or a section about expressing faith without emphasizing the vital importance of church involvement. The church is not perfect, but it is the absolute best place possible for believers to learn and grow and be accountable to one another. In my experience, the believers who thrive are involved in a local church; the believers who struggle without success typically are not. Simply put: we need each other.

It Takes a Community

The basketball game pitted one of the state's perennial powerhouse teams against a small school of overachievers. The press was billing it as a blowout.

As I watched the game, I observed some of players on the underdog team trying to do too much all alone. One of their guards would bring the ball down court, move toward the basket, shoot the ball, and then go in for the rebound. To the casual observer, he appeared ambitious, aggressive—a hard worker. But while he appeared to be almost heroic in his attempts, he was, in fact, hurting the team by trying to do everything on his own.

He dribbled the ball. He shot the ball. He even attempted to do all the rebounding. And by the time he decided to start passing the ball, sharing the shots, and pulling back on defense, it was too late. His team was too far down to catch up.

As I watched the game, I thought, *That's the same way it is in the Christian faith.* We look at the enemy, the world around us, and we know it's large and it's intimidating. So we grab our faith, we dribble toward enemy territory, we push, we shove, and—what happens? We lose. And in the process, we end up feeling disconnected from God.

You cannot go through the faith and handle it all alone. The walk is too dangerous, and you're bound to get tripped up.

The Power of Other People

If you're going to really connect with God, you need a Christian community to lift you, encourage you, help you, and sustain you.

I think one of the biggest sins in the contemporary evangelical church is that we have grossly overindividualized our experiences with God. We talk about our personal salvation, and we discuss "*my* quiet time," "*my* faith," "*my* walk with God." In the process, I fear we sometimes isolate ourselves from each other.

Look at it like this: here we are, diving deep into the murky waters of a sinful world. I have the protection of the diving suit of God, and I have a lifeline that goes up to that great white ship on the surface above. You have your suit and your lifeline as well. And every once in a while, as we're trying to get out the kinks or keep the oxygen coming, we might wave at each other, or smile at each other, or bump into each other. But in that kind of situation, I don't think we'd really believe we *needed* each other to remain connected to God.

Beware! _____

Some folks say that because God is everywhere, they can worship just as well on the golf course as they can in a church on Sunday morning. Frankly, they're fooling themselves. Although they certainly can communicate with God on the golf course, they're distracted, focused on things other than his voice. They also rob themselves of the benefits of being part of a true community of believers; they also rob that community of their own presence to encourage and inspire.

Of course our relationships with God are personal and unique. But we mustn't forget the value of the church. We need each other to stay in touch with God.

The life of faith is not about "God and *me*." It's about "God and *we*."

Church Essentials

We can't stay connected to God unless we are in life with each other. And that means more than just enjoying time together in Sunday school or cheering on the women's softball team or attending a men's retreat. As you seek a church community in which you can really put down some serious spiritual roots, find nourishment for your journey of faith, and truly flourish, keep the following essentials in mind.

Faith 101 _____

If you're looking for a community of believers to join, start your search close to home. You'll be more likely to get involved in more than just worship services if you can get to the church or other members' homes with only a short drive or a walk.

Integrity

Integrity in the Christian community is demonstrated in a church's obedience to the Word of God.

I don't know exactly what issues John was dealing with in the first-century church, but a quick reading of 1 John reveals even to the most casual reader just how concerned he was that these Christians be involved in a community of integrity. That's why he continually reminds his readers that to be a community that connects people to God, they must practice integrity through obedience.

Show me a community absent of integrity, and I'll show you a community that will sidetrack you from a connection with God. Show me a community of Christians for which integrity is their hallmark, and I'll show you a community in which connection to God can happen.

Integrity is demonstrated in the content of the songs being sung, the sermons or messages being preached, and in more behind-the-scenes ways: in the church's sensitivity to its handling of its children's ministries, the counseling being offered by the church staff, and the way staff and volunteers treat one another.

Confession

People won't feel connected to God when they're involved in a community in which everyone is always putting on the pretense of perfection. (In fact, it's such church communities that have given rise to the old cliché "the church is just full of hypocrites.") Connection with God often happens by denying the pretense of perfection and encouraging confession.

Behold!

Confession was a big thought on John's mind, too. In fact, in 1 John 1:8–9, he rips to shreds the idea that in the community of Christians, we ought to pretend we have it all put together. "If we claim to be without sin, we deceive ourselves and the truth is not in us. But if we confess our sins, he is faithful and just and will forgive us our sins and purify us from all unrighteousness."

When we confess our sins, our imperfections, the barriers come down. We feel refreshing renewal. We experience God's presence in a profound way when we are involved in a community in which confession is allowed and even encouraged to occur without the fear of condemnation, retaliation, or rejection.

When evaluating a congregation's attitudes toward confession, listen to the prayers being said and the attitude of the pastor and lay leaders as they speak about church life from the pulpit. Does the church feel "holier than thou," or does it feel "faithful by God's grace"?

Love

Again, we have no idea what was happening in the church to which John was writing, but it's clear that whatever it was, it wasn't very loving. John tells them that if they're not being loving toward one another, there's no way they'll stay connected to God. In 1 John 3:10, he says, "This is how we know who the children of God are and who the children of the devil are: Anyone who does not do what is right is not a child of God; neither is anyone who does not love his brother."

Then, in chapter 4:19, he continues with, "We love because he first loved us. If anyone says, 'I love God' yet hates his brother, he is a liar. For anyone who does not love his brother whom he has seen, cannot love God, whom he has not seen. And he has given us this command: Whoever loves God must also love his brother."

John makes two very serious indictments here. If you say you are connected with God but are unloving, you are a liar. Then, if you say you are connected to God but are unloving, you are a child of Satan.

Faith 101

There may be no greater challenge for the Christian life than living out the love we proclaim with our lips. Some days, we may not feel like reaching out in love to others. And some people can be especially difficult to love or even may refuse to be loved. As we make the effort to love others—even when loving feels like a burden—we demonstrate the reality of our faith, we draw closer to being the people God wants us to be, and we mature in our Christian faith.

Tragically, some people in churches today seem to work overtime at participating in unloving activities, becoming spiritually distracted themselves even as they lead others to become sidetracked by petty issues and trivial matters.

If a church is to empower people to stay connected to God, the church must be loving. Of course, each church member and every attendee shares in fulfilling that responsibility—just as they all play a part in a congregation's attitudes toward integrity and confession.

As you prepare to align yourself with a body of fellow believers, it can help to evaluate just how loving you are yourself. How can you tell if you are acting out of love in the church? Ask yourself the following questions:

- *Am I patient?* Sometimes we need to realize that God's grace is a process that takes time. People don't change instantly.

- *Do I show respect?* I never cease to be amazed at how some Christians don't even stop to think about what they're saying. Maliciously, we can participate in gossip, put-downs, accusations, and more without even batting an eye.

- *Am I tolerant?* Sometimes in the church, I don't understand all the fuss and commotion over secondary matters. In the church, we may not always agree, but there is a biblical call to be open and receptive to diversity.

- *Am I gentle?* Bulldozing, manipulating, and overpowering have no place in life of a lover of God.

Need more descriptions for what a Christian's love should look like? See 1 Corinthians 13 for a list—a *challenging* list, it must be said—of just what Christian love *should* look like.

The Least You Need to Know

- No congregation of human beings will be a perfect reflection of God.

- Nevertheless, the church is an essential ingredient in the life of a faithful person.

- Church informs and educates believers while building community and nurturing spiritual growth.

- Essential elements in a godly church include integrity, confession, and love.

Part 3

Living Faith

The book of James makes it clear: "Faith by itself, if it is not accompanied by action, is dead." (James 2:17) By contrast, a *living* faith shines out through every part of our lives—sometimes subtly, sometimes very obviously.

In Part 3, you get a close-up look at how faith can be lived out in some of life's most important areas, from our finances, friendships, and marriages, to our jobs and our parenting. You also get an honest appraisal of how we can rely on faith even as we experience some of life's most painful or challenging moments. A *living* faith isn't just for the good times; a living faith is relevant for *all* life.

Chapter 13

Faith and Friends

In This Chapter

- ◆ Realizing the value of friendship
- ◆ Being a faithful friend
- ◆ Changing lives
- ◆ Faith that divides

Living our faith in the real world can bring special challenges in lots of different areas, from our marriages to our jobs, from the way we raise our children to how we handle our money. But perhaps the toughest challenge is to live faithfully with our friends, especially if we're new believers.

Our friends know us well—maybe even better than we know ourselves. They can spot our shortcomings in a heartbeat; they know when we're not being honest with ourselves. Yet these close relationships can also enrich our faith, even as our faith can lead to even stronger ties with our loved ones.

In Need of Friends

The apostle Paul placed an incredible value on friendship: Aquilla and Priscilla, his mentors and teachers; Luke the physician; Onesimus the slave; Peter, his colleague. Paul knew what so many of us have come to appreciate: friendships are vital to healthy living.

Several years ago, a survey was taken among the people living in a major metropolitan neighborhood that offered an incredibly high standard of living. The community consisted of shopping malls, elegant restaurants, major department stores, top-rated educational institutions, excellent hospitals, expanding businesses, and more. From a material perspective, the community had a lot going for it.

Yet this survey of 1,000 residents revealed something interesting. The greatest need that existed among the population? The need for friends! Driveways were filled with nice cars, big boats, and top-of-the-line RVs. Houses held entertainment centers, plasma TVs, game rooms, spas, and personal computers. Yet none of it was enough to supplant the basic human need for friendship.

There's an amusing exchange between Charlie Brown and Lucy in one of Charles Schultz's *Peanuts* cartoons. Charlie Brown tells Lucy, "I need all the friends I can get. I don't have any friends.

"Define *friend*," Lucy says.

Charlie Brown then lists some of the attributes of a friend:

- ◆ "A friend wants to watch the same television program you want to watch."

- ◆ "A friend can't stand the same sort of music that you can't stand."

- ◆ "A friend sticks up for you when you're not even there."

- ◆ "A friend accepts you for what you are."

Lucy assures Charlie Brown that she is none of those things.

"Poor Charlie Brown," she says, walking away, "I feel so sorry for him. I don't care if I have any friends or not—just so I'm *popular!*"

She may not have realized it, but Lucy needed friends just as much as Charlie Brown did. And just as much as you and I do.

True Friendship

What are the grounds for being a real friend? Lots of friendships are described in the Bible, but I want to look particularly at the relationship between Paul and one man, Onesiphorus. (After all, a man named "Onesiphorus" could probably use all the friends he could get!)

In 2 Timothy, chapter 1, Paul is writing to his friend Timothy about being genuinely moved by the pattern of friendship he sees in Onesiphorus.

Behold!

Bible scholars tell us that Onesiphorus became a convert to the Christian faith during one of Paul's earlier missionary journeys to the city of Ephesus. Although some have suggested that he is also known by another name, Onesimus the slave, we really don't know for sure. The one thing we do know, from Paul's words here, is that the apostle considered Onesiphorus a true friend.

Let's look at some of the qualities that make for an authentic, lasting, and faith-based friendship.

Friendship First

Friends make each other a priority. We know from Paul's words that Paul made his friendship with Onesiphorus a priority. And we know from Onesiphorus's actions that Paul was a priority for him.

Commissioned to spread the gospel, Paul maintained a demanding pace of travel and ministry. And yet his writings indicate a life that was neither too busy nor too important to cultivate close relationships with his friends. Sometimes he wrote from prison. At other times, he wrote while traveling. At other times, he wrote from another continent, miles removed from those he loved. Yet in spite of the conditions, obstacles, and distance, Paul was eager to maintain contact with his friends.

Because friendship was a priority with Paul, it also became a priority with Onesiphorus. In 2 Timothy 1:17, Paul expresses his heartfelt appreciation to his friend for his diligence in finding him during an earlier journey to Rome. "He searched hard for me until he found me," Paul says. There were no e-mail addresses, no cell phones, no Blackberries, GPS, or text messages. Onesiphorus had to invest time and energy to find his friend. But he did it. Friendship was a personal priority.

I've seen this exemplified in my own life. When I was a young boy, my parents took our family on a vacation to Washington, D.C., where we hoped to see our former next-door neighbors who'd moved to the area. When we arrived in D.C., though, we discovered we didn't have their address. To complicate matters, their phone number was unlisted. How could we find them?

My parents called some friends back home, who shared our former neighbor's address. We then went to a city building to purchase a map. Wouldn't you know it: the street was not on the map! So we drove to a police station and requested directions. Finally, after getting lost several times during the next few hours, we found our friends.

Behold!

Thanks to e-mail, cell phones, inexpensive long-distance telephone rates—not to mention the good old U.S. Post Office—it's never been easier to stay in touch with friends near and far. Consider sending a card to a friend for no reason whatsoever. Pick up the phone just to say hello. Make it a point to take advantage of the many ways we can maintain and build our relationships. You'll not only brighten someone else's day; you'll bring a smile to your own face as well.

Why keep pursuing these friends, even when the situation got increasingly ridiculous? Because the friendship was a priority. Friendships are never accidental. They require a sense of intentionality, which in turn demands that choices be made.

"Okay," you say, "that's great. Friends are good. Got it. But how does faith come into the picture?" Read on, my friend.

Getting Better All the Time

Faithful friends practice the art of encouragement. In 2 Timothy 1:16, Paul shares a blessing: "May the Lord show mercy to the household of Onesiphorus, because he often refreshed me."

The word *refreshed* literally means "to brace up a person." Onesiphorus was instrumental in alleviating Paul's material needs and provided Paul with financial support. But he also supported Paul's ministry by providing emotional and spiritual support.

When you develop a friendship with someone, you will find yourself strategically positioned in the other person's life to cheer them on—believing in them when others may not, encouraging them in the face of obstacles, listening when they are in pain, rejoicing at their achievements.

One of my closest friends is another pastor who is one of my biggest boosters. I have more confidence in him than he has in himself, and he seems to have more confidence in me than I have in myself. That has made for a terrific combination. Any time he calls me and shares a personal struggle, a doubt, an obstacle, or a problem he might be facing with a church member, I tell him what it is about him that causes me to believe in his ability to handle the situation. He does the same for me. Friends encourage. Friends push each other on.

Behold!

Lee Strobel, a pastor at Willow Creek Community Church in suburban Chicago, has said, "When you are specific with your affirmation of your friends and you offer it consistently, when you accentuate the positive while dealing constructively with the negative, you will infuse your friends with the confidence and courage to go the next step in their endeavors!"

Every now and then, it can be helpful to take a sort of "friendship inventory" and ask yourself if you're being an encouraging, uplifting presence in the lives of your friends:

- When was the last time you told your closest friends how important they are to you?

- How long has it been since you painted a compelling vision for them of what you believe God might accomplish through their unique talents, personalities, and temperaments?

- When did you last play the role of a vocal and unabashed cheerleader for a friend?

Support in the Hard Times

Evidently, there were those in Paul's circle of acquaintances who had become embarrassed by his predicaments. Arrested on the charge of civil disobedience and creating societal unrest, Paul was writing to Timothy from a prison cell. And there were people who felt a sense of personal humiliation by that fact.

Not Onesiphorus. "He was not ashamed of my chains," Paul notes at the end of 2 Timothy 1:16. And you can almost hear Onesiphorus saying, "Paul, others may laugh at you. They may scorn you, criticize you, and refuse to believe in you or your mission any longer. But not me. I believe in you. I see possibilities emerging from the time you are spending in prison. I see opportunities for you to share your faith with the entire Roman prison guard and others! Keep the faith, brother. God has a purpose in mind for you."

All-Season Friendship

Faithful friends demonstrate loyalty. Paul clearly had his share of fair-weather friends, the followers and disciples who were willing to stay with him while life was easy. But as soon as life became difficult (read: *imprisonment*) and the road became rocky, what happened? They bolted for the door.

Paul writes in 2 Timothy 1:15, "You know that everyone in the province of Asia has deserted me." Okay, *everyone in the province of Asia?* Even in Paul's day, that was a lot of people. And that word *deserted* is the most powerful term in the New Testament that could be used to describe a disloyal act. It's a word that captures the essence of what Judas did when he betrayed Jesus and sent him to die on the cross. Paul's fair-weather friends were playing the role of the traitor, the friend turned foe.

In one of Dostoevsky's writings, one character says to another, "I can accept the tragedies in our world. But it's the tragedies of relationships that I don't understand." War, disease, natural disasters: we have come to expect these things in our world. But what continues to catch us by surprise is when friend turns against friend.

Contrast that with the words of the writer in Proverbs 17:17: "A friend loves at all times, and a brother is born for adversity." This is the kind of friend that faith calls us to become.

Behold!

I've heard a story about a man who ran for sheriff in his community. He was disappointed to discover that he had been overwhelmingly defeated at the polls. The next day, he was seen on the streets with a pistol strapped to his side. An acquaintance cautiously approached him and asked, "Why are you wearing that pistol? You lost the race for sheriff, you know." The man replied, "Oh, I know I lost the race. That's why I'm wearing this gun. I figure that any man who doesn't have any more friends than I do had better carry a gun to protect himself!"

Celebrate Good Times

Friends rejoice over each other's successes. They hope for the best for one another.

Let's be honest. From time to time, when we hear that something good is going on in somebody's life, it can be difficult to rejoice. Sometimes it can be difficult to sit and hear someone share how good things are in their lives.

You're looking for a job, and your friend says, "I got a promotion!" You're struggling financially, and your friend says, "I just inherited $50,000!" Your dating life is going through a rough period, and your friend tells about an exciting new relationship. On the inside, you feel torn. You want to rejoice in their blessings, but those twinges of envy make it difficult.

Faith 101

Want to help a friend celebrate some good news? Depending on the news, you may want to throw a surprise party in your friend's honor. Put an announcement in the local paper. Rent one of those embarrassing message signs to stick in their front yard. Whatever else you choose to do, thank God for blessing your friend in this way.

Faithful friends find a way to sort through their emotions. We find a way to rejoice with those who rejoice. We find a way to express authentic gladness when good news comes.

I still remember one of the first times when this quality of friendship was tested in me. One of my best friends and I were seniors in seminary, desperately hoping some church would be willing to take a chance on hiring a recent seminary graduate.

I was the first to find a church, and I felt fortunate. It was a small, rural church in a tiny community of 1,800. I'd start at $13,000 per year plus a few benefits. (That wasn't such bad starting pay, back in the day.) A few weeks later, my friend received his own good news: a 500-member church in Minneapolis was offering him a full-time position as an associate pastor. The salary was nearly 40 percent more than what I would be making. Plus, he'd be living in one of the most beautiful metropolitan areas in our country.

When he told me the good news, he was excited. On the outside, I smiled and tried to act excited, too. I *wanted* to be genuinely glad. But deep down inside, I was being tested. Would I share in his joy? Would I be able to celebrate with him? Or would I allow my professional envy to drive me into petty jealousy?

That isn't always an easy hurdle to get over. But faith gives us the strength and perspective we need to celebrate with our friends even as we continue to trust God to meet our own needs.

Do You Have Enough Friends?

If you're a person of faith, maybe you're wondering, *Well, is it okay to still hang out with people who don't share my faith?* Maybe you've even heard the idea that Christians are to be "in" the world, not "of" the world. That is, believers are to be an active presence in the world—"salt and light," to use two biblical images—but we're not to get so caught up with worldly things that we lose our spiritual effectiveness.

Knowing where to draw that in/of line can be challenging. It doesn't help that the line is different for each of us; there's no set of absolute rules that covers every activity, every situation. The call is up to us, our consciences, and the Holy Spirit's leading.

Beware!

Friends come and go throughout our lives as a result of changing circumstances, interests, and more. If you are new to faith, chances are that some of your current friends won't understand your new choices and priorities. At the same time, you'll be meeting new friends as you plug into a community of faith. There's nothing wrong with working to maintain all of your friendships, even as you increase your circle of friends to include new faith-based relationships. However, don't be surprised if some current friends decide to pull away as a result of your faith commitment.

Our tendency, though, is usually to pull back from the world, to set ourselves apart as believers. Do that, and you'll certainly keep your faith intact. But you'll be robbing your nonbelieving friends of the benefits of your faith. You also may be robbing yourself of relationships with others that could prove personally rewarding.

A number of years ago, my co-author, Bob, felt stuck in that situation. He had a full-time job at a Christian publishing company. He taught junior-high Sunday school on the weekends. As a result, he had been bothered by a nagging thought: "I spent my days going from work to home to church and back again. As a result, I never had any contact with non-Christians," he says.

"I was yearning to step out of the 'safe' zone and share my beliefs with other people. I wanted to be someplace where I might really make an eternal difference in someone else's life." So he headed to the local mall. There, he got a part-time job at a men's gift store.

"Conversation came easily with just about all of the other six part-timers," Bob says. "Between helping customers, setting out stock, and dusting the display cases, we talked about family, hobbies, significant others, hopes for the future, and our 'real' full-time jobs that paid the bills. If something was important to us, it was bound to come up after a couple of four-hour weeknights or seven-hour Saturdays. Everyone knew I worked for a Christian company during the day, so it was only natural to talk about faith. I feel certain that God used me at that store. And I think I had an impact on the lives of some of my co-workers.

"Ultimately, I believe I was able to be Christ's presence for my co-workers, a person who shared their struggles and rejoiced at their successes. Someone who believed sincerely in redemption and salvation and the resurrection—and who was still willing to take out the trash" (*willing*, Bob emphasizes—not thrilled about it).

Bob's experience at the shop showed him that he could develop close relationships with people who didn't necessarily share his beliefs, and that he could draw on his faith to be a positive influence for his friends.

Behold!

Jesus was not afraid to invite criticism from the religious leaders of his day by spending time with people who were considered "unworthy." When he shared a meal with Zacchaeus, a despised tax collector, onlookers criticized him for visiting a sinner. (Luke 19) When Jesus spoke to a Samaritan woman at a well in John 4, she herself was shocked; Jews typically shunned Samaritans. Jesus, though, didn't look at someone and see "tax collector" or "Samaritan." He looked and simply saw people in need.

When Faith and Friendship Collide

I have to warn you, though, that all is not sunshine and roses when it comes to being a friend as a person of faith. If you're a new believer, chances are the majority of your closest friends may not share your beliefs. They may be cool with your new direction, or they may resent the new role faith is playing in your life. Even as God is changing you into the best person you can be, your closest friends may be missing the "old you," the person they knew and loved.

Sometimes, all it takes is time—time for friends to see that your faith is real and something you're committed to for the long haul; time for them to adjust to the new you; time for them to figure out where—or if—they fit in your new life.

I don't want to suggest that people of faith should only associate with like-minded people. That's clearly not something the Bible ever teaches. And that would rob us of so much of life's richness; it would also rob the people around us of our faithful influence.

But there might be times where your faith and your friendships collide.

"Keith was my best friend in high school," a good friend told me. But when these two friends met up again midway through their college years, Keith had some news to share. He told my friend he was gay.

"I know you think that's a sin," Keith said.

"Well, yes, I do," my friend replied. "But I don't think it's any different than any other sin. The results are the same: a broken relationship with God. But the good news is that God is willing to forgive and heal his people."

Keith didn't say anything at that point.

"You're still my friend, Keith," my friend added. "You know your being gay doesn't change that."

But it did change things. Knowing how my friend felt, Keith simply felt more comfortable spending time with people who didn't have any problem accepting his lifestyle. When they did talk, it was like a wall had risen up between them.

Jesus says in Matthew 10:34, "Do not suppose that I have come to bring peace to the earth. I did not come to bring peace, but a sword. For I have come to turn 'a man against his father, a daughter against her mother, a daughter-in-law against her mother-in-law.'" So why not friend against friend as well?

"I regret the loss of Keith's friendship," my friend says now. "Since we last talked, I've learned a lot about God and about people. But if I had the chance to relive that conversation, I'd probably deliver the same message today. Because the truth of the gospel hasn't changed for me.

Faith 101

If you're working to live faithfully among friends who don't share your beliefs, pray about your situation and ask for God's guidance. If you're a new believer, let your friends know that you still love and care about them. But also don't be afraid to ask that they respect your beliefs.

"I still think of Keith as my friend, even though I haven't seen him in about 20 years now. I hope to see him again someday and discuss God's love with him one more time. And I hope that, if such a reunion does not occur, then someone else will talk with Keith, someone who cares enough to speak the truth out of love and friendship."

Faith 101

As long as you both still breathe, it's not too late to heal a broken friendship. It doesn't matter what led to the break. Reach out in faith. Forgive your friend or, if necessary, ask your friend to forgive you. Even if the wounds are too deep for your friend to overlook, pray about the relationship and ask God to bless your efforts to reconcile.

The Least You Need to Know

◆ Faith has the power to enrich and deepen our friendships.

◆ Faithful friends make friendship a priority.

◆ Faithful friends support and encourage each other.

◆ Faith enables us to make a difference in friends' lives.

◆ There may be times when our faith causes rifts in our human relationships.

Chapter 14

For Better and Best

In This Chapter

♦ Made in God's image—and for one another

♦ Intimate relationships and God's love

♦ The power of a promise

♦ Facets of a faithful marriage

No area of life is unaffected by our faith—including our marriage. Basing our love life on faith doesn't mean that suddenly everything about our relationships will be perfect from here on out. Every marriage requires commitment and trust to work. But with commitment to—and trust in—God as our model for marriage, this most intimate of human relationships takes on even greater significance and richness. Our marriage relationship can beautifully mirror our faith relationship with God.

Made for Each Other

Marriage can mean much more than the messages we find in love poetry or Hallmark sentiments. At its best, it joins the kind of enthusiastic expressions of love you might see in a marriage proposal on the electronic scoreboard during a basketball game half-time with the more enduring aspects of devotion, trust, respect, and desire.

According to Genesis, God laid the groundwork for modern marriage when he created Adam, the first man, in his own image after creating everything else. Here's how the Bible describes it: "When the Lord God made the earth and the heavens … the Lord God formed the man from the dust of the ground and breathed into his nostrils the breath of life, and the man became a living being." (Genesis 2:4, 7)

In other words, people were to be God's crowning creation. Sun, moon, oceans—yeah, they're really nice. But it's *people* who were made in the image of God.

God's crowning achievement would have ended fairly soon, though, if it weren't for Eve. God recognized that his man should not be alone in the world. He needed companionship. So in the words of Genesis 2:21–22, God "caused the man to fall into a deep sleep; and while he was sleeping, he took one of the man's ribs and closed up the place with flesh. Then the Lord God made a woman from the rib he had taken out of the man, and he brought her to the man."

It's significant that woman was created out of man. Eve shares the privilege of being made in the image of God, but she also shares part of Adam's flesh. And Adam, in turn, would be a lesser human being without Eve at his side. This is the single most important idea about marriage between a man and woman: they both share God's image, but they share something from each other as well. Men and women were made for God. But they were also uniquely made for each other. No other living creature had such an auspicious beginning.

When we pursue our marriages from an attitude of faithfulness, we recognize this miraculous situation for what it is—and strive to bring blessing to God as well as to our spouse.

Sex: Invented by God

Obviously, sex is a significant element in any healthy marriage. Some people believe, though, that sex is dirty or shameful or sinful. If this reflects how you were raised or what you have come to believe, this attitude will affect aspects of your marriage that go beyond the bedroom. So I want to make a point about this belief before we get too far along in this chapter.

The truth is—and I'll try not to blush when I say this—God made sex. It didn't originate with Dr. Ruth or any other "sex guru." Sex started with God. It isn't dirty or shameful; it isn't a sin. So when you're engaged in sex with a spouse, you're acting in precisely the way God meant for you to act. There's no reason to feel guilty, embarrassed, or ashamed about it.

Behold!

When the King James Version of the Bible says Adam "knew" Eve (Genesis 4:1), it meant they had sex. This used to be a great source of snickering back when the King James Version was *the* translation to use in church. Even though modern dictionaries consider that use of "know" archaic, "to know" someone isn't such a laughing matter. It takes time, communication, and real motivation to truly know someone. It requires a level of intimacy that goes far beyond simple sexual intercourse. To really "know" someone is an amazing thing.

For some wonderful reason I can't fathom—alas, I haven't found *all* the answers to life's big questions yet—our sexual relationships were designed to reflect God's relationship with us. When those two relationships are in sync, something amazing happens. We'll be looking at this point more as we make our way through the next few pages.

Beware!

Some folks have the mistaken impression that sex is what's meant by the phrase "original sin." Don't believe it. The "original sin"—that is, the first break in humanity's relationship with God—was Adam and Eve's decision to disobey God's instruction to not eat the fruit of the Tree of Knowledge of Good and Evil.

Promises and Pledges

I tried doing an Internet search to find out just how many songs have been written about falling in love. Computers around the world didn't exactly crash when I did this, but they might as well have, because the number of love songs is huge—and it's growing every day.

No wonder. Love can inspire some of the most wonderful, most heart-wrenching, and most complex feelings we will ever experience. Mature love isn't just about feelings, though. (That would be infatuation.) It's also about promises and pledges, which can have eternal significance.

Virtually every marriage begins with some kind of pledge. No doubt, you've heard or even said something along these lines: "I, Juliet, take you, Romeo, to be my husband; to have and to hold from this day forward—for better, for worse, for richer, for poorer, in sickness and in health, to love and to cherish, as long as we both shall live."

Modern wedding vows take all shapes and forms, of course. But most acknowledge that, no matter what might come, good or bad, these two people are pledging to stay together and see it through together. When you think about it, this is a pretty amazing promise to make to another person. Some things about the future are fairly predictable: we'll probably all lose some hair, gain some wrinkles, and worry if we've planned well enough for our retirement. But none of us knows what's really going to happen in the coming weeks, months, and years. It could be wonderful—or not. The miracle of marriage is that, either way, it doesn't matter; regardless of what might happen to us, we promise we'll weather it together.

Behold!

The vows we now call "traditional" closely follow a ceremony described in the *York Manual*, published in the 1400s. We've updated the spelling (no "wedded wyf" for us), and we don't often include the final "thereto I pledge thee my troth" anymore. (Probably because we have no idea what a "troth" is.) In all other respects, though, many couples today repeat a promise that has endured about 600 years.

To be honest, I'm surprised that any couple without a shared faith is able to make and keep such a promise. It's not easy in the least. We all naturally change and grow over time. And as I discuss a bit later, our relationship should be changing and growing as well. Balancing all those changes with our unchanging commitment to each other can be quite a test. That's when faith comes to the rescue. It gives us a real foundation for living out the marriage pledge we've made.

A faith-based marriage draws its strength from mirroring God's loving relationship with the world. And God has given us his promise that he is absolutely in this for the long haul: "Never will I leave you; never will I forsake you," he says in Hebrews 13:5. God's devotion to us is constant and unchanging, a covenant promise from the Creator that has nothing to do with our changing circumstances or how devoted *we* might be feeling at any given moment.

It can be a big relief to approach our own marriage relationships with this same perspective of faith. We don't have to worry seriously about our future together simply because we might be experiencing a rough spot today. We have God's pledge of steadfast love as our model for keeping the pledges we've made.

Faithful people make the choice to trust in God without having scientific proof of him in hand. Over time, as they experience God working in their lives, they build up their own personal stockpile of proof. It can be the same in a marriage. At the outset, we have no idea what the future will bring. But we trust that *this* is the person we are meant to be with, and we pledge ourselves to living out that commitment to the best of our abilities.

Growing Together

A friend once told me, "I'm tired of the same old 'same olds'!" When I asked him to explain, he said, "Well, every day, I climb out of the same old bed. I walk into the same old bathroom and look at the same old face. Then, I go to the same old kitchen. I sit down in the same old chair and eat the same old breakfast. A few minutes later, I drive to work in the same old car, down the same old highway to the same old office. Throughout the day, I work at the same old desk, seeing the same old people doing the same old jobs. At the end of the day, I drive home in my same old car to my same old house where I repeat the same old routines."

Battling the same old "same olds" can be one of life's greatest challenges. Our routines become predictable. We act without even thinking. Like Pavlov's dog, we subconsciously respond to life's demands—on the job, in the home, and in our marriages. When everything in a marriage becomes predictable, though, vitality evaporates. The relationship becomes lifeless. Boredom sets in.

> **Behold!**
>
> Maybe you've seen the survey: if you had to do it all over again, would you marry the same spouse? According to one poll, 80 percent of the men said yes, while only 50 percent of the women said they would choose the same man again.

These feelings are a signal that we've lost intimacy with our spouse. Reviving that sense of intimacy can move a marriage from mediocre to meaningful. In a healthy, vital, growing marriage, the partners are developing intimacy together.

There are at least five key areas where intimacy plays an important role in a faith-filled marriage.

Emotional Intimacy

Emotional intimacy means getting in touch with your emotions and your loved one's emotions. It means going beyond the typical, "How are you?" and "I'm fine" level of conversation. It means sharing from your heart.

This is not exactly every man's strong suit. But just because some males aren't always great at verbalizing their emotions, that doesn't mean they don't have them. Wives might have to work harder at drawing them out, understanding that men may actually have nonverbal ways of communicating exactly how they're feeling.

And just because women are often considered more open about their emotions doesn't mean their feelings don't need additional interpretation as well. The typical male response to a wife's statement about her bad day, for instance, usually leads to a well-meaning suggestion of how to fix the problems. Not good. In situations like this, women often want and need to vent. They probably already know exactly how to fix the problems; they just need to blow off steam to a compassionate, thoughtful listener. (Note to husbands: that "compassionate, thoughtful listener" means you.)

Faith 101

Stumped about ways to build faithful intimacy? The following three *T*s can help create an environment that encourages intimacy:

- ◆ Talk—about anything and everything.
- ◆ Spend Time together, even if neither one of you says a word.
- ◆ Thank each other. Think of ways each day to express your gratitude for your spouse.

Financial Intimacy

Bring up the topic of money, and suddenly folks get anxious. No doubt about it, financial issues can touch a nerve. They're especially worthy of our attention.

We'll explore the bigger impact faith can have on our finances later in Chapter 18, but it's worth discussing here as well. I've learned in years of pastoral counseling that the number-one reason marriages suffer or even fail—even otherwise loving marriages between Christian partners—comes down to a lack of financial intimacy.

Financial intimacy refers to the sharing of financial goals, to having mutual financial dreams:

- ◆ How much money do we spend on our summer vacation?
- ◆ How much can we spend without consulting the other person?
- ◆ How much should we be saving?
- ◆ How much do we give away?
- ◆ How do we invest?
- ◆ Do we use credit cards?

Choices about money are often the result of our upbringing. If our parents were careful and thrifty, we'll likely follow their example. But if we were lavishly showered with gifts—or, on the other hand, if we felt deprived of life's basic necessities—as adults, we may find it difficult to control our spending (or we easily justify overspending). Building financial intimacy requires gaining an understanding of and appreciation for each other's money-handling tendencies, coming to mutual compromises for the sake of your financial health as a couple.

Intellectual Intimacy

Intellectual intimacy refers to the bonding of two minds. It doesn't mean both partners have to possess the same level of education. It does mean that even if they possess different levels of education and knowledge, each has mutual respect for what the other knows.

Let me tell you about one interesting marriage I've heard about. The wife has a Ph.D. in nuclear physics. She heads the physics department at a leading university. She travels around the world, speaking at conferences and presenting papers. The husband is employed by the same university, but he works as a custodian. Some folks have questioned the marriage: "A nuclear physicist married to a custodian? Won't work." But it has, for more than 35 years. Why? Because they have a mutual respect for each other's insights and knowledge. He will tell you, "My wife is brilliant. She can share incredible insights about science. She's amazing." Likewise, she will tell you, "He's brilliant. He's saved us thousands of dollars during our marriage. When there's a leak in the plumbing, he can fix it. When we have an electrical malfunction, he repairs it. Our house is in wonderful condition because of him."

Intellectual intimacy leaves out words such as *stupid, incompetent,* or worse. Instead, it focuses on mutual respect for each other's unique intellectual gifts and abilities. Respect builds intellectual intimacy.

Sexual Intimacy

For many couples, sexual intimacy at the outset of their relationship becomes the most intense bond of all. Yet this is where the danger lies. Sexual intimacy can bond, but it can also blind.

A couple once came to a colleague of mine for premarital counseling. The counselor encouraged them to refrain from sexual expression until after marriage. But they were convinced sex would only bring them closer as a couple in love. Six months into the marriage, the husband was consulting a lawyer and his wife was trying to figure out what went wrong. As she later said, "We convinced ourselves that because we had achieved sexual intimacy, we had already taken care of the most difficult part of marriage. We thought we were guaranteeing ourselves a good marriage. We made a major mistake!" They mistook sexual experience for true sexual—and marital—intimacy.

Behold!

When the Apostle Paul talks about the marriage relationship in his letter to the church at Ephesus, he describes it like this: "A man will leave his father and mother and be united to his wife, and the two will become one flesh." (Ephesians 5:31) One flesh? You can't get any closer than that.

True sexual intimacy involves physical closeness, of course. But it also involves real communication, the sharing of our hearts and minds as well as our bodies.

Some couples are able to improve their intimacy in this area on their own. But if you're like most of us, it can help to talk things over with a trusted counselor. If you'd feel comfortable discussing something this private with a member of the clergy, let me encourage you to do so. However, don't avoid finding help for this area of your marriage—or any area of your marriage—simply because you don't feel comfortable talking about it with a pastor. Seek out a trained Christian counselor or therapist who shares your faith perspective and is extensively trained and experienced in helping you find a solution.

With practice and patience, vitality can be restored.

Spiritual Intimacy

True spiritual intimacy occurs when both partners share and celebrate a mutually vital and growing relationship with God. It's the level of spirituality you enjoy by praying together, reading the Scriptures together, worshipping together, and directing your children through life in a faithful way.

I'm amazed at how many couples don't think of spiritual intimacy as being important. In fact, a lot of men blow it off: "Ah, that's a 'woman' thing." But think about what "getting spiritual" means. In many ways, it involves the same things that create a good relationship of any kind: openness, honesty, transparency, vulnerability. And when a couple is connecting with God together ... well, it makes for a connection that can seldom be achieved any other way.

Faith 101

Looking for ways to build spiritual intimacy? Try the following:

- ◆ Join a Bible study together.
- ◆ Keep a marriage journal, where you each take turns writing down your thoughts and feelings.
- ◆ Read a religious book together and then set aside time to discuss it.
- ◆ Go on a mission trip together.

Because our spirituality is often a quiet, personal undertaking, simply talking about your spiritual life with your spouse can be a boon to building spiritual intimacy. Start the conversation with some of the following questions if you like:

- ◆ What have you been praying for?
- ◆ What have you been reading in the Bible that has made a particular impression on you?
- ◆ Are you struggling with something in your walk of faith?
- ◆ Have you had any great faith successes lately?

Behold!

Part of nurturing a faith-based marriage involves working to bring out each other's best.

Share these and any other kinds of faith thoughts, simply to keep your spouse in the loop about what's happening in your walk with God. Then take the time to listen when your spouse chooses to open up about his or her own spiritual life. As you each share the challenges and successes, you will naturally become an inspiration to one another.

For Better and Best

In Ephesians 5, Paul explains that the marriage relationship parallels the relationship Jesus Christ has with all those believe in him, his church. Verse 26 says: "Christ loved the church and gave himself up for her to make her holy, cleansing her … and to present her to himself as a radiant church, without stain or wrinkle or any other blemish, but holy and blameless." He is working with us and through us to make us into the people he knows we can become: holy, cleansed, radiant, blameless.

Holy? Radiant? Blameless? Those aren't always the words we associate with marriage. But that doesn't mean we can't aspire to those kinds of marital heights.

If you want to restore life to your marriage—or build a faithful marriage from that first "I do"—ask yourself, "Am I working to bring out the best in my spouse?" Speak words of encouragement. Perform acts of kindness. Demonstrate your love. And consider whether the words you're preparing to say or the thing you're just about to do will bring you closer together … or drive you a little farther apart.

Love is a feeling, sure, but it is also a choice. When you choose to love and to show that love, your loving actions inject new life into your feelings. And I believe that when you show that love because God has shown his love to you, you can dramatically change the tone of any marriage relationship. Struggling marriages can take on renewed life. Good marriages can go to that next level, becoming great.

Trust me, your efforts will be rewarded.

The Least You Need to Know

- The story of Adam and Eve clarifies God's love for people, as well as the deep relationship God intends between the sexes.

- ◆ God's promise of steadfast love is a model for faith-based marriage.

- ◆ Faithful marriages nurture at least five kinds of intimacy: emotional, financial, intellectual, sexual, and spiritual.

- ◆ Commitment based on faith makes marriages work.

Chapter 15

Faith from 9 to 5

In This Chapter

- ◆ Doing work you can love
- ◆ Finding worth beyond work
- ◆ Working faithfully

Work is what we do, but it's also a reflection of who we are: what we value, what we believe, and where our interests and abilities lie.

Being faithful from 9 to 5 involves remembering what we're working for. Of course, paying the mortgage each month is great! But by bringing our faith to work with us, we can gain something more than a paycheck and health benefits. We can get a fresh perspective on how we do the work we do—from how we handle office politics to how we climb the corporate ladder.

Passionate Pursuits

I'm passionate about my job. I think you can be, too. In fact, I think it's one of the keys to building a successful career. I also think that approaching our work from the perspective of faith gives us an advantage in finding fulfillment and satisfaction in the workplace. And why shouldn't we enjoy our work? That's where most of us end up spending most of our waking hours.

Some people think ideas like "following your passion" are only for creative types. For them, "passion" sounds too intangible and undependable. "You're better off just finding a good job and sticking with it," they say.

But that's the problem. In today's workplace, there are no employment guarantees. The old model of the worker who hires on at a company straight out of high school or college and stays with that company straight through to retirement is long gone. In today's business world, "change" is the mantra, and those changes are usually not in the employee's best interest. Companies routinely downsize and restructure, laying off hundreds—if not thousands—of workers at a time. For those who remain, the pace of work is faster than ever before, and the pressure to "produce" just builds and builds. For many, there's never any escape: thanks to cell phones, e-mail, instant messaging, wireless communication, and home offices, a lot of people are finding themselves on call 24/7.

> **Behold!**
>
> Are you struggling to figure out what you really want to be doing in your work life? Pick up Linda Gale's book *Discover What You're Best At* (Fireside, 1998), and work your way through the self-surveys. Chances are, you'll find far more appealing career suggestions than you ever imagined.

Given the state of today's workplace, if you're not passionate about what you're doing, you'll likely burn out or turn cynical. And you won't be the only one paying the price: your job stress is bound to affect your family and friends, not to mention the quality of your work. By contrast, following your passion actually leads to a greater sense of personal fulfillment, enriching us as individuals and as members of our larger communities.

Work Worth Doing

When it comes to doing your job as a faithful believer, the Bible offers several general, helpful guidelines. Consider these verses:

"Love the Lord your God with all your heart and with all your soul and with all your mind." (Matthew 22:37)

"Love your neighbor as yourself." (Matthew 22:39)

"Go into all the world and preach the good news to all creation." (Mark 16:15)

Whatever you do, work at it with all your heart, as working for the Lord, not for men, since you know that you will receive an inheritance from the Lord as a reward. It is the Lord Christ you are serving. (Colossians 3:23–24)

Each of these essentials helps guide and direct us as we try to figure out and follow God's will for our lives as people of faith.

If you're on a job hunt, these essentials will lead us away from jobs and career goals that simply don't fit with living a moral, biblically based life. (It's kind of hard to reconcile being a mob hit man if you're committed to following what Jesus taught.) At the same time, these ideals help lead us toward those activities and attitudes that will fulfill us as human beings and bring glory to our Creator.

Beware!

Some folks believe that becoming a person of faith means you suddenly have to leave your current job and start doing something "religious" or "Christian." Although there's always a need for full-time Christian professionals, God absolutely will use you right where you are now. He wants to see people of faith having an impact on every industry, every business.

All sorts of motivational and self-help books and speakers talk about "following your bliss," discovering your purpose in life, and making a living by doing what you love. But I believe it's only when we go after those ideals from the foundation of Christian faith that our efforts will yield anything worth holding on to.

Where God Wants You

An anonymous writer recently posted a note on a website in which he (or she) said, "Trying to determine what God wants you to do with your life is extremely tough. (That's an understatement!)" I think this writer found it so tough because he or she was going at it backward.

God is concerned more with who we are as workers and what we accomplish for his kingdom rather than what kind of vacation package we have or what our title is. Remember Colossians 3:23–24: "Whatever you do, work at it with all your heart, as working for the Lord, not for men, since you know that you will receive an inheritance from the Lord as a reward. It is the Lord Christ you are serving."

A friend told me about an experience he and his wife had when signing the paperwork to buy their first brand-new car. After they chose their vehicle, they were ushered into the credit manager's office. The man was like human electricity, talking nonstop as he keyed their information into his computer, zoomed his chair back and forth between his desk and printer, and dealt out a growing collection of documents for their signatures. At the same time, he also answered several phone calls and a page from the public-address system. It was after 9 at night, and the man was a blur of frenzied motion. He told the couple that this was pretty much how he spent every working hour.

"My wife hates my schedule," he said, "but, hey, I just tell her that we'll be able to retire in style by the time I'm 40."

Yeah, my friend remembers thinking, *if you're lucky enough to live that long! And if she hasn't packed up and left you by then!*

Obviously, I have no idea what this man's relationship with God was. But I feel fairly safe in saying that God probably didn't intend for him to sacrifice family and, possibly, health for the sake of an early retirement. I think it's probably safe to say that his job was helping him become someone less than he could be.

Life is too short to be doing work that makes you miserable or bores you or somehow detracts from your growing relationship with God. If you're going to be doing work, you might as well be doing something you care about, something worthwhile that's going to count for something in the world. That's where the joy is.

Work and Worth

I'm not sure any other environment can have a more powerful impact on our sense of self-worth than the workplace. After all, companies literally put a price tag on just how valuable we are to the business. And then there's our position in the company, our frequency (or lack) of raises, those annual evaluations with our supervisor. It all seems designed to affect our perception of personal value—to the world at large, as well as our co-workers and colleagues.

Or consider your choice of career. In our cultural pecking order, certain jobs are considered to be more prestigious than others. Acquire one of those positions, we think, and what will happen? You'll feel great! You'll *be* somebody. But accept a position that holds less cultural prestige, and what happens? People just aren't impressed.

> **Behold!**
>
> Climb high
> Climb far
> Your goal the sky
> Your aim the star.
>
> —Inscription at Williams College, Williamstown, Massachusetts

Or consider the effect of retirement. When you work, you feel wanted, valued. You have a purpose. But leave the company, and you can lose your sense of who you are and what your role is in the world.

This was an issue in Jesus' time as well. In Mark, chapter 9, Jesus is walking along with his disciples from Galilee into Capernaum. During the journey, the disciples begin to have a conversation among themselves. Trying not to talk too loudly, the disciples are bickering over who is the greatest disciple of all.

When they reach Capernaum, Jesus asks what they were arguing about. They are too embarrassed to reply. But Jesus knows their minds and hearts. "If anyone wants to be first, he must be the very last, and the servant of all," he told them. (Mark 9:35)

One might expect the discussion to stop there. But one chapter later, James and John, two of the members of Jesus' inner circle, catch Jesus alone. "Teacher," they say, "we want you to do for us whatever we ask." But Jesus won't give an answer until the request is laid on the table. "Let one of us sit on your right hand and the other on your left when we go to glory," they ask him. In other words, they were playing office politics. They wanted a promotion to a position of prestige and honor.

Jesus' reply? "You don't know what you're asking."

The fact is, they weren't going to reach heights in God's kingdom by asking for favors. As Jesus had told them only days earlier, God treasures an attitude of servanthood, an attitude that puts "self" aside and allows God's power to shine through.

Moving up a rung or receiving a career kick isn't necessarily the guarantee to personal worth and satisfaction. Or to put it another way, self-worth is affected more by *how* you work than by where you work or what you do.

Faithful Attitudes

Like so many topics we explore in this book, workplace issues are affected by our spiritual beliefs and our attitudes regarding God. Three key attitudes from Scripture can help you live out your faith on the job.

An Ambitious Servant

First, God wants us to be ambitious in the workplace. But here's God's twist: he wants us to be ambitious about *serving* in the workplace. Jesus never condemned ambition. He simply redefined what we do with it and how we use it. What is the proper role of ambition? Jesus puts it clearly: to serve.

When Jesus' disciples came to him asking about a "promotion" when Jesus came into his kingdom, he never told them, "Your ambition is a sin." Instead, he told them their ambition was misplaced. "Wanna be great?" he asked. "Be a servant. Wanna be first in my kingdom? Be a slave to all."

That was a radical idea in Jesus' day, and it's no less radical for us. *The Apprentice?* Sure! A servant? Uhhh ... not so much. Servanthood doesn't exactly fit our idea of contemporary corporate culture. In fact, in some businesses, the culture tells us to aggressively elbow our way to the top without a concern about who we might hurt in the process: "It's not personal; it's business." Some companies reward influence and favoritism. Some see servanthood as a shortcoming.

Jesus recognized the need for people to feel as if they are getting ahead in life. He knew how that can affect our sense of self-worth. But he wanted to make certain our need was met the right way. No matter where you are in the career track, you can find self-worth right where you are when you are ambitious to serve.

Behold!

My friend David Thompson is a good example of living servanthood. Having graduated from a prestigious U.S. medical school, he decided to forgo a comfortable doctor's life in the States and instead take his skills to a third-world nation. There is no upscale income. There are no club memberships. David spends 14 hours a day, 6 days a week working with people who are dying of the typical diseases that ravish life around the world. But ask David, "Are you happy? Do you feel fulfilled? Are you content?" Without hesitating, David would tell you, "Absolutely! I'm serving. I'm touching lives. I'm bringing about change in the world."

You don't have to move to another country or even change jobs to serve. Begin right where you are. Consider all the everyday ways you can be a profoundly positive servant influence in the workplace:

- Offer to help a co-worker complete a rush project.

- Ask your boss for practical things you could be doing to make her job easier.

- Give a listening ear to a co-worker's personal struggles.

Opportunities such as these arise every day. When possible, take advantage of the chance to demonstrate a servant attitude—and you might be surprised to see your workplace transformed by your acts of faith.

Doing It for God

I've often wondered what sort of a difference it would make in our work ethic—how our attitudes might be changed—if, every morning when we rolled out of bed, we all remembered to say, "I am going to work today for God!" (Yes, even pastors and seminary presidents sometimes have to be reminded of that!)

One particular Bible verse comes to mind here. In writing to the church at Colosse, Paul is addressing a group of Christians who are convinced that their spiritual lives and their day-to-day lives are miles apart. "Our faith doesn't affect the way we live," they think. And yet in Colossians 3:23, Paul reminds them that their faith impacts a very practical area of life: their work. "Whatever you do, work at it with all your heart, as working for the Lord, not for men," he writes.

That phrase "as working for the Lord" means to give someone something special, to present a gift. In other words, work as if your work were a gift being given to God himself.

I don't know about you, but that really jump-starts my sense of satisfaction in my work. It restores excitement to even routine jobs. It makes handling even those must-do drudge tasks—say, filing—something more rewarding than they could be if God weren't part of the equation.

I once overheard a conversation during a high-school basketball game. Behind me, two men who were obviously managers for major companies were talking. Speaking about the lack of zest many of their employees demonstrate, one man lamented, "It used to be that one hour of pay meant one hour of work. But today, I swear we end up giving one week's pay for only one hour of work." He then went on to list a number of problems he sees: tardiness, intentional absenteeism, extended breaks, longer lunch hours.

What kind of an impact might it have on our jobs if we would remember that our work efforts are a gift to God? Would we work with more diligence, more care? Would we be more energetic, positive, and excited about the tasks we perform? And if so, just think of the impact that kind of attitude would have on our work environment—our colleagues, co-workers, bosses—as well as on our own sense of purpose and self-worth.

Working with Integrity

People of faith aren't exempt from the temptations in the workplace. Maybe that means taking a pen or a pad of Post-it Notes home, taking frequent breaks to surf the Internet and e-mail friends, or padding an expense account or overcharging a customer. Sometimes, we think we have it coming. *After all*, it's easy to think, *you just raised my insurance co-payment; the least you could do to compensate me is to let me copy this software onto my computer at home.*

The reasons don't really matter. Whether we're pocketing a cheap pen or taking the credit for a co-worker's work, the issue comes down to workplace integrity.

In Ephesians 4:28, Paul lays out a basic principle that needs to impact every area of our work: "He who has been stealing must steal no longer, but must work, doing something useful with his own hands, that he may have something to share with those in need." Paul's main point is to turn from lawless pursuits—"Don't steal"—and embrace honest work, but the underlying principle goes deeper. That's right: *integrity*.

I have to marvel at a man like the prophet Daniel. In his workplace, he faced endless opportunities to participate in actions inconsistent with God's plan for his life. And yet, when his enemies plotted against him, they did everything within their power to find a reason to put him to death. And as Daniel 6:4 tells us, "They could find no corruption in him, because he was trustworthy and neither corrupt nor negligent."

> **Faith 101**
>
> No matter what you do, strive to end each workday with a prayer: "Here, God, this is my gift. I've done the best I can do, and I give you this gift with pride."

That's the sort of indictment I would love to have leveled against me! "Well, Chuck, we looked as hard as we could into your work practices. We hired our spies. We talked to people who know you. We followed you, and we read all the notes in your daily planner. But we found nothing. In all your work, you're trustworthy and on top of things."

People who practice integrity in their work have a greater sense of self-worth than people who don't. They can look themselves in the mirror. They don't have to avoid their employer's watchful eyes.

Even more important, no misdeeds stand in the way of their relationship with God. When we compromise our integrity, we start to build barriers that eventually cut us off from having an open and honest relationship with God. We create areas of our life we don't want God to see. We rationalize the actions we don't want God to question. In the end, we sacrifice closeness with God.

When you seek to live out your faith in the workplace, it doesn't matter what you do, where your office is located, or how much you're paid. You will hear God say, "Well done! You have been a good and faithful servant."

Could there really be any better performance review than that?

The Least You Need to Know

◆ Regardless of what we do for a living, God wants us to approach our work from a perspective of faith.

◆ God is more concerned with our motivations and attitudes toward our work than the specific kind of job we find ourselves doing.

◆ We find our greatest sense of self-worth and meaning in the workplace when we work as if we were working for God.

◆ Faithful workers demonstrate servanthood and integrity in the workplace.

Chapter 16

Powerful Parenting

In This Chapter

- ◆ Giving them to God
- ◆ Parental prayers
- ◆ Practicing what we preach
- ◆ A faithful foundation

All of us who are parents probably like to think that our children will inherit our prized possessions after we're gone, appreciating and caring for them just as much as we do. But one of the greatest possessions we can pass along to them isn't a physical object at all. It's our faith. Faith will give our children the strength they need to face whatever may come over the course of their lives. It will help them respond to life's challenges even as it provides a profound source of joy and satisfaction.

Being *people* of faith means that, naturally, we desire to be *parents* of faith as well, nurturing the gift of godly belief.

Prized Possessions

Someone once asked me the provocative question, "What is your most prized possession?" I gave it some thought and then I replied, "Without a doubt, my children." No, they're not possessions in the sense that I own them. And they're not possessions in the sense that I think of them as material things, as I do a car or a microwave oven.

But when I think about the adjective *prized*, I have to say that my kids are the most valuable gift God has given to me. And because I do prize them, I am absolutely committed to passing on my faith to them.

Have you ever seen the movie *My Life*, starring Michael Keaton? It's a heart-wrenching film about a young man who discovers he is dying of cancer. His wife is pregnant, and he is forced to come to grips with the fact that he will not live to see the birth of his son. So he videotapes some significant segments of his life. He doesn't want to be forgotten, and he doesn't want his values to be forgotten either. He desperately wants to pass on important life lessons and beliefs to his child.

I've often asked myself what I can do to pass on my faith to my children. How can I prepare them to counteract the philosophies of our culture, in which they may be tempted to compromise their faith or, worse yet, to walk away from it completely?

Adopted by God

No matter how old your children are—whether toddlers, teenagers, or adults—we never stop wanting what's best for them. The story of 1 Samuel 1 offers some great advice about how to ensure that they have it.

When the book of 1 Samuel begins, a woman named Hannah is spending her time hanging out in the temple, begging God to bless her with the birth of a son. As a part of her cultural background, she believes she hasn't done her job as a woman unless she gives birth to a son. At this point in her life, is still hasn't happened, and she's "deeply disturbed." But then it does happen. According to 1 Samuel 1:19, "Elkanah lay with Hannah his wife, and the Lord remembered her prayer." Hannah conceived and gave birth to a son. She named him Samuel, which means, "I asked the Lord for him, and God answered."

In time, Hannah and Elkanah take Samuel to the temple, where they dedicate him to God. There, in a moment of celebration, they praise God for what he has done. In verse 28, Hannah says, "Now I give him to the Lord. For his whole life he will be given over to the Lord."

That's a tough thing to say as a parent. It's hard to give up our sense of control and give our children over to God. But it's a crucial step in being faithful parents.

I can remember when my daughter, Melissa, was getting ready to leave for college. At that point, I also realized that my twin boys, Mike and Josh, would soon be following her and leaving home to start their college careers. And it hit me: they would all soon be facing a bundle of critical choices that would impact the rest of their lives. And they'd be facing them without me standing at their side, pointing them in the right direction—assuming I'd even know what the right direction would be for them!

> **Behold!**
>
> Many churches today have infant-dedication services, where parents bring their newborns to be blessed and dedicated to God. But Hannah's statement implies something more. She wasn't simply asking God's blessing for Samuel. She was basically giving him up to be adopted by God.

Thankfully, I don't *have* to be at their side 24/7. I can entrust them to God's infinitely wiser care.

Dedicating our children to God is a way of celebrating life. It's a way of affirming that each tiny creature has been made in God's image and has a God-given destiny. And it's a way of taking the always-difficult step of releasing control and trusting in the wisdom of their Creator.

Into God's Hands

One of the best ways to instill godly values in the lives of our children is to release control and to just let God be God. Frankly, I'm not sure how it works, but I know it does. For evidence, you only have to look at the relative lack of success experienced by overly controlling, manipulative parents who seemingly work day and night to instill godly values in the lives of their kids.

I can point to hundreds of cases in which parents have asked, "Why aren't our children carrying on our values? We taught them differently!" In some cases, the issue is simply that the children have chosen differently. (That's *always* going to be a possibility.) But in many other cases, I have witnessed parents who—with good intentions—have actually attempted to control their children, forcing or manipulating them into following God.

But where does that control take their children? Down the road to rebellion, where the values they were trying so desperately to pass on are lost.

Beware!

Some people point to the Old Testament words, "Train up a child in the way he should go: and when he is old, he will not depart from it." (Proverbs 22:6) "See?" they say. "It's a promise from God. If you push your kids enough, God guarantees that even if they check out for a while, they'll eventually return to the faith." But that verse could also be translated this way: "Steer your children toward their God-given bent, and when they grow older, they'll reach their God-given destiny." The writer is reminding us that faith-filled parents help their children tap into their God-given gifts—realizing that, given the right environment of nurture and love, they'll live out their God-given inclinations in the future.

I know parents who think they have to make every decision for their children. They start a college fund at their alma mater on the day their child is born. Why? "Because my daughter is going to attend the college I graduated from!" I once spoke with a young father who said he fully expects to pick out his son's wife. My first thought when I heard that: *I wonder if you'll also try to pick out your son's second wife, too.*

Somehow, some of us have gotten the mistaken idea that disciplining, shaping, and guiding—all important aspects of our role as parents—means *controlling*. But when we start controlling rather than nurturing our children, we actually take the reins away from God.

Dedicating our children to God means placing their control and care firmly into God's hands. That means ...

◆ God gets to decide what my children will do with their lives.

◆ God gets to decide where my children are going to live.

◆ God gets to decide if—and who—my children are going to marry.

God gets to choose these paths—and all the rest. That doesn't mean we shouldn't continue to share our hopes and concerns directly with our

children. We should also continue to take these hopes and concerns to
God in prayer.

Praying as a Parent

Praying is sometimes the last thing we do. We treat it like calling 911
after the fire has started. Or we think of it as our last resort: "Well, I
guess all we can do now is pray." But according to Hannah's story,
prayer shouldn't be the final thing. Prayer should be the first thing.

Faith 101

You may be at the point where you feel you've already lost the battle
for your children's spiritual lives. Maybe you feel your relationship with
your children is damaged or even completely shattered. But do you
know what you can do for them right now? Hold them, by prayer,
continually in the presence of God. God can heal relationships. God
can change lives.

What should our prayers involve? Everything! Ever since our children's
birth, Marilyn and I have diligently prayed for the key choices they are
about to make. And I make sure my children know I'm praying for them:

- I pray that God will keep them sexually pure.

- I pray for their eventual spouses, whoever they might be.

- I pray that God will give them a clear sense of their God-given
  destinies.

- I pray that God will bring friends into their lives who hold similar
  Christ-centered values.

I like to think of prayer as the best preventive maintenance there is for
parents.

Show and Tell

Assuming Samuel grew up in a typical Jewish home, he would have had
no doubt about his father's faith in God. Sitting around the table, working out in the fields, before going to bed at nights—he would have
listened as his father told him the stories of his faith.

Faith 101

Many Christian families set aside time each week for reading a short Bible passage together, talking about what the verses mean for their daily life, sharing concerns to pray about, and then praying together. Such a time can have a powerfully positive impact.

Elkanah would have known and treasured an important teaching of the Law, from Deuteronomy 6:6. After giving Moses the commandments, God gives the prophet these words: "These commandments that I give you today are to be upon your hearts. Impress them on your children. Talk about them when you sit at home and when you walk along the road, when you lie down and when you get up."

What would your children say if someone were to ask them, "What do your parents believe? What are their core values?" Sometimes we think our children can pick up our values through osmosis. But in truth, the only way they'll learn—really learn—is if we show them and talk about them.

With all the time commitments the typical family faces these days, it's easy for us to live in the same house without ever really taking the time to communicate all that much. We pass each other while we're on the way to somewhere else. And in the process, our values aren't communicated. Or worse, we communicate something we don't intend: that our jobs or our hobbies or our sports take precedence over our families, over our faith.

As a father, I have to work hard to be sure that doesn't happen. I'm committed to talking about anything and everything with my children. I want my children to know my wife and I refrained from sexually expressing ourselves until marriage. I want my children to know I am so committed to a life of biblical stewardship that I will always give at least 10 percent to the ministry of the church—whether I'm a pastor or not. I want my children to know that in my younger years, I made some mistakes (like nearly flunking out of college because I didn't study!).

Behold!

Remember the definition of a *conservative parent*: a liberal with a teenage daughter.

I want my kids to not only see the faith, the lifestyle of values I practice. I want them to hear it from my lips.

One of the more encouraging aspects of my baby boomer generation is that many of my fellow boomers, having adopted a somewhat turbulent lifestyle in the 1960s, have decided they don't want their children following their example.

Many of my fellow boomers are returning to churches to provide their children with some moral backing—which is great. But sometimes in sending their children to church, they're hoping that the professionals will do for them what they need to be doing firsthand: passing on values that will impact their decisions.

This simply isn't enough. We need to be participating parents, teaching and talking about the important role God is playing in our lives.

Beware!

When pressed for time and resources, we can fall into the trap of handing our children over to educational institutions, saying, "Teach them," without checking on their homework or their tests. We can rely on medical professionals to "make them better" without taking an interest in what they're eating or how much they're exercising. And we can hand them over to the church and say, "Guide them." To truly succeed in passing along our faith as parents, we need to be more plugged in.

A Faithful Family

At this point, I have to share a major concern. Several years ago, I took a hard look at the church where I was serving as senior pastor. I didn't like everything I was seeing.

I noticed that some of the parents in our church were looking at church as just one option on their Sunday-morning menu. Church was definitely on their list of activities, of course, but it was sandwiched between karate classes, swimming classes, music lessons, soccer camp, football practice, and more.

And worship? I noticed that some families did choose to worship God as a family—but only when nothing better came along. If there was a chance to jump in the camper, drive to the cabin, go to the amusement park, or head to the woods during hunting season, they took it. Worship was just another option.

Now, don't get me wrong. I don't have anything against karate, swimming, music, amusement parks, or any of the rest of those things.

But for me, if I have to decide whether my child will be an Olympic-level swimmer, a black belt in karate, a first-chair violinist, or an authentic follower of Jesus ... Well, I take my chances with Jesus anytime.

Our children have an unerring way of sniffing out hypocritical behavior, particularly when it comes to the way their parents "practice what they preach." Kids can smell an inconsistency a mile away. That's why children need not only to have parents bring them to church; they need to have parents join them in this community of faith.

Our children need to see consistency in our spiritual lives. In fact, they beg for it. They want to see the real deal.

> **Beware!** _____
> Please, don't just drop your children off at the church's front door before heading to Starbucks for a relaxing hour with the Sunday paper. No matter how good the church is, we just can't afford to use the Sunday school, the Wednesday night youth program, or any other church ministry as some kind of spiritual baby-sitting service. Make church a whole-family affair.

The Joshua Rules

In our home, we have nurtured a set of "Joshua" rules for years. We call them the Joshua rules not because we have a son named Joshua (which we do), but because it was Joshua who said, "Choose for yourselves this day whom you will serve .... As for me and my household, we will serve the Lord." (Joshua 24:15)

So what are our Joshua rules? There are just three:

- **Rule #1:** The members of this family will maintain a daily and active quiet time with God and, at times, do so as a family.

- **Rule #2:** This family will worship together regularly.

- **Rule #3:** This family will engage in at least one midweek spiritual activity during the course of each week, a group where encouragement, support, and prayer take place.

Are we being too tough? Are we bordering on legalism? You might think so. But when my doctor says to me, "Chuck, if you want to lose weight, exercise and watch what you eat," what do I do? If I want to lose weight, I follow the rules!

Sure, they may be rules. But they're rules with a real purpose. They're rules that will help instill values that will last a lifetime.

No Guarantees

Okay, you've done absolutely everything right. You've followed the rules. You've lived your faith to the best of your ability. But are there any guarantees?

Unfortunately, there aren't. We can dedicate our children, surrendering control. We can pray for our children, before and after they're born. We can teach them from our experiences and our knowledge. We can bring them to God's presence through prayer. Will they make all the right choices—every time and all the time—as a result of our efforts? Probably not. After all, they're human beings, not computers. (And let's face it: even computers crash now and then.)

But the chances for your children's spiritual success are certainly much higher as a result of your efforts on their behalf. And even when they make poor choices or bad decisions, they have the grounding they need to find their way again to the welcoming and loving grace of God.

Maybe you've heard Jesus' parable about the prodigal, or lost, son told in Luke 15:11–32. I'll briefly recap it here: a father had two sons, one of whom requested his inheritance early. The father provided it, and the son took the money, headed for the big city, and quickly squandered it. Then a famine hit the land, and the son had nothing to live on. He ended up becoming a hired field hand, eventually so hungry he was tempted to eat the food he was feeding the pigs.

He realized things were better back home, even for his father's servants. So he "came to his senses" and went home, begging his dad's forgiveness and asking to become one of his hired men.

Even though the son had stopped loving himself, his father had never stopped loving him. Even when his son was a long way off, his father recognized him. And he ran to him with open arms. "This son of mine was lost!" the father said. "Now he is found!" The celebrating began in earnest.

The father had no assurance he would ever see this errant son again. He had no idea what had happened to him since he left. But the seeds of faithfulness he had planted in the young man's life eventually began to grow. And even though the son had fallen far since leaving his father's household, he was still able to "come to his senses" and turn his life around.

Faith 101

Every year for 15 years, we planted eight broccoli plants in our family garden. And for 15 years, our approach had been successful. But one year—despite watering, fertilizing, and weeding the same way we always had—all the plants died. It was a reminder that we can do all the right things, but sometimes our efforts still fail. The same is true with our children. Still, 14 good crops in 15 years is an incredible average. And this year, I'm taking my chances by doing the same things again.

God doesn't say, "Do this, and I'll give you a money-back, iron-clad guarantee." But he does say, "Do this and then trust me."

Passing on values to the children we value—that's a pretty weighty responsibility and, frankly, it scares me to death. Their choices, their decisions, may depend on *me*. I couldn't begin to face that kind of parenting pressure without God's help.

The Least You Need to Know

♦ Faith is a great inheritance to pass on to our children.

♦ Faith grows in our children when we give up control and turn them over to God.

♦ Faith grows in our children as we seek to live out and speak honestly about our beliefs.

♦ Faithful practices need to be a whole-family pursuit.

♦ There are no guarantees for our children's future, yet we can help to build a foundation of faith for them.

Chapter 17

Students of Faith

In This Chapter

- Education and self-worth
- Meaningful information
- Weighing worldviews
- Building faithful foundations

From public prayer to the posting of the Ten Commandments, the role faith can and should play in America's schools is at the top of the hot-button list. Ever since the 1925 *Scopes* trial—in which a Tennessee high school football coach and science teacher was prosecuted (successfully) for teaching evolution—there has been public debate about the extent to which spiritual beliefs should affect what gets taught in America's public schools.

All the discussion is important, to be sure. But it can be useful to consider the bigger picture, which tends to get overlooked. I'm talking about the way faith affects our approach to education and the way education can affect our faith—whether you're a high school or college student, a teacher, or a parent concerned about giving your child the best and most responsible education possible.

Putting It in Perspective

I have a friend who's fairly successful in his chosen career. He's in his early 40s, owns his own business, has made a modest name for himself, and holds a high elected position in an association devoted to his profession. What's more, he loves his work.

Yet almost every year, as September rolls around, he feels a tiny urge to go back to school for a Master's degree. My friend is self-employed and plans to stay that way. There's no way an M.A. could possibly help him earn more money or increase his reputation. In fact, I doubt whether he'd even learn much he doesn't already know in the process of acquiring another degree.

For now, his own doubts about the value of a Master's degree—not to mention the time commitment it would take—have kept him from enrolling at a local university. But it continues to be a struggle for him. Why? Because he has so many friends who have advanced degrees.

"I figure, if they could make it through a Master's program, I certainly could!" he says with a laugh. In other words, he's a little envious. For him, a Master's degree is a further endorsement that he's "made it" in his particular field of endeavor. The fact that he doesn't have one while so many of his acquaintances do makes him feel somewhat inadequate, like he's less of a "someone." Never mind that he's wholly successful without that piece of paper hanging on the wall. He still has those twinges of not quite measuring up.

Not surprisingly, the Bible says that sort of thinking is wrong.

More Than Learning

I have to say, for the record, that I believe in the profound difference education can make. I'd say that even if I weren't the president of a seminary.

But I also have to say there's more to living than just learning. In the words of the writer of Ecclesiastes: "Of making many books there is no end, and much study wearies the body." (Ecclesiastes 12:12)

Many Bible scholars think this verse was written at a time in which there was massive literary activity taking place in the world. Scholars were digging, philosophers were searching, and authors were writing it all down. And yet against that backdrop, the message is clear: there is no end to the acquisition of knowledge. No matter how much you learn, there will always be something you don't know. And the harder you study, the more weary you will become.

When I was in college—pulling the all-nighters, staying up late for the final exams—I knew what he meant. I had a strange way of getting ready for exams during my 4 years of college. I would go to my room after dinner and sleep for 2 hours, from 6 until 8 P.M. Then I'd wake up and study until 6 o'clock the next morning, take a shower, eat some breakfast, and take the test. And then I would crash.

> **Behold!**
>
> Think book publishing might be slowing down? Not a chance. More than 50,000 books are published every year in the United States alone. Worldwide, more than 300,000 new books appear every year. (I think a good percentage of them wind up on my bookshelves.)

When I worked my way through graduate school, I went through a similar process. The only difference was that I was part of a study group. That meant *three* of us would all follow this schedule together.

It worked great, but I came to a new appreciation of what that verse in Ecclesiastes meant. It seemed as though no matter how hard I studied, there was always something about the material I overlooked or forgot; I hadn't been able to learn it all. And after it was all over, I was dead tired!

Beware!

You can read, you can study, you can fall asleep to books on tape—all in the hope that you'll someday acquire enough information to help you to feel like a better person. But no matter how high you climb on the intellectual ladder, and no matter how many degrees you attach to the end of your name, it won't help your sense of self-worth. There's more to living than just learning.

A Doctor in the Family!

A few years ago, my father shared with me a form that I'd completed when I was in the seventh grade. One of the questions on that form was, "What is the highest degree you wish to attain?" followed by a list:

- ❑ High school diploma
- ❑ Bachelor's degree
- ❑ Master's degree
- ❑ Doctorate

Of course, now I look back and wonder, *What sort of question is that for a seventh grader?!* But also, I was amazed at how I'd responded. I had checked "Doctorate." Now, why in the world would a seventh-grader ever say he wanted a Ph.D.?

This is what I think happened: my father was a mathematics and physics teacher for 38 years. He taught full-time at the high school level and part-time at Penn State University as well as at various other colleges in western Pennsylvania. I can still remember hearing him lament, "I should have completed my dissertation and received my doctorate degree." He had completed all his other coursework for his Ph.D., but he wasn't able to complete the dissertation because of some family-related issues.

I'd grown up hearing his lament. My conclusion as a seventh-grader: if you really want to be happy, fulfilled, and worthy, get the doctorate degree. And eventually, I did it. I got my own doctorate.

A few months afterward, someone came to my office at the church I pastored, noticed the nameplate my brother bought for me ("Charles W. Moore, Doctor of Ministry"), and said, "Boy, Chuck, you must feel great about yourself." And for the first time, I thought about it.

Sure, it felt great to finally get the whole thing over with. But did it affect the way I felt about myself? Not really. Who I am as a person—a person loved and accepted and treasured by God—has nothing to do with the titles in front of my name or the degrees that follow it. It has nothing to do with the level of education I've completed.

Beware!

If you're in the process of getting a degree, or if you're thinking of undergoing a period of intense ongoing education in hopes of giving your sense of self-worth a boost, be careful. Accomplishing a task like that could be very helpful. But it will not be enough, in and of itself, to fill any inner hunger you might have for an increased sense of self-worth.

By the same token, if you've felt discouraged because you've never obtained the degree you might have checked on your own seventh-grade evaluation form, stop kicking yourself about it. God's love for you doesn't depend on how far you've gone, or how much you know, or how much you'll learn in the future.

Information Overload

I am amazed at how much useless information is available to the public these days. (Thank you, Internet!) For example, did you know ...

- The average a person will drink nearly 347 cans of soda every year?

- Antarctica holds 90 percent of the world's fresh water?

- There are 1 million ants for every person in the world?

I realize that one person's "trivia" may be another person's life work. (You can bet the folks at Pepsi and Coca-Cola don't think our per-capita soda consumption is trivial information!) I also admit it can be a lot of fun to know little facts about the world around us.

But never before has so much information been so easily available to so many of us. And it's quite possible that there's even some trivial information being taught in your classes and required on your tests. It's one thing to be able to pass your coursework successfully. But in the process of acquiring a broad range of information for a class, you'll certainly need to weed out the trivial from the truly meaningful.

What is meaningful information? It's information rooted in God's Word. It's information that emerges from his eternal truth.

My grandmother never went beyond a high school education. She was a bright, intelligent woman with a keen mind. But she saw her place in life to be alongside her husband, who was a career farmer. She had no titles, no degrees. But she also didn't suffer from the debilitating sense of self-worth (or maybe I should say "self-worthlessness") that seems to affect so many modern people.

Grandma amazed me. One evening, I walked into the living room to find her reading her Bible. I asked her, "Grandma, what are you doing?"

"Studying for my final exams," she said.

Behold!
Bibles are more often used to adorn coffee tables or press flowers than to feed souls for disciplined lives. —Charles Colson

That's focusing on meaningful information. It doesn't mean you throw out the *Encyclopedia Britannica* or you tune out your teachers. It means you ground yourself in the essential information of life and then rely on that foundation of truth to help you make sense of everything else.

It's Who You Know

In our age of information and education, it's worth remembering that, as faithful people, it's not *what* you know that counts. It's *who* you know.

Proverbs 2 calls us to hunger for a knowledge that really counts. And it's not a knowledge of facts; it's a knowledge of someone:

> Store up my commands within you, turning your ear to wisdom and applying your heart to understanding, and if you call out for insight and cry aloud for understanding, and if you look for it as for silver and search for it as for hidden treasure, then you will understand the fear of the Lord and find the knowledge of God. (Proverbs 2:1–5)

I clearly don't want to discourage anyone from educating themselves. I mean, I'm the president of a seminary—I believe very strongly in the value of education! But I also think it's important to put our learning into proper perspective. We can know facts. We can acquire information. We can be brilliant thinkers. But in the end, these are not our yardsticks for measuring our own value—and they certainly aren't the best measures of anyone else, either.

Please don't spend all your time chasing facts, pursuing information, and climbing the academic ladder until you know the One who can really make a difference in your life. When you do have a relationship with God, that relationship will—or should—have an impact on how you approach day-to-day life in the classroom.

True to Your School—or Your Faith?

In John 14:6, Jesus says, "I am the way and the truth and the life." Jesus is truth. And that idea has led faithful people throughout history to the understanding that "all truth comes from God" or, to put it another way, "All truth is God's truth."

Faith 101

For some Christian families, the solution for dealing with controversy in the classroom is to enroll their children in Christian schools. Others take a more dramatic step, choosing to home-school their kids. Still others believe Christians can have the greatest impact if they are active in public schools. The choice is a personal one. Regardless of your own choice, I encourage you to pray about the implications and then take whatever steps you need to, to ensure that your kids, no matter where they attend school, get the broadest and richest education possible.

As students, you don't have to worry about what you'll learn from your studies. You don't have to be afraid about discovering facts about the world that might alter your preconceptions. You don't have to be anxious about discovering new or even uncomfortable truths. God holds them all in his hands.

That said, it can be valuable to enter the classroom with at least some skepticism. One way to really understand new information is to probe it, ask questions, test it to see if it really holds up under scrutiny. I don't recommend being a cynic, but I also don't recommend just being a sponge.

One of the first things a faithful student should be skeptical about is your own approach to the classroom. How you view your spiritual life in relation to your school life can affect other students, teachers, and your own spiritual growth.

I want to look at four basic responses students might make.

Separation

Some students see no connection whatsoever between their studies and their faith. Art, science, mathematics—none of them seem to have any relevance to their spiritual lives. They see the dots, but they don't connect them to their faith.

As a result, their influence on campus may be nonexistent or limited to a small group of like-minded believers. They write their papers and take their exams without ever considering how the topics might challenge or enhance their spiritual beliefs.

Accommodation

Some students find their beliefs modified and shaped with every new class, every new lecture.

Don't misunderstand: our faith can deepen as we educate ourselves. I mean, we all carry around misconceptions about the world and about our faith. No matter how mature we might be in our beliefs, education can help bring us closer to God's truth. But some Christians end up accommodating their faith whenever it is challenged by their studies, and that can be potentially harmful.

Beware!

Don't get me wrong: psychology and comparative religions are great subjects to study. The danger lies in allowing their assumptions to obscure what you already know to be true about God.

For example, studying psychology might lead some students to see prayer as a merely helpful psychological event in which we're basically talking to ourselves, making ourselves feel better in the process. Studying comparative religions might lead others to water down Jesus' claim to be the way, the truth, and the life.

Faithless

Sometimes students respond to the challenges of high school and college life by giving up their faith altogether. Maybe they become friends with peers who don't hold any specific spiritual beliefs. Or maybe their studies lead them to the conclusion that God doesn't exist. Or that he doesn't care. Or that his people have been so messed up through the centuries that they should be rejected.

And so they also reject God.

Faithful

And then, of course, some students remain faithful—and grow even more so—over the course of their school years. Unwilling to separate, accommodate, or abandon their faith, these students integrate their faith with their studies. They strive to think and act faithfully.

Students who think faithfully understand Jesus' claim over all aspects of life, as described in Colossians 1:16–17:

> For by him all things were created: things in heaven and on earth, visible and invisible, whether thrones or powers or rulers or authorities; all things were created by him and for him. He is before all things, and in him all things hold together.

Notice how many times the words *all things* occur throughout these two verses. Jesus is the Creator of all things, he is before all things, and all things are reconciled to him. There isn't any curriculum, any class assignment, any school activity that lies outside his jurisdiction.

What does that look like? Let's take a look.

Faithful Students

Here's something easy to miss as you're reading the Bible: the Bible shows men and women as inherently religious creatures.

"Duh!" I can hear you saying. "It's the Bible, after all."

Yes, it is. But it's incredibly easy to forget—or to minimize—the fact that each of us is a spiritual creature in need of something beyond ourselves to worship. Most of the people in the Bible lived their lives in an environment where that was never even questioned. That's not necessarily the world most of us find ourselves in today.

World(view) Turning

If we don't reflect God, we'll mirror something else. (And in Bible terms, that "something else" would be called an idol.) Paul puts it this way:

> Although they claimed to be wise, they became fools and exchanged the glory of the immortal God for images made to look like mortal man and birds and animals and reptiles.... They exchanged the truth of God for a lie, and worshiped and served created things rather than the Creator. (Romans 1:22–23, 25)

The Bible's pretty clear about this: either we serve God, or we serve something he created. Simple.

Everybody places confidence in someone or something. I guess, in that sense, everyone is "religious." Whether or not we come right out and say it, we all interpret the events of life within some framework that tries to make sense of what's going on. Naturally, our decisions and choices flow out of this worldview.

Faith 101

In Jesus' famous sermon on the Mount of Olives, he tells believers we are to be salt and light for the world. Believers give the world flavor (like salt) and point the way to truth (like a light shining on a hillside). If we cease to do either of those things, we've lost some of our value for the people around us. Staying faithful requires diligence in the face of opposing beliefs and worldviews.

Mapping Our World

If you're a student, everyone on your campus has a view of the world that affects the way they think and approach their studies.

A worldview is kind of like a road map. It tells us the "lay of the land" and how to get from one place to another. But we all operate according to different maps, which show the world differently and suggest different routes through life. We're best able to mesh our education and our faith when we get a handle on the road maps being used by those teaching us.

Here's what I'm getting at: a professor walks into the college lecture hall at 8 o'clock on Tuesday morning. When she begins to lecture on electrical engineering, the literary criticism of a play, or the molecular structure of a cell, is she simply giving us the bare facts? Is her lecture totally divorced from who she is as a person and what her fundamental beliefs might be?

No. She brings to her lecture all the baggage that comes with her worldview. As faithful students, we need to ask questions about our professors' and textbooks' underlying presuppositions, such as ...

◆ Does what's being taught assume that God plays no role at all in life?

◆ Are theories and hypotheses treated as theories and hypotheses— or are they given the weight of proven fact?

◆ Do any statements about God jibe with the God described in the Bible and the God I've experienced as real in my own life?

Questions such as these help to get at the worldview roots of what's being taught. That doesn't mean you should reject the teaching or the teacher; it just means you'll understand, going in, what assumptions are at the heart of what's being taught.

As a faithful student, you can weigh the information and better sift out the facts and the truth from the maybe-not-so-true beliefs of the teacher or the textbook authors.

A Faithful Foundation

Of course, the whole idea of asking worldview questions is beside the point if we're not all that sure about what we believe ourselves.

To successfully integrate our faith with our studies, we need to be thoroughly grounded in the Bible and in a biblical understanding of life. We can only tell what's false if we understand what God has revealed to us to be true.

Faith 101

Don't be bashful about banding together with other Christian students, seeking out Christian professors, and studying Christian authorities in your fields of interest. Such relationships can help you develop a Christian perspective—and live it out in the classroom.

Bible study and the support of other Christians on campus is important. But neither one of these things is something you have to do alone. I have no doubt you'll be able to find groups of fellow believers on any high school or college campus. And together, you can meet to read and study the Bible, pray for one another, and discuss the challenges and successes you've had in integrating your faith with your studies and social lives.

The Least You Need to Know

◆ Self-worth is rooted in our relationship with God, not in our educational achievements.

◆ Faith gives us a filter for weighing new information and making sense of the world.

◆ Faithful students integrate their beliefs with their studies.

◆ We can only judge truth when we're grounded in the Bible and working to live a faithful life.

Chapter 18

Money, Money, Money

In This Chapter

- ◆ Who owns the money?
- ◆ Treasures here and there
- ◆ Financial freedom
- ◆ Giving, saving, and spending

Preachers often can talk all they want about prayer, Bible reading, evangelism—even sin—and most people don't feel too threatened. Raise the issue of money, though, and suddenly everyone reaches protectively for their wallets and purses!

We get nervous when someone tries to tell us what to do with our hard-earned dollars. It's a hot-button topic for most of us—and why not? Money plays a uniquely important role in our daily lives. It's something we like to keep private, whether we have a little or a lot.

Being faithful, though, means opening up the dollars-and-cents side of our lives to God. It means following, financially, where he leads us.

What Do You Want?

One of my co-author Bob's favorite movies is the classic 1940s drama *Citizen Kane*. Critics have called the film one of the best (if not *the* best) American movie ever made. If you haven't seen it, rent it and judge for yourself. And if you'd like some insight into money and motivation, watch for the scene between the unnamed reporter and a man named Mr. Bernstein.

The reporter is in Bernstein's office, asking about the rise and fall of Bernstein's former boss, Charles Foster Kane. The reporter is a little awed by Kane's multimillion-dollar fortune. Mr. Bernstein, someone who knew what Kane was really like, isn't so impressed.

"It isn't hard to make a lot of money," Bernstein says, dismissively, "if all you want is to make a lot of money."

Think about that: "It isn't hard to make a lot of money, if *all you want* is to make a lot of money."

I realize this is just a line of dialogue from a movie. But there's an incredible amount of insight in it. Obviously, cash flow is important. Unless we decide to be an entirely self-sufficient hermit, we all need money. But the fact that you're reading this book makes me think making a lot of money is not *all* you want. You also yearn for meaning in life. You want to feel like a whole human being. You want to know that there is a God who created you and cares about you.

In *Citizen Kane*, you could argue that Kane at one time or another sacrificed all those things. For nearly all his life, his sole goal was to make more money so he could, as he says, "buy things." He relied on his purchasing power to fill a void in his life that had existed since his childhood. In the end, he died surrounded by thousands of *things*—but not a single friend.

> **Behold!**
>
> The man who dies ... rich dies disgraced.
>
> —Andrew Carnegie

Whose Money?

Don't misunderstand: there's nothing inherently bad about money. It's all just metal and paper, after all (plus all those modern anti-counterfeiting devices). But because money enables us to do so much—buy a home, see the world, feed the hungry, fund an education—it can exert a powerful influence over how we live our lives.

Ask yourself, "Who owns my money? To whom does it really belong?" Chances are you might be tempted to answer, "Well, whose wallet is it in? Obviously, I own it. I earned it, and it's mine to spend, invest, and use as I want."

Faith suggests a better answer. Faith says, "I have what I have because God has given it to me." In fact, faith goes one step further and adds, "It doesn't really belong to me at all. I've been entrusted with this money to manage it for God. It's on loan to me."

Psalm 24:1 reads, "The earth is the Lord's, and everything in it." From a money standpoint, that includes everything from the loose change sitting on our bedroom dresser to our 5- or 6- or 7-figure salary. It's all God's. What difference does that make? It means we are expected to handle that money with wisdom, with more than simply our own immediate needs at the forefront of our minds. The biblical concept for that is called *stewardship*.

def•i•ni•tion

Stewardship is the human responsibility, entrusted to us by God, to care for his creation. Being good stewards of the money that has been entrusted to us means demonstrating wisdom in how we give, how we save, and how we spend—remembering every step of the way that the money we have is merely on loan to us from God.

Wallet and Heart

So if there's nothing inherently bad about money and God just wants us to remember that all we have belongs to him, why do so many Bible verses cast such a negative light on money and riches?

> A man who has riches without understanding is like the beasts that perish. (Psalm 49:20)

> Do not wear yourself out to get rich; have the wisdom to show restraint. (Proverbs 23:4)

The sleep of a laborer is sweet, whether he eats little or much, but the abundance of a rich man permits him no sleep. (Ecclesiastes 5:12)

That's just a small sample. Kind of makes you wonder: what's God got against having money?

Well ... nothing, actually. What God *is* against are the sinful attitudes that all too often come with riches: greed, entitlement, an inflated sense of self-worth, abuse of power. When money leads to these kinds of responses, it starts to become something more than mere paper and metal, a tool with which we've been entrusted. It begins to take on the weight of a god in our lives.

Beware!

Raise your hand if you believe the Bible says, "Money is the root of all evil." Don't believe it for a minute. This is one of the most misquoted passages in the Bible. In fact, the Bible, in 1 Timothy 10, says, "*The love of* money is the root of all evil." Why? As 1 Timothy 10 continues, "Some people, eager for money, have wandered from the faith and pierced themselves with many griefs." (Okay, you can put your hand down now.)

That's what Jesus was getting at when he said, "It is easier for a camel to go through the eye of a needle than for a rich man to enter the kingdom of God." (Mark 10:25) Jesus knew just how tight money's grasp could become in our lives. If we fall into the trap of believing that money is all we need, money becomes our guiding light and God doesn't have any choice but to slip into the backseat of our lives.

The alternative—and it's important whether our bank accounts are healthy and thriving or on critical life support—is to be sure our allegiance never strays from God. Never settle for a runner-up god such as money. "Provide purses for yourselves that will not wear out, a treasure in heaven that will not be exhausted, where no thief comes near and no moth destroys," Jesus said. "For where your treasure is, there your heart will be also." (Luke 12:33–34)

God wants our treasure and our hearts to remain rooted in him.

Master and Servant

Many of us might think that if we can get our hands on enough money, then we'll really be free: *If only I had enough money, then I would be free from anxiety, worry, and fear.* But is it true? Does it work?

For many people, having enough money isn't the tough part. They grab every investment opportunity that comes their way. They meticulously monitor their investments. They follow the trail from paycheck to checkbook to budget spreadsheet like an ant following the crumbs on a picnic. Nothing gets by them. They're determined they will have enough.

But what really happens? Preoccupied by their need to have "enough," they become imprisoned by their preoccupation. Instead of becoming free, they become trapped. They may get the "having enough money" part of the equation right, but they still struggle to get past the worry.

Of course, planning for the future is important. And there's nothing wrong with putting enough money aside for the proverbial "rainy day." But here's an axiom I've learned: ultimate freedom doesn't come through what you're hoping to get; it lies in what you already have. Freedom from the fear that you won't have enough doesn't come when you get enough, however much that might be. Rather, freedom from fear comes when you realize what you have in your relationship with God.

Faith 101

A few years ago Marilyn and I took a trip to Florida. Marilyn had to leave early while I went on to attend a conference at a five-star resort. The last night before Marilyn left for home, we stayed in a "starless" motel, equipped with a hard mattress and poor air conditioning. The next day, I moved into my conference hotel accommodations: a luxurious room with a view of the sparkling Atlantic Ocean. You know what I thought, though? *I'd rather be in an inexpensive hotel with the bride of my dreams than in a five-star resort all alone.* Besides the obvious fact that I love my wife, we're meant to live in relationships. Money is useful for buying many things, but it's helpless when it comes to providing that kind of relationship.

Consider Howard Hughes. If you saw the movie *Aviator*, you may remember a Hughes who was always preoccupied with a new worry. His wealth didn't free him from worry; it actually created more worry.

When, as Hughes did, we allow money to occupy our thoughts to the extent that it becomes an obsession—or the driving force for how we live—then it becomes our master. Faith helps us view money in its proper perspective—as a tool, a servant that assists rater than a ruler that demands we bend to its will.

A Faith Perspective

When we turn our finances over to God, our faith naturally affects everything we do with that money—from how and when we give it away to how we spend and save.

Giving

We learn at a young age that if we want to get ahead, we have to be on the taking side of things. As children, we learn how to fight for what we think rightfully belongs to us.

In Luke 9:24–25, Jesus had something interesting to say about that position: "Whoever wants to save his life will lose it, but whoever loses his life for me will save it. What good is it for a man to gain the whole world, and yet lose or forfeit his very self?" That word *save* literally means to clutch, to grab, to hold on so tightly that one is unwilling to share control—like little kids fighting for toys in a sandbox.

But Jesus tells us that God's way is different. The secret to fulfillment doesn't lie in clutching—it lies in releasing! Or to put it another way: it's better—more fun, more fulfilling, more enriching—to give than to receive!

Faith 101

Not sure how much you can reasonably afford to give away? Consider these verses from Luke:

> As he looked up, Jesus saw the rich putting their gifts into the temple treasury. He also saw a poor widow put in two very small copper coins. "I tell you the truth," he said, "this poor widow has put in more than all the others. All these people gave their gifts out of their wealth; but she out of her poverty put in all she had to live on." (Luke 21:1–4)

Faith turns people into givers, not takers. Faith, focusing on what we have and who we have in God, causes a person's heart to swell with thanksgiving and to look beyond their own private worlds. Faith—far from clutching, grabbing, hoarding, or keeping—opens its hands to share.

Faith is a reminder that we have what we have because of God. With that thought in mind, it makes it a lot easier to give what we have away. When the postal service holds its annual food drive for the homeless, we don't give reluctantly. Faith joyfully gives it away. When the United Way comes and asks for an annual gift, faith joyfully reaches into its pocket. When a church youth group sends a group of teenagers on a mission trip, faith doesn't respond, "Let them pay for it themselves." Faith joyfully gives money away, including *tithes*, realizing that we have what we have because of God.

def•i•ni•tion _____

A **tithe** represents 10 percent of our income, given over to God for his use.

Do *joy* and *giving* seem mutually exclusive?

There's an incredible story about giving in the Old Testament. In Exodus 35 and 36, a group of people from Israel are constructing a tabernacle, or holy place of worship, for God. The people couldn't run to their local building-supply superstore to pick up the materials; they had to share what they owned if they were going to make the tabernacle a reality.

Beware! _____

Nothing could be more logical than believing we cannot give away money if we're struggling to meet our own needs. This is one of those areas, though, when logic is often miraculously confounded by God's power. Many believers have discovered that God blesses their giving and continues to meet their needs. Before you dismiss the idea of giving money away, try it—and ask God to bless your efforts. You may be surprised at the results.

Here's the amazing part: they gave much more than was needed to complete the construction project. Their leader, Moses, had to step in and tell them, "Stop giving! We have enough."

That's pretty remarkable. And that's how faith affects our giving.

Saving

It's no secret that I *love* a good bargain. But have you ever really thought about how we sometimes use the word *save* to actually mean "spend"? We clip coupons, go on a shopping spree, and come home from the store to announce, "I just saved $50!" If you find yourself buying items you don't really need or wouldn't otherwise purchase just so you can "save money" with coupons or special sales, you're not really saving anything. You're just spending.

Some people think having real faith means you never have to worry about saving. Their perspective is: "If God says he takes of the birds and the trees and the flowers"—which he does, in Matthew 6:26—"why should I worry about money? He'll take care of me."

Yes, he will. But as we've seen from the very first chapter of this book, God's perspective is eternal. Because God sees our lives from here to eternity, his notion of "care" for us will not always mesh with our own, more immediate perspective. And as we've seen in this chapter, money is not God's number-one priority.

In other words, how we handle our finances is our responsibility. Being wise spenders is just another facet of our role as good stewards of all God has entrusted to us. Faith believes that God looks out for our needs, yes. But faith also believes that God provides for our future by asking us to exercise personal responsibility today.

Faith believes that the gifts we have today are God's way of preparing us for tomorrow. So being a good steward means setting aside some money for the future—both the knowns (like a child's education) and the unknowns (illness or temporary job loss). I'm not talking about stockpiling our investments while not sharing anything with others. And I'm not talking about relying on our riches instead of our relationship with God. I'm talking about reasonable saving that's informed and intelligent.

Of course, this raises a question: "Then how much should I save?"

I believe savings should be divided into three categories:

- ◆ Emergency needs
- ◆ Short-term goals
- ◆ Long-term destinations

Behold!

There's a story told about a man whose house was flooding. A neighbor stopped by to help. However, the man refused, claiming, "God will save me." Eventually, the man was forced to his roof. While he waited on the roof, a woman rowed up in a small boat. "Can I give you a ride somewhere?" she asked. The homeowner refused her help, claiming, "God will save me." A few minutes later a helicopter hovered above the man's roof while lowering a ladder. Again, the man rejected the help, claiming, "God will save me."

The waters continued to rise. A few hours later, the man drowned. When he stood before God, he was indignant. "Why didn't you save me?" he demanded.

"Don't blame me!" God told him. "I sent you a neighbor, a boat, and a helicopter."

An emergency need is something like a refrigerator that breaks down or the deductible on your medical insurance. These are the unexpected surprises that come around every so often.

The short-term goals are things such as holidays, birthdays, and anniversaries. The kitchen remodel you want to do. That special vacation you've been dreaming about. Those property taxes you don't want to think about.

And the long-term destinations? They're events and experiences that are 10 years and beyond. They're things such as the cost of college, purchasing a house, or saving for retirement. They're life's "big-ticket" items. They may take a bit longer to prepare for, but ignoring or neglecting them won't make them go away.

> **Faith 101**
>
> There is desirable treasure, and oil in the dwelling of the wise, but a foolish man squanders it. (Proverbs 21:20, New King James Version)

Spending

Open the Sunday newspaper in practically any city, and what do you find? Ads, ads, and more ads! (I recently weighed my Sunday *Chicago Tribune* only to discover that the 4-pound newspaper contained

---

Behold!

Money will buy a bed, but
  not sleep;
Books, but not brains;
Food, but not appetite;
Finery, but not beauty;
A house, but not a home;
Medicine, but not health;
Luxuries, but not culture;
Amusements, but not
  happiness;
Religion, but not salvation;
A passport to everywhere but
  heaven.

—Author unknown

2.5 pounds of ads!) What do the ads say to us? "Live the American dream!" "Trade up your lifestyle." "Pursue your passions!" "Get what's new—before it's old news."

In our consumption-inundated culture, companies fight for their share of your money, whether they're pushing designer clothes, gourmet coffee, or the latest iPod. It's the American dream: life, liberty, and the pursuit of a little bit more!

But when faith enters the picture, what happens? We begin to understand the deeper value of limits and restraint. A faithful person can look boldly into the face of the advertising culture and respond, "I don't need you to count." Realizing that ultimate satisfaction, freedom, and fulfillment are the byproducts of a faith relationship, the buying beast is suddenly tamed.

The Least You Need to Know

◆ The money we have is entrusted to us by God.

◆ God wants our hearts to remain rooted in him and not be drawn away by a love for money.

◆ Faith enables us to see money as a tool or a servant rather than an all-consuming master.

◆ Faith has an effect on how we give away, spend, and save money.

Chapter 19

Strength in Times of Trial

In This Chapter

- A firm foundation
- God's love, power, and faithfulness
- Ever-present help
- Strength in God

You know it's going to be a bad day when your twin brother forgets your birthday. Or you turn on the TV and see a map of emergency routes out of your town. Or you have that dream where you show up to class for a test, completely unprepared—and then you realize you're wide awake.

Humor can help us cope with some of life's minor traumas, but there's nothing funny about the fact that all of us are going to have some bad days—days that range from anxious or stress-filled to days that feel like one long, hard, uphill struggle.

We might even have some days when the world is pulled out from under us and we're left wondering just how we're going to make it through.

For Christians, God is our ultimate source of strength in tough times. But that doesn't mean we just have to say the magic words and—*poof!*—our problems disappear. All of us, regardless of our beliefs, struggle. Faith helps us realize, though, that we don't walk alone through life's valleys.

Changing Times

In the summer of 1997, moviegoers got to see their world dramatically changed by two surprise volcanic eruptions, in *Dante's Peak* and *Volcano*. And then, to highlight just how original Hollywood is, a similar situation happened again the very next year: in the summer of 1998, *Armageddon* and *Deep Impact* both told the story of what might happen if a giant meteor were on a collision course with Earth.

Whether the disaster is a high-rise fire, a global climate shift, or an upside-down cruise ship, movie audiences seem to enjoy weathering dramatic events—if only to see that people really can cope, no matter how bleak the situation might look. After all, if these characters can deal with meteors and volcanoes, surely we can face our own less-than-earthshaking trials without giving in to confusion or fear.

You don't have to look far to see evidence that instability is a major part of our lives:

- ◆ Nearly 40 percent of all new marriages end in divorce.

- ◆ Most of us will work seven different jobs and explore at least two completely different careers.

- ◆ The majority of Americans will move at least eight times over the course of their lifetime.

I've read surveys that said two thirds of all Americans are concerned about deadly violence in our schools. Thirty percent are worried about mad cow disease. Add in the very real concerns about terrorism, the stock market, serious illness—even war—and you might wonder how anyone could feel anything *but* confusion and fear these days.

To see how real people dealt with such situations, we can turn to the Bible. The Bible is kind of like the ultimate disaster movie; it chronicles a lot of very serious trials over the course of thousands of years. But it also has the ultimate solution for every one of them: as people of faith, we can turn for strength and stability to the God who does not change.

Unchanging God

In theological circles, we have a 25¢ word for the unchanging nature of God: *immutable*. It means God is consistent, changeless. His character, unlike our human society, is the same yesterday, today, and tomorrow.

Because Scripture is so packed with prime examples of people—and nations—facing trials, I'm going to bounce around from book to book more than usual in this chapter. But I think the rewards are going to be worth all the page turning. (You *are* following along with a Bible of your own, right?)

I think the prophet Malachi, writer of the last book in the Old Testament, offers some important facts about God's unchanging nature. Keeping these facts in mind can give us a strong foundation as we seek to face our own trials in faith.

def•i•ni•tion

God is **immutable**. He does not change and cannot *be* changed. What was true about God 5,000 years ago will still be true about God 5,000 years in the future. This aspect of God's character can be a great source of strength in the midst of our own constantly changing circumstances.

Unchanging Love

In Malachi 1:2, the prophet begins his prophecy by announcing the best piece of good news humanity has ever heard: "'I have loved you,' says the Lord." That's almost childish in its simplicity. Still, it's important. God wants his people to remember his past love in spite of current, unstable times.

Yet notice the next phrase that appears in that verse, "But you ask, 'How have you loved us?'" This is pretty close to our modern, dismissive response: "Yeah, whatever." The people in Judah were wondering, in the depths of their hearts, "Is God's love for real? Are you sure we can count on it?" These are the questions that naturally rise to the surface when we're struggling in life, when things aren't going the way we hoped or planned.

The answer is a resounding "Yes!" God's love *is* real, and it will never stop.

Behold!

A few years ago, I was on an airplane returning from a trip to the west coast. As we were coming into Chicago, we hit some bumpy weather. The pilot told everyone to return to their seats and fasten their seatbelts. Then we really hit it: stomach-churning turbulence.

As I looked around at the other passengers' faces, I could see concern, fear, and anxiety. Yet what fascinated me was a young child in front of me. Never once did he cry. He sat relaxed, quiet, apparently content—looking as if he weren't concerned in the least; maybe he was too young to even make sense of the situation. I couldn't help noticing that he sat cradled in his mother's arms. She was calm, and I think he could tell she was not about to let him go.

God says, "No matter what you face or encounter, relax in the turbulence. I will never let you go."

Unchanging Power

In Malachi 1:11, Malachi reminds his audience that ultimate power rests in God alone. "My name will be great among the nations," God says, "from the rising to the setting of the sun. In every place incense and pure offerings will be brought to my name, because my name will be great among the nations."

Given the times in which we live, we might think there are other things that hold ultimate power—technology, biological science, weapons of mass destruction. No matter how powerful these and other "powers"—both good and bad—seem to be, God makes his point perfectly clear: I am the only source of ultimate power.

I want to jump briefly from the last book in the Old Testament to the last book in the New Testament, Revelation. In Revelation 4:6–7, the apostle John gets a glimpse of heaven. As he looks up at the throne of

God, he sees "four living creatures, and they were covered with eyes, in front and in back. The first living creature was like a lion, the second was like an ox, the third had a face like a man, the fourth was like a flying eagle."

For us today, it just sounds like John saw some kind of weird zoo exhibit. But in John's day, this vision had great significance. The Jewish rabbis taught that the mightiest of wild animals is the lion, the mightiest of domestic animals is the ox, the mightiest of birds is the eagle, and the mightiest of all is man. Yet the idea that Revelation conveys is that none of these "mightiest powers" compares to God.

Revelation 4:8 goes on to tell us that even these powerful creatures are constantly acknowledging the supreme power of God: "Day and night they never stop saying: 'Holy, holy, holy is the Lord God Almighty.'"

Unchanging Faithfulness

Okay, back to Malachi. He is writing to a group of people who have become somewhat sloppy in certain elements of their faith. One area was the tithe. God had instructed his people, in response to his generosity and kindness, to reciprocate by giving 10 percent of their income to him. But they've been failing.

God offers them a challenge:

> "Bring the whole tithe into the storehouse, that there may be food in my house. Test me in this," says the Lord Almighty, "and see if I will not throw open the floodgates of heaven and pour out so much blessing that you will not have room enough for it." (Malachi 3:10)

Test me in this, God says. Bring your gifts like I ask. And what will occur? I will be faithful. You can count on me.

Recently I read this statement shared by a pessimistic cynic (assuming that's not redundant): "You will know you have reached the stage of adulthood when you realize that everyone in your life who *could* have disappointed you *has*." Maybe, sooner or later, most people do let us down. After all, we're human, not perfect.

Yet that truth doesn't have to leave us despairing. Despite the erratic responses of human beings, there is one who can be counted on completely: God.

Knowing all these great facts about God doesn't mean they're easy to apply when we find ourselves caught up in a current struggle or trial. Let's look at some ways we can make these beliefs about God a regular part of how we face dark times as faithful believers.

The Taxing Problem of Worry

I have a good friend—I'll call him Ross—who had a particularly bad March day not too many years ago. He knew he and his wife would owe money to the IRS come tax time, and he'd put off filling out his 1040 form as long as he could. When he finally got around to doing the paperwork, he discovered, much to his shock, that they were $1,500 in the hole. That was about $1,500 more than they could afford to pay.

He broke the news to his wife the next morning. "How are we ever going to pay our taxes?" Ross asked. His wife gave him a look that *really* made him start worrying. "Do you expect me to tackle this by myself?" he asked, panicking.

"Of course not," she told him. "But you know we approach situations like this differently. I don't see any point in worrying about money when God knows what we need."

Ross knew in his heart that she was right. But he'd been a worrier for as long as he could remember. "Worrying is my active response to seemingly overwhelming problems," he told me later. "Worrying means I'm not standing idly by, twiddling my thumbs. I'm *doing* something."

But worrying is not exactly the *best* "something."

God doesn't want our vision to be so clouded by worry that we forget to look for his saving hand in the situation. "Look at the birds of the air; they do not sow or reap or store away in barns, and yet your heavenly Father feeds them." Jesus says in Matthew 6:26. "Are you not much more valuable than they?"

Then Jesus goes from birds to buds, pointing at the lilies that "do not labor or spin" yet are clothed in finer garments than Solomon himself. (And Solomon had the finest garments money could buy.) The conclusion? "Seek first his kingdom and his righteousness ... Do not worry about tomorrow." (Matthew 6:25–34)

For many of us, that's easier said than done. Ross knew in his head that God was in control of *every* situation. But as he says, "It's still a struggle for that message to work its way down to my heart."

So Ross prayed about the situation. He asked God to calm his spirit. And then he boldly asked God to help him solve the problem. God came through. On April 14, Ross and his wife had been able to do enough freelance work to earn the extra $1,500 they needed to pay their tax bill.

"We got there by grace—not worry—using the gifts God has given us," he now admits. "I got a valuable refresher course in trusting God."

> **Beware!**
>
> Despite being quoted a lot, "The Lord helps those who help themselves" never once appears in the Bible. In fact, the Lord helps those who *can't* help themselves. That, of course, means all of us.

In the Pits

Now, I want to go back to the Bible's first book, Genesis. (I warned you about the page turning!) The story of Joseph and his brothers offers a perfect example of the power of faith to help us overcome adversity in life.

Joseph was a 17-year-old with a lot of brothers and step-brothers who, not surprisingly, didn't like hearing about his dreams he was convinced were prophetic—the ones where they all bowed down to worship him. His brothers didn't care for the implication. They were jealous. So they plotted to kill him.

In Genesis 37:21, we learn that Joseph's brother Reuben disagrees with the plan: "No, let's not shed his blood. Let's just toss him into that cistern over there and leave him there."

And so Joseph is tossed into a deep desert well. His brothers, feeling satisfied and probably famished from all that work, sit down for something to eat.

As they are eating, a group of Ishmaelite travelers pass their way. That's when brother Judah gets an even better idea than the cistern: "Let's sell Joseph to them. We'll get rid of our problem without having to kill him. And in the process, we'll even make some money!" Two birds. One stone.

So Joseph is sold into slavery.

I can't imagine the thoughts that must have been plaguing Joseph at that moment. He was a complete victim, with every circumstance working against him. And yet …

We know—because we get the rest of the story in Genesis—that God was with Joseph. He rescued Joseph from all his troubles. He gave Joseph wisdom to handle his situation. And he enabled Joseph to eventually become the godly leader of a nation.

> **Behold!**
>
> Life is like an iceberg: we see only the top, and only God knows what lies under the surface.

There are four powerful lessons we can take from Joseph's story and apply to our own trials today.

God Is Ever Present

Whether Joseph was in the cistern at the hands of his brothers or in the courts of Pharaoh as Egypt's ruler, God did not leave him alone for a second.

No matter what you find yourself going through right now, God will never close his eyes to your problem or predicament. I can't begin to understand it or explain it. But this is the awesome fact of God's existence: in addition to being *omniscient* and *omnipotent*, God is omnipresent. He knows all, he is all-powerful, and he is present everywhere.

God never sleeps or becomes preoccupied with someone else's situation. Even when we're in the pits of life, God has told us, "I will not leave you. I will not forsake you." Others may abandon you, question you, doubt you. But not God.

def•i•ni•tion

Part of what makes God God is the fact that he is both **omniscient,** knowing everything that can be known, and **omnipotent,** all-powerful and above all creation.

I know it doesn't always *feel* as if God is beside you. But he is. As Romans 8:38 says, "Neither death nor life, nor angels nor demons, neither the present nor the future ... nor anything else in all creation, will be able to separate us from the love of God that is in Christ Jesus our Lord." That word *separate* here means to be apart by as little as one single inch. When you're a follower of Jesus, nothing is powerful enough to take God even an inch away from your life.

We Are in God's Care

God promises that, no matter what, we are in his care. Others may seek to do us harm. Circumstances may come tumbling down on our heads. Yet through it all, God is there to walk us through the trials and bring us into his perfect will.

"But wait a minute, Chuck," I can hear you saying. "Bad things *do* happen to God's people. God's people do get hurt. God's people do encounter tragedy. God's people die."

Faith 101

Genesis 37:24 contains a statement that almost seems incidental: "There was no water in the cistern" into which Joseph was thrown by his brothers. That's important. It was unusual that the cistern was dry. After all, the whole point of a desert cistern is to provide water. Why was it dry? I believe God prearranged for the cistern to be dry so Joseph wouldn't drown. God was providing the means for Joseph to live out his promise, despite his brothers' evil actions.

You're right. Disasters and tragedies do happen to God's people. And yet we have the very real promise from God that we can turn to him for strength, for healing, for understanding. And even when confronted with our own death—our ultimate "valley"—we can face it with the knowledge that we are passing completely into God's presence. He has not abandoned us.

Beware!

Some people preach a gospel that claims God wants all his followers to be healthy, wealthy, and successful in the world's eyes. The implication? If you're *not* healthy, wealthy, and even more successful than the next guy, you're falling short as a believer.

Don't believe this myth. God will care for you, but his perspective is much bigger than what we see in this life. He isn't impressed by the size of your bank account or how "successful" you are in the world's eyes. These are not God's priorities.

We Have a Purpose to Fulfill

Joseph's time in the well was only the first scene of a lengthy series of events that would enable his prophetic dreams to come true. Joseph did become ruler over Egypt. His brothers did, in fact, bow down before him.

Consider this: Joseph lacked complete understanding while in the cistern and, later, while serving as a slave. This experience probably made no sense to him. He knew in the end that somehow he was destined to possess power over his brothers, yet God never told him the route he would have to take to get there. God had a purpose and a plan, even if Joseph didn't understand what it was.

Some situations in life may make absolutely no sense at all. We may try to understand and explain what's happening to us, and yet no matter how hard we try, we fail to come up with a logical and legitimate explanation. That's okay. Even though we may not understand, God is working.

We Can Draw on God's Power

How did Joseph manage to cope while in the well? I believe he relied on the same power he would rely on when he was ruling in Egypt. In Acts 7:10, we read, "God gave Joseph wisdom and enabled him to gain the goodwill of Pharaoh."

Bear with me for a moment, because I think this takes us to a really important fact about what it means to have faith. In Colossians 2:9, Paul notes, "In Christ all the fullness of the Deity lives in bodily form, and you have been given fullness in Christ."

Follow the logic: God lived in Christ. If you are a follower of Christ, God lives in you, too.

Consider one of the many implications. If God lives in you, that means the power of God lives in you also. You possess an incredibly powerful coping mechanism that is stronger than any alternative this world can offer. Nothing can compete with the power of God.

That's the power Paul had in mind when he reminded the Corinthian Christians that God's grace was sufficient for him. God's power "is made perfect in weakness," Paul notes. "Therefore I will boast all the more gladly about my weaknesses, so that Christ's power may rest on me." (2 Corinthians 12:9)

In other words, when we are at our weakest points, facing our most desperate trials, Christ's power is most able to shine forth in our lives.

The Least You Need to Know

- ◆ God's unchanging character gives us a firm foundation.
- ◆ God loves us and will be faithful to us.
- ◆ Regardless of our situation, we are in God's care.
- ◆ As believers, we have strength to cope through Jesus Christ.

Part 4

Expanding Your Faith

A living faith grows and changes with us over the course of our lives. But it takes a little "care and feeding" of our faith to ensure not only that it remains vibrant and relevant, but actually matures and deepens.

In Part 4, you find encouragement, inspiration, and practical suggestions for your lifelong journey of faith. There are chapters on deepening your ongoing relationship with God through prayer, investing yourself in a community of believers, reaching out to those around you, and dealing constructively with the inevitable periods of doubts we all experience. To finish up, we look at the best steps to take to nurture your faith in the years ahead.

Chapter 20

Listening to God

In This Chapter

- A deeper relationship
- Making room for God
- Myth-busting
- Benefits of being still
- How to listen

Busyness, self-assurance, other priorities—many things can draw us away from spending time with God. Yet meeting God through prayer may be the most powerful tool we have for enriching and expanding our faith.

Once we open the door to regular, ongoing communication, God can speak to us in new ways. Our faith deepens. Our lives change. And our impact on the world increases. With benefits like those, we may find that we're too busy and too committed *not* to take the time to pray.

Slipping Away

One Christmas while I was in Pennsylvania on vacation, a man I didn't recognize approached me in a movie theater and said, "Hey, aren't you Chuck Moore?"

I was a little taken aback. "I am," I said cautiously.

"You don't recognize me, do you?" he asked.

I gave up. "I'm sorry. I don't know who you are."

"I'm Mike Tagg!"

I looked at his bald head and his oversize stomach, and I thought, *You're not Mike Tagg.* The last time I saw Mike Tagg, he had hair down to his shoulders. He had a body like the arm of a goalpost: tall and skinny.

But of course, he *was* Mike Tagg. Why hadn't I recognized him? For one thing, we hadn't seen each other in 19 years.

Unless you stay in regular contact over the weeks, months, and years, it's easy to forget the changes that happen to all of us. We lose touch. In the process, the relationships we once had can slowly slip away.

It can happen in our relationship with God, too. In fact, the longer we walk in faith, the more we need to work at keeping our relationship with God current, alive, and relevant. If we don't, we can start to take him for granted. And when we do that, we'll miss out on his best for us.

Relationships Take Work

Many of us are living very busy, cluttered, committed lives. We spend our time doing a lot of things—a lot of very good things. But to use the words of one writer, we allow the tyranny of the *urgent* to block out the *important.*

There are always going to be other good and needful things that clamor for our attention. So as we consider ways we can enrich and expand our faith, we have to look at one of the most productive steps possible: listening to God. And that happens through prayer.

No Room at This Inn

I was preparing a sermon once when I ran into two experiences that summed up my life. The first occurred as I was sitting at my computer, typing my Sunday sermon. I went to save my latest changes, and a message suddenly appeared on the screen: "WordPerfect Drive Is Full. Cannot accept additional information." My hard drive was saying to me, "I'm stuffed to the max. Put one more bit of information into my already clogged-up lines, and I'll explode."

Okay, maybe it wouldn't have exploded. But you get the idea.

A few minutes later, I walked to my filing cabinet to retrieve a file on servanthood, my sermon topic for that Sunday. When I went to pull the file from the drawer, I couldn't get it out. There were so many papers, articles, drafts, and documents in the drawer, the folder was stuck.

I had to laugh. *This is my life!* I thought.

Like my computer and my filing cabinet, I'm overcrowded, pushed to the point that sometimes I think I'm going to burst. Yes, I would love to pray. I would love to spend a few minutes every day simply enjoying God. But sometimes I feel like all those innkeepers who had to turn away the traveling Mary and Joseph so long ago. Sorry, there's just no room at Chuck's Inn.

Too Little Time

Think of all you do in your lifetime and how much time you already invest. Over the course of a lifetime, the average person will spend ...

24 years sleeping.

4.5 years eating.

20 years watching TV.

9 months doing homework.

22 weeks talking on the phone (although I think most of our calls occur between the ages of 12 and 17!).

That doesn't count all the other parts of life, like washing the car, cleaning the house, mending pants, making dinner, driving the children, enjoying recreation, going to church, mowing the yard, balancing the checkbook, commuting to work, taking a vacation, and on and on. So maybe you're thinking, *Just look at my schedule! Yes, I would love to spend time in prayer. But when can I do it?*

Prayer Busters

I am convinced that the reason many of us don't spend more time in prayer is because we tend to believe one of the following three myths, or what I'm calling "prayer-busters."

Busyness = Effectiveness

First, we believe the myth that busyness is a sign of effectiveness. We convince ourselves that if only we can do enough things and perform enough tasks, we will be effective people.

We insist on convincing ourselves that if we're busy, we're contributing in a positive way. That's not necessarily so.

Behold!
Management guru Peter Drucker once stated, "Busy people are not necessarily any more effective than people who are less busy. Sometimes, in fact, people are busy because they have failed to plan out their schedule, think out their priorities, or zero in on their purpose."

Working = Becoming

Second, there's the myth that working is the key to becoming. Or to put it another way: *If only I can do enough things, I will feel as though I am someone important. My inner life will be fulfilled. I will gain an improved sense of self-worth. If I work hard enough, I will become more.*

Really? The stress studies are in. They conclude exactly the opposite, that sometimes people who work more actually become less. Addicted to the craving for work, they work until they drop.

Working is not necessarily the key to *becoming*. Sometimes it's the key to becoming *ill*.

Doing Is Better Than Talking

I stopped and thought about my past schedules and took a look at one of my typical weeks when I was serving as a church pastor. Here's a rundown:

Monday: All day at the office. In the evening, six telephone calls and a hospital visit.

Tuesday: Another day at the office. In the evening, a visit to the funeral home and several meetings at church.

Wednesday: A day spent preparing: for a funeral, for a Bible study, for Sunday's sermon. Later, there was the funeral to do, another hospital visit. In the evening, I led a Bible study.

Thursday: Preparation for Sunday night's service and studying for an educational class.

Friday: A day off, because on Saturday morning at 7:00 the routine begins again.

When God says, "Speak to me. Spend time listening to me," I'm tempted to protest, "What do you mean, God? I'm too busy *working* for you! Being a Christian is a full-time assignment."

But doing isn't always better than talking—especially if we're doing instead of talking *with God*. No matter how cluttered our lives may be, faith only grows as we experience God. And you can't experience God unless you spend time in prayer.

Dr. John Pippo, former campus pastor at Michigan State University, told me of something he has been doing every week for more than a

> **Behold!**
>
> What the soul has to do in the time of quiet is only to be gentle and make no noise.... Let the will quietly and prudently understand that one does not deal successfully with God by any efforts of one's own.
>
> —St. Teresa of Avila

dozen years. He goes out every Tuesday morning, leaving his work environment for maybe several hours, and prays in isolation.

During that time, God descends from John's mind and is able to enter his heart. And the sometimes-brittle parts of his soul that are broken are suddenly healed. Doesn't that sound a whole lot more beneficial than sitting in an office, answering e-mails and phone calls and shuffling papers?

Listening to God comes before working for God.

Be Still

Maybe it all comes down to a difficult choice, a choice that runs in direct contradiction to our culture's clarion calls and even our personalities: the choice to consciously work at spending time with God. The choice to take a break, ease up on the accelerator, and slow down to be with God.

Let's check out Luke 10:38–42: Jesus and his disciples came to a village where a woman named Martha opened her home to them. Martha's sister Mary sat at Jesus' feet listening to what he said. But Martha was busy playing the perfect hostess. After all, it isn't every day that one has the privilege of entertaining a celebrity for dinner.

Finally, Martha got fed up. "Lord," she said, "don't you care that my sister has left me to do the work by myself? Tell her to help me!"

"Martha," Jesus answered, "you're worried and upset about many things, but only one thing is needed. Mary has chosen to do what is better. She has chosen to spend time with me, and I'm not going to take that away from her."

For all we know, Martha had planned to listen to Jesus just as much as her sister. But she got distracted by everything else that needed doing (or she *thought* needed doing). But like the choice to become more physically fit by exercising and dieting, it's a choice you won't regret.

Faith 101

Be still before the Lord, all mankind. (Zechariah 2:13)

Make no mistake about it—that choice can be tough to make. Like a married couple who wants to work for a great marriage, as soon as you make the choice to work for something more, you can almost count on distractions and disturbances to get in the way.

Whose Voice?

Of course, one of the questions you might be asking yourself is, *How do I know when it's* God *talking and when it's* me *talking to myself?* For example, let's say I'm walking in the woods, trying to listen to God. All of a sudden, an idea comes into my head. Something like, *Quit school. Marry Bethany. Move to Montana and raise elk!*

How do you know if that's God's advice or just your own wishful thinking (assuming you actually like Bethany and think elk are cool)?

Here are some clues:

♦ **Read the Bible.** When you're listening to God, God will never ask you to do something that's inconsistent with his teachings in the Bible. He'll never ask you to rob the neighborhood 7-Eleven. He'll never ask you to cheat on a test to get an A, just so you can pursue the career you think he wants you to pursue. When in doubt, begin with the Bible.

♦ **Talk to trusted friends.** One of the best gifts God gives us are friends who are looking out for our best interest. True, they're not God and they don't always know what God is saying to us. But I've discovered that talking to friends who share your faith—and who are willing to be honest with you—can be helpful.

♦ **Give it time.** If God is asking you to do something, he won't back down. He's incredibly patient, and he will keep coming back. If you have a fantastic idea that isn't from God, there's a good chance it will eventually disappear. But if it's God who is doing the talking, that thought may keep coming back until you act on it.

♦ **Check out your abilities.** When God asks you to do something, he'll also give you the ability to carry it out. One of the easiest ways to determine if it's God talking to you is by asking, "Do I have the gifts and abilities to pull this off?" For example, I never had to stop and ask, "Is God asking me to be a professional football player?" When I was a young boy, I loved football. I always wanted to play football. But when I graduated from high school, I weighed all of 140 pounds. I could have been the football! I may have had the will, but there was no way I could have pulled off a professional football career.

Better Things in Store

When we take the time to listen to God, we discover benefits we can't get by "doing" or staying busy. I'd like to highlight four "better things" that are especially important in today's high-stress, fast-moving world:

- ◆ **Peace.** In Luke 22, when Jesus was wrestling with his eventual encounter with the cross, he prayed. You might think that if anyone in history didn't need to pray, it would be Jesus; however, he knew just how important prayer was to maintaining a strong relationship with his father. When he needed God's peace, Jesus prayed.

- ◆ **Power.** There isn't a problem so monumental that God can't handle it. If he can create the planets, raise the dead, and heal the afflicted, don't think for one second that your problems are either too big or too small for him. Whatever your crisis may be, God can do anything or change anything.

- ◆ **Presence.** Connecting and conversing with God serves as a vivid reminder that he is there. You are not a miniscule object that has gone unnoticed. You have not been plopped down on this planet and then forgotten. He walks and talks with you every second of every single day. Prayer reminds you of that, deepening your relationship with God like nothing else can.

Faith 101

In the unpredictability and instability of our culture, when we find our inner lives craving tranquility and quietness, prayer offers us a pathway into peace.

- ◆ **Perseverance.** Many of us have felt like giving up or giving in at one point or another. But when you pray, you gain purpose and direction to keep going, knowing that God is with you to support, to guide, to comfort.

Faith 101 _____

Linda Schultz was working at the cosmetic counter at Macy's department store in New York City when the telephone rang. Another employee answered it. When Linda was told the call was for her, she
replied, "Tell them I'm busy. I'll be there in a second." Minutes passed.
Eventually, Linda got to the phone. To her shock, the voice on the other
end said, "Please hold for the president of the United States. He received
your letter and would like to talk with you." Ronald Reagan soon came
on the line. Imagine the once-in-a-lifetime experience Linda would have
missed if she had continued to put off taking that call. And now imagine
how much we may forfeit when we believe we're too busy to pray.

Making the Most of Prayer Time

You don't have to follow a precise formula to spend time with God. In
addition to your usual prayers, you might consider some of the following alternative approaches to spending time with God:

- Listen to a favorite piece of Christian music and then discuss the
  lyrics with the Lord, telling him what's in your heart.

- Listen to a taped sermon and then respond to it personally
  through prayer.

- Construct a "joy box." Collect items that remind you of experiences that have brought authentic joy to your life. Open it weekly,
  and give God thanksgiving.

- Meet the Lord with someone else: your spouse, your roommate,
  or a co-worker.

- Interact with the news. When you have a strong emotional reac-
  tion to something you've just read or seen, stop and commit it to
  God.

- Take a hike, celebrating God's goodness in creation.

- Consider your own do-it-yourself spiritual retreat. Once every 3
  months, escape from life for a day: read a Christian classic or dig
  deep into God's Word.

Your commitment to pray is a journey—both a journey *with* God and a journey *toward* him. And the benefits you experience are simply indescribable to those who have not yet discovered them.

Growing Through Prayer

In Joshua 7, we read how Joshua's attack on the city of Ai was met with defeat. Joshua fell into despair, tearing his clothes and falling face-down to the ground (which is how they did things back then).

In Joshua 8, though, the man is ready to try again. He surrounds Ai with thousands of troops. Eventually, the people of Ai are destroyed and Joshua is victorious. He has bounced back even though he had been badly beaten.

Bouncing back. Does that describe the way you handle a setback? When a marriage has gone bad? When you've been released from a job? When the bank says no to your loan application? When you've flunked the test?

How can you bounce back in life? How can you really grow your faith in times like these?

Listening to God

Keep listening to God. Joshua learned from his first experience. Prior to attacking Ai the first time, Joshua made a serious strategic mistake. He forgot to pray. In forgetting to pray, he neglected to listen to God. He jumped into the battle with both feet—but without God at his side.

Contrast chapter 7's events with those described in chapter 8. Joshua 8 begins with God talking: "Then the Lord said to Joshua, 'Do not be afraid; do not be discouraged. Take the whole army with you, and go up and attack Ai.'"

This time, Joshua didn't budge until God did the talking. He'd learned his lesson. Listening to God is a vital ingredient if we want to move forward.

I know what it's like to be like Joshua. I know what it's like to want to move into high gear, to plunge ahead too quickly without listening to God: when I was in seminary, I injured my ankle during a basketball game. At the emergency room, the doctor told me to use crutches for the next 2 weeks. I used crutches for 2 days and then decided they were a nuisance. I set them aside. You can probably guess what happened: my ankle didn't heal properly. Several years ago, an orthopedic surgeon told me that sooner or later I may need surgery to repair the damage.

The same can happen when we refuse to listen to God. Overly anxious or a bit too aggressive, we can end up causing problems. Over time, the damage can get worse.

Take your time. Slow down. Know that you can grow your faith by following the advice of Psalm 46:10: "Be still and know that I am God."

Beware!

Rushing ahead without listening to God can easily make matters worse. When we listen to God, he gives us guidance. He may show us other options. He may reveal insights and alternatives we never before considered.

The Least You Need to Know

- Prayer is a vital part of a growing faith relationship with God.

- Prayer must be a priority in our lives.

- We can choose to be still and listen to God.

- Listening leads to peace, power, a deeper sense of God's presence, and a spirit of perseverance.

Chapter 21

Wrestling with Doubt

In This Chapter

- ◆ Doubting is natural
- ◆ Why we doubt
- ◆ Asking questions
- ◆ Seeking answers
- ◆ Living with doubt

Doubting is a natural part of having faith. I've yet to meet a person who is serious about their faith who hasn't had some doubts. In fact, when a person tells me, "I've never doubted—not once," I often think, *You've either been blessed with an incredibly easy life, or you're lying!*

Doubt doesn't mean we're giving up on faith or we're turning our backs on God. In fact, we can approach doubt positively, using our questions to deepen our understanding of who God is and building spiritual muscles that can help us weather all of life's storms.

Natural Doubt

The world is filled with doubters. In fact, we even have a state whose motto is built on the concept of doubt: Missouri, the "show me" state. (I have a friend in Missouri who reminds me that Missourians aren't really skeptics; they're intelligently cautious people who have learned not to fall for every trick that comes down the track—or so he wants me to believe.)

You've met the doubters. They don't believe a man ever landed on the moon; it was all staged in Hollywood. They don't believe Elvis ever died; he lives in Kalamazoo, Michigan.

We smile at those doubts, but what about a person who doubts their faith? A person who says, "Sometimes I wonder if God really loves me!" "Sometimes I question if God is really involved in my life." "Sometimes I struggle to believe that God is listening."

Is it wrong to doubt? Are people who doubt "bad people"? Is doubting an indication that your faith is weak? Should a person "just believe" and question nothing?

"No," to all the above.

Faith 101

Some believers think denying doubt is a sign of superspirituality. But read even a little bit about faithful people—from the writers of the Bible to Billy Graham—and you'll find that they've all wrestled with their faith. Wrestling with doubt can help us grow in our faith, moving toward a deeper level of spiritual maturity.

Recently I had lunch with a pastor of a large, thriving congregation. He's a great pastor who's passionate about his faith. He believes the Bible, reads the Bible, teaches the Bible. I don't question his faith in God. Yet he's been through a lot. A few years back, his daughter went through a period of public rebellion. His family nearly fell apart. Then, his other daughter was diagnosed with a disease that could take her life. He told me he's preaching a series of sermons on the topic "Disappointed with God." He confessed to me that the sermon came from his personal doubts.

Doubting Thomases, Etc.

Some of the greatest people in the Bible doubted God:

◆ When Moses was called by God to be a leader, he second-guessed God, wondering, "Are you sure you have the right guy?"

◆ When Gideon was called by God to be a leader, he protested, "Get somebody else, God."

◆ When Thomas heard that Jesus had risen from the dead, he said, "I'll believe it when I can touch the nail holes in his hands."

Were any of these giants of the faith second-class citizens in God's family? Were they feeble or, worse yet, fakes of the faith? No. They were human.

Each of them was straightforward about his questions and misgivings. God heard them. In fact, one of the most poignant scenes in Scripture is when the resurrected Jesus appears to Thomas, holds out his nail-scarred hands, and says, "Put your finger here; see my hands … Stop doubting and believe." (John 20:27) God had similar "close encounters" with Moses, Gideon, and many others. And then God went on to lead them through the valley of their doubt and use them dramatically.

When a person has a relationship with God, God doesn't remove his or her brain. God doesn't say, "Come to church, but check those questions at the door." As rational individuals who like to look for answers, doubting comes naturally.

We were born to ask questions, to ask "Why?" when what we're told doesn't seem to match what we see. It's not unusual for those questions to actually lead us to doubt the truth about what we believe.

The Problem of Pain

Some people doubt because of personal suffering. Maybe they've been assuming that if they have enough faith in God, they'll never suffer. Or maybe their suffering reaches such a level of intensity that they begin to believe that God must have abandoned them.

Of course, believers do suffer. To paraphrase a pop song from the 1970s, God never promised us a rose garden filled with nothing but bliss and blessing. At times, the life of faith is like guerrilla warfare, pitting us against the day-to-day realities of living in the real world. It can be a heart-wrenching battle filled with plenty of pain.

Take Job as an example: Job was a wealthy, successful man. But God allowed his faith to be tested. As a result, Job lost everything: his live-stock, his servants, his possessions, even his children. At one point, Job is so overwhelmed that he says, "God has turned me over to evil men and thrown me into the clutches of the wicked." (Job 16:11)

Suffering like this is real. Loss goes hand in hand with being human. And sometimes we can feel pain, anger, and disappointment so strongly that those feelings blot out the voice of God and lead us to question his relevance in our lives.

Did Job make it through his period of questioning God? You'd better believe it. The book of Job ends with Job prospering again, with "twice as much as he had before." (Job 42:10) Even in the midst of his darkest hours, he was never outside his Creator's care.

Behold!

Consider this: suffering is like holding a penny up to one eye while look-ing at the sun. (Don't try this at home!) Imagine being unable to see a huge ball of fire 870,000 miles wide simply because you're holding an object that measures less than 1 inch in width! Our emotions can work the same way. When we're going through tough times, it's easy to get so caught up in our troubles that we don't see God. He's still there, vital and involved, but we've shut him out.

That's Unbelievable!

Other doubts are caused by our human tendency to rationalize, to dismiss the elements of faith we simply cannot understand or explain logically.

I'll admit that a number of things in the Bible defy human reasoning. Does it really make sense that Jesus resurrected from the dead? (I've served at hundreds of funerals and never witnessed a resurrection yet.) Does it make any sense that Jesus could restore sight to the blind or heal the paralyzed? In our sophisticated world of science, miracles don't make sense to many people. They defy human reasoning. In fact, some people are willing to pay anyone who can prove that miracles *do* exist.

The Show-Me State

Some people, to put it bluntly, are born doubters. They say, "I don't believe what I think I just saw with my own eyes." They doubt everything and accept nothing. They find it much easier to doubt than to believe, to be pessimistic rather than optimistic. When anything good happens in their lives, they're convinced something bad is just around the corner.

These folks are like spiritual Missourians: they live in a perpetual state of "show me." And when they see? Well, even then they're not so sure.

Doubtful Experiences

Some people doubt because of the situations they've experienced in their lives. I know of a very gifted young man who struggles to believe that God will never leave him because his father left him at the age of 4. Then his mother passed him off to a foster-care agency when he was just 11. With two parents who had "checked out," he struggles to believe that God won't be the next one to abandon him.

Limited Visibility

Others doubt simply because they don't have a good understanding of God. In their minds, God is like the resident police officer whose primary job is to enforce the law, dishing out justice at our every mistake. They just can't believe in a God of love or mercy. When it comes to seeing the whole character of God, they have limited vision.

Several years ago, a pastor was talking with a young woman who said, "I don't believe in God." So the pastor said, "Tell me about this God you don't believe in." The woman proceeded to describe a God of anger who stepped on people every time they got out of line. At that point the pastor said, "You know something? I don't believe in that God, either."

Signs and Symptoms

Frankly, doubting isn't a big deal. It's part of daily life—ever doubted the advice of a parent, teacher, plumber, or investment counselor? It's definitely part of the Christian life.

Doubting isn't the issue, though. The issue is what do you do with your doubt?

Questioning Doubt

Doubt is a little like pain. When my tooth hurts, the pain is an indication that something's wrong. Maybe it's indicating that a cavity is developing. Maybe I just need to floss and brush more often. When the pain comes, I need to listen.

Granted, some of us like to ignore the things we'd rather not face. My friend Bob says it's amazing how many potentially serious car problems completely disappear if you just turn up the volume on the car stereo!

The problem with ignoring doubt—and car problems, too, I might add—is that the problems only get worse over time. If we simply let doubt develop without any kind of response, our faith is going to dry up and deteriorate. If faith has come to mean anything at all to us, we need to give it a chance to thrive.

When doubt shows up on the scene, we need to pay attention. We need to be willing to ask ourselves some questions about how we got to this point in our faith:

- ◆ What has happened in my life that has led me to doubt?

- ◆ Am I doing anything differently in my spiritual life that has helped to open the door to doubt?

- ◆ What, exactly, am I doubting now?

It pays to face your doubts head-on, moving past the signs and symptoms to find a solution.

Behold!

If a person constantly admits his doubts, won't it lead to instability in his faith? Isn't there the danger that he'll give up on his faith? Good questions. But let's consider the alternative. Isn't it possible that if a person believes without doubting, she'll become so casual in her faith that when it's stretched or tested, she'll collapse under the pressure? Wrestling with doubt actually builds spiritual muscle.

Go to God

It's important, too, to take your doubts to God. Some people think they have to play "make believe" with God. They think they can't tell God the truth. But that's funny when you think about it, because God already knows us better than we know ourselves. He knows our thoughts before our thoughts are ever translated into words. We can't tell God anything he doesn't already know.

And yet Scripture nevertheless encourages us to go to God with our every request. By taking that step, we open up our hearts to his response and we nurture our relationship with him.

Faith 101

I know it might seem counterintuitive to pray to God when you may be questioning his very existence. But who better than God to prove to you that he exists and cares about you? If you close yourself off from the one who is best able to answer your question, you'll be stuck with second-rate responses. I have no doubt—no pun intended—that God will prove himself to you if you approach him in a spirit of honest questioning and give him the opportunity to answer.

The writer of the book of Hebrews tells us to approach God "with confidence, so that we may receive mercy and find grace to help us in our time of need." (Hebrews 4:16) That word *confidence* also means "openness." We don't have to wear a mask when we talk with God. We don't have to play games. God doesn't frown on our doubt. He is big enough to handle our honesty without punishing us or turning us away.

Seek Answers

If you're doubting the facts about faith—the historical truth of the people and places described in the Bible—you can turn to numerous resources for insight. I highly recommend Josh McDowell's *Evidence That Demands a Verdict* (Nelson Reference, 2004) and Lee Strobel's *The Case for Christ* (Zondervan, 1998). *Biblical Archaeology Review* is also a great magazine featuring the highest level of scholarship in its examination of the Bible's history.

Faith 101

Some chapters and even whole books of the Bible can be a challenge for modern readers. To help you get through the Bible, check out a devotional guide that provides a daily reading plan to take you through the whole Bible in a year or two.

If you're questioning the character of God or how God works in people's lives, there's no better place to turn than the Bible. This actually may be a good time for you to consider reading the Bible through in its entirety. There's no better way to get as complete a view of God's character as possible.

If your doubts are more personal or experiential, consider investigating them by attending a church where you're not judged because you doubt—where you're welcome to openly question and struggle in a faith community where you're accepted and affirmed.

In a church I pastored, a man regularly attended who wasn't a person of faith. Once he even told me, "Chuck, I don't agree with anything you're saying. I think it's all make believe." I couldn't help noticing, though, that he continued to come to church.

I was intrigued. So one day I said, "Paul, why do you come to church? Why do you show up even though you don't agree—and you haven't hidden the fact that you don't agree."

I'll never forget his response. "Because," he said, "someday I might choose to believe. But in the meantime, I know you won't reject me while I'm still considering my options."

Faith 101 _____

Sometimes nothing is as helpful as simply talking about your doubts with a trusted spiritual adviser. Don't be reluctant about sharing your questions and frustrations with a pastor. You also might want to confide in a close friend who is spiritually mature. You might be surprised to discover that even those who have devoted their professional lives to following God have experience with doubt.

Weigh Your Doubt

My guess is that when we die, we all enter the next life with at least a few unreconciled doubts. I think that's okay. I've never read anything in the Bible that says, "Doubters: Keep Out!"

I do, however, believe that a person must believe in God and possess a life-changing relationship with Jesus Christ. But most of us will die with some unanswered questions. Some of those questions can wait. Some doubts need to be placed in a tiny box in the rear of our mind that's labeled, "To be studied later."

I have a personal library of hundreds of books. A few weeks ago, a friend stopped by my office. While looking at my books, he asked, "Have you read all these books?" I assured him that I have many books that I've never opened. I've read good reviews about many of them; several have been recommended by friends. So I buy them and keep them around, often taking them with me during my travels or to read while on vacation. In the interim, they sit on the shelves gathering dust, waiting to be read and studied later.

It's okay to have a "to be examined later" file in our mind of faith questions that can't be answered easily. You don't have to have all the answers to believe!

The Least You Need to Know

- We all do or will experience periods when we question God's work in our lives.

- Doubting is not a sign that you've lost your faith.

- God welcomes our questions.

- Understanding why we doubt can lead us to find answers.

- The search for answers ultimately can strengthen and enrich our faith.

Chapter 22

Growing in Community

In This Chapter

◆ God with us

◆ Transformed by his presence

◆ Visionary worship

◆ A Christian community

Faith is a personal thing, but it's also something we share with millions of believers throughout the world—and with hundreds of others right in our own community. When it comes to living and growing our faith, there's no such thing as a "lone ranger." We need each other.

Communities of believers are just like any other communities, though; they take work. The ebb and flow of personalities and changing circumstances sometimes causes friction. Yet the rewards that come from worshipping together, studying Scripture together, and sharing our deepest feelings with one another can make the struggles and setbacks worth every step of the journey.

Where Two or Three Are Gathered ...

When Jimmy Carter occupied the Oval Office, he attended a Baptist church every Sunday morning. I've often wondered what it was like to be the pastor of that congregation, living with the reality that the most powerful man in the free world was listening to every word? Would it have influenced the choice of sermon topics? Would it have affected the way the pastor interpreted Scripture? What effect would it have had on the worshippers who were present?

Every time we come together as believers, though, we have someone who is even more famous in our midst. It's Jesus Christ, who said generations ago that "where two or three come together in my name, there am I with them." (Matthew 18:20)

That's not wishful thinking. It's not something we say to make ourselves feel good. It's the truth. As we come together, Jesus is a part of our worship. What difference does that make as we come together as a *community of faith?*

def•i•ni•tion

A **community of faith** as I'm talking about it here is any gathering of believers that meets to expand their faith and deepen their relationship with God. Whether your community consists of a small group meeting for Bible study and prayer or a congregation of 2,000, God will meet you where you are and help you become the people he intends you to be.

A Living Christ

Walk with me through the story of Christ's *transfiguration*, which appears in Matthew 17:1–13, Mark 9:1–13, and Luke 9:28–36: Jesus had been speaking to his disciples in vivid terms about his impending suffering and death. With that on their minds, he took Peter, James, and John up onto a mountain for a time of prayer. (This was probably Mount Hermon, known for generations as "the sacred mountain.")

In his account, Luke mentions that the disciples were sleepy. (It was a long walk up the mountain, and it's pretty certain there were no

Starbucks stops along the way.) But all thoughts of sleep faded away when the disciples noticed a remarkable change coming over Jesus. "His face changed, and his clothes became as bright as a flash of lightning," Luke notes. But that's just the beginning—then the vision arrives.

In the vision—which Peter, James, and John all experience together— they see the Old Testament prophets Moses and Elijah. The prophets have come to point out the fact that Jesus Christ embodies all that they taught in the Law.

def•i•ni•tion

The **transfiguration** of Jesus refers to the specific event in the Bible when he underwent a miraculous change of appearance in the presence of the disciples Peter, James, and John. The event was a confirmation that Jesus truly was God's son, come to fulfill the Old Testament prophecies.

Their lives and ministries had been the "preshow," if you will. They laid the foundation for Jesus' arrival; they prepared the way for him. Now that Jesus has come, they have appeared to point to Jesus as the fulfillment of all the Old Testament had promised.

As if this sight weren't enough, a cloud descends upon the mountaintop and the voice of God suddenly thunders from the heavens: "This is my Son, whom I have chosen; listen to him." (Luke 9:35)

Not surprisingly, the disciples were terrified, and they threw themselves to the ground.

Jesus came and touched them. "Get up," he said, according to Matthew 17:7. "Don't be afraid." And when the disciples looked up, they were alone with Jesus.

Okay. Maybe you're wondering what this Bible scene has to do with coming together as a community of believers. I'm glad you asked.

Sharing the Vision

What kind of impact would it have on us if we had that sort of mountaintop confrontation with the living Christ? What difference might it make in our worship if we remembered that the very same Jesus is with us today?

I'm sure it would make a profound difference in the way we worship:

- We wouldn't stare at the clock during church and say, "Isn't it done?" We would say, "Give me more, more, more."

- We wouldn't sing the songs of faith with an attitude of boredom. We'd be filled with enthusiasm, joy, and praise.

- Worship wouldn't be something we do because that's what we always do every week at 10 o'clock (or whenever). We would look at worship as a privilege.

- Scripture readings would be vital and alive, like hearing about something exciting that happened yesterday rather than something dry and dusty from the pages of ancient history.

- We'd give our tithes and offerings with delight, happy to play any part we can to help further God's work in the world.

- The preaching would be filled with passion.

- Worshippers would lay their fear to rest and openly share the deepest desires of their hearts.

Imagine what would happen if we would rediscover the love of worship and worship God with "first love" enthusiasm. The Gospels' transfiguration accounts share some clues what this would be like.

Behold!

C. L. Culpepper wrote a marvelous book called *The Shantung Revival* (Crescendo Book Publications, 1976). In it, Culpepper explains what happened when, one day, a group of Chinese Christians experienced the reality of Christ's presence:

> There was continual singing.... Old people who could not read or write memorized the songs and sang with their eyes closed, with their bodies swaying in rhythm to the music.... Entire congregations bowed in silent meditation for several minutes and suddenly whole churches were filled with spiritual power.... What I saw was the Spirit of God renewing the hearts of his people.

This can be our experience of God today as well.

Fear Not

If we worshipped with enthusiasm, we would experience a greater sense of peace as a community of believers. When Jesus went over and touched the disciples, he said to them, "Don't be afraid."

Many churches—my own included—call the place where we hold Sunday worship services "the sanctuary." Frankly, I don't like the word *sanctuary* to describe an area in the church. It smacks too much of an image of escape, of a criminal on the run who's looking for a secret place to hole up. It's as if the real world never passes through the church doors. But I've got news for you: it does.

We can try to convince ourselves that church is the place to which we come to escape the pains of our world. But in reality, it isn't that place at all. Yes, we can come to find peace in our pain and rest in our chaos. But we can never enter into a sanctuary hoping we can close the curtain on reality. We bring the family crises in with us. We bring the cancer with us, the unemployment, the debt, the pregnancy, the divorce, the depression.

However, peace is waiting when we realize that the resurrected Jesus is with us as we worship. The same hand that reached over and touched Peter, James, and John can touch our lives, too. The same voice that said, "Do not be afraid," can comfort our hearts today as well.

Several years ago, a young lady confided in one of my colleagues that she had been involved in an extramarital relationship. She knew God had forgiven her. The problem was that she wrestled with forgiving herself.

One Sunday morning she decided to attend a small country church. There were only 17 people present. On that particular Sunday, the church celebrated the Lord's Supper, or *communion.*

def•i•ni•tion

Communion, also called the Lord's Supper or the Eucharist, is the celebration of Jesus' last meal with his disciples, when he gave them bread (to symbolize the sacrifice of his body) and wine (to symbolize the sacrifice of his blood) and told them to remember him each time they shared this meal in the future. Today, communion is a way for a body of believers to collectively reflect on Jesus' sacrificial death for our sins and his subsequent resurrection.

It was a rustic older church building. Both the preaching and the singing were more than a little rough around the edges. However, as communion was served, the young lady sat in her pew and reflected on everything Jesus had done for her. She realized, for the first time in her life, how much God really loved her.

She didn't have to *work* for his forgiveness. She didn't have to beat herself up. The work was already done—completed by Christ on the cross and memorialized in the Lord's Supper celebration. Suddenly, a feeling of tranquility washed over her. Suddenly, what happened in her past didn't seem so limiting.

This woman didn't need a stadium-size church or a camera-ready congregation. In this small country church where only a handful of worshippers gathered, she found the peace of God.

That's what can happen in our midst every Sunday as we worship together. It doesn't matter whether we have the latest technology or the most talented praise band or the most well-read pastor. When we fix our minds and our attention on the amazing reality that Jesus is with us, our lives can find rest in Christ.

Listen Up

Second, when we recognize the presence of Christ as we gather together, it causes us to listen. "Listen to him," God told the disciples on the mountaintop. Perhaps more than anything, that's what Jesus asks of us every time we come together to worship, to celebrate, to pray. Yes, he wants our worship, our praise, our prayers. But perhaps the greatest offering we can give him are ears that are open to hearing his voice and spirits that are receptive.

Let me make some concrete suggestions as to how you can hone your listening skills when we worship together. Pardon me if some of these seem like no-brainers; I've found that we all can benefit from refresher courses every now and then.

   ◆ **As much as possible, arrive on time for worship.** It will give you time to take a breath, let the responsibilities of the world fall away for a moment, and turn your attention wholly to God.

- ◆ **Be attentive.** I realize that some of us haven't seen each other for a week and we need to catch up. Some of us also come to church with children in tow, and that can make for some distracting moments. But make it a priority to give worship your total attention.

- ◆ **Participate.** Don't simply hold the hymnal or look at the lyrics on the overhead screen; sing the songs with joy. Don't simply take the pastor's word when reading Scripture; open your Bible and follow along. Take notes.

- ◆ **Respond.** When the sermon begins to wind down, start asking yourself questions: *What kinds of changes should I make in my life as a result of what I've heard this morning? What is God asking me to do? How do I need to respond?*

There's an old saying: "Talk can arouse, but, of itself, it cannot heal. To be healed one must listen." How true that is in worship! We must not only talk to God. We must not only tell God our needs, our desires, our wants. We must take the time to listen for his voice.

An Awesome God

Finally, when we recognize the presence of Christ in our community of believers, we will approach him in awe.

It's interesting that when Jesus went over to rouse the disciples from where they'd thrown themselves on the ground, he didn't chastise them for their prostrated position. He simply corrected their attitude.

The fact is, there was nothing wrong or inappropriate about their response. Falling to the ground was, in fact, a natural response when they confronted their Creator.

A number of churches these days use kneeling pads so worshippers can fall to their knees when they come before God in prayer. Although I'm not advocating that for everyone (I have to confess that kneeling pads are noticeably absent in my own denomination), I think the *attitude* of kneeling in the presence of God should be more prevalent in our churches—as well as in our personal spiritual lives.

The Lord of the universe is with us. Yet we sometimes nonchalantly breeze in and out of church rather than enter with reverence and humility. Is it possible that we have grown too accustomed to our Lord? Is it possible that we take his presence for granted? Is it possible we've grown too casual in our approach to worship? I think it's likely that, over the course of our faith journey, all these "possibilities" will actually be true. And I'm no different in that regard.

As we come together as a community of believers, we need to make a point of remembering that we are coming together before the Almighty God, the Creator and Sustainer of the universe, a holy and righteous God who truly is awesome—and worthy of our awe.

The Mark of a Christian Community

Maybe your current Christian community is six friends who meet to study the Bible. Or maybe your community of faith is a mega-church with thousands in attendance every week. Whether your community is big or small, young or old, or anything in between, God has several traits that he wants all his people to develop and display.

Following are just a few of the hallmarks of a Christian community. Work at nurturing these characteristics, and your faith can't help but grow.

Reverence for God

Note the relationship that existed between Jesus and God, his father. Even though they were both one—in a truly unique way—Jesus respected his father and never failed to revere him.

Jesus never once tried to steal his father's thunder. He never once tried to draw people's attention to himself and away from God. When tempted by Satan (described in Matthew 4:1–11), Jesus never once attempted to elevate himself to a position of prominence or power. He allowed God to be God. He lived in humble recognition of exactly who his father was.

Sometimes I'm afraid to ask whether we really revere and respect God today. Have we been guilty of attempting to bring God down to our level? Have we tried to become so familiar with him that we no longer treat him with a sense of dignity? I think the answers to those questions are pretty obvious.

Jesus knew absolutely nothing of a "down home" relationship with the Creator of the universe. He knew God as friend and confidant, certainly. But Jesus never ceased being awestruck by God's greatness. He could be intimately close to God without ever crossing the line into irreverence. Is that the sort of a God you worship? Are you constantly and continually amazed by who he is? Or have you permitted your understanding of God to become a little too common?

Consider these steps for building an attitude of reverence for God in your own spiritual life:

- Pray that God will give you a deeper understanding of his character and a growing sense of reverence.

- Study the various names for God and their meanings. The names of God encompass the many awesome facets of God's holy character.

- In addition to your regular (and spur-of-the-moment) prayer times, set aside a special time and place to go to God in prayer. Think of this as your own "holy of Holies"—the area in the tabernacle where God met his High Priest—and reflect on God's nature when you go there to meet him.

Share these ideas—and any others you might come up with yourself—with your community of believers.

Gentleness of Spirit

Jesus was a great pastor. He knew perfectly how to relate to the real-life needs of his people. In Hebrews 5:2, the writer is comparing Jesus with the High Priest who interceded for the people during the days of the Old Testament. "He is able to deal gently with those who are ignorant and are going astray," he writes.

He deals gently. He doesn't force, coerce, overpower, or dominate.

The ability to "go gently" is one of the greatest marks of the Christian faith. And notice with whom Hebrews says we are called to deal gently: those who are described as being ignorant and going astray. The "ignorant" are those who have yet to hear the Good News of Christ's love. Those who are "going astray" are the people who are vacillating in their commitment to Christ.

I have discovered that, as Christians, we sometimes struggle to relate to such people. We wonder, *What's wrong with them? Can't they see it? Why don't they just accept the truth and turn their lives around?* Sometimes the steps others should take are so blatantly obvious to us—and so bafflingly obscure to them—that we just want to give them a swift kick and set them straight about what's what.

But contrast that to the model exemplified with Jesus. No manipulative techniques were geared at getting people to make quick decisions. There was no kicking. Jesus practiced patience, tolerance, compassion, and understanding. He knew the people who had rejected him or who weren't sure about him weren't the enemy. They were *victims* of the enemy. Gentleness was the hallmark of his life.

Beware! _____

Gentleness doesn't imply *spinelessness*. Yes, gentleness was a hallmark of Jesus' life and ministry, but he could also demonstrate truly righteous anger when the situation warranted it. Check out Mark 11:15–18. When Jesus discovered that people were doing business in the temple—and cheating the people who came there to make sacrifices—he overturned their tables and drove out the thieves. There are times when being a faithful follower of God requires decisive action.

Focus on developing your own spirit of gentleness when you talk with ...

♦ The person who doesn't understand your faith because he or she hasn't experienced it.

♦ The colleague who sometimes makes a snide remark about your beliefs.

♦ The friend whose faith was once active and vibrant but is now stale and stagnant.

♦ The teenager who has put her faith on hold until she "figures things out."

Gentleness may not be our first response, but as we seek to respond to those around us with a gentle spirit, this trait will take root and grow.

Humility

Virtually everything we've covered so far in this chapter—and virtually all the traits covered elsewhere in this book—arise from one simple word: *humility*.

When we have an accurate, humble understanding of who we are and what we need in relation to God, faith can begin to flourish in our lives. We are humble when we ...

♦ Recognize that we haven't chosen God; God has chosen us.

♦ Worship God in all his glory.

♦ Enthusiastically respond to God's call.

♦ Confess that we can't make it by ourselves.

> **Behold!**
>
> C. S. Lewis has noted that a proud person can never demonstrate authentic Christian faith, because as long as you're busy looking down on things and other people, you can't see the one who is above you.

What is your attitude before God and within the circle of believers who make up your faith community? Authentically humble is the mark that Christ has given for Christians to wear in the world. It doesn't mean we don't respect or love ourselves. It doesn't mean we put ourselves down. It means we recognize God as God and we acknowledge our need for his love and salvation.

Christ has modeled for us the marks of the Christian faith. We can do nothing better for the sake of our spiritual health than to imitate his example.

The Least You Need to Know

◆ Jesus is present when we gather together as believers.

◆ Encountering the living God transforms our worship.

◆ Christian communities are marked by reverence, gentleness, and humility.

Chapter 23

Reaching Out

In This Chapter

- ◆ Talking friend to friend
- ◆ Overcoming reluctance
- ◆ Going and doing
- ◆ Reaching the world

Faith is such a personal, private thing that it can be daunting to think of actually talking about our faith with family, friends, co-workers, or even total strangers. But here's the thing: as we discuss our spiritual beliefs, those beliefs can develop and mature. And our discussions can also help others explore their own faith responses to God, enriching the world around us in ways we can't begin to imagine.

Telling the Truth

I have a friend who will tell anyone who will listen how much he loves TiVo. If you're not a TiVo devotee yourself, I'll explain: TiVo is a hardware unit—a bit like a VCR—that can record television programming. But it's smart: you never have to program it. You don't even have to figure out how to set the clock. You just tell TiVo what shows you want to see—by name—and TiVo will automatically record them, even if the shows change time slots, run longer than usual, or appear on more than one channel (can you say *Law & Order?*). If you're an *American Idol* fan, just let TiVo know, and it'll automatically record all of the episodes in the series. And if "American Idol" appears in any other show listings—say, "'American Idol' Carrie Underwood performs on *Today*"—TiVo will get those, too. TiVo will also record shows it *thinks* you'll like based on what you've recorded in the past.

My friend thinks TiVo is the best thing to ever happen to television. He is a dyed-in-the-wool, eager TiVo evangelist. And why not? He's found something he thinks is fantastic. In fact, I don't think he'd consider it a stretch to say TiVo has actually made his life happier. Who wouldn't want to talk about something like that in their life? Who wouldn't want their friends and acquaintances to know about it?

A Different Story: Evangelism

It can be a much different story when it comes to our faith. We may think it's fantastic. We can probably say, in all honesty, that it has made our lives happier and more joyful. And unlike TiVo, it has eternal benefits. But for a variety of reasons, many of us are reluctant to talk about what we believe about God.

I think a lot of that has to do with how we think about the word—ready for it?—*evangelism.*

def•i•ni•tion _____

At its heart, **evangelism** is the act of communicating— through both our actions and our words—the message of God's love to those who do not yet believe.

I realize *evangelism* is not a popular word in some circles these days. I also realize that you don't have to look too hard to find examples of bad or even offensive evangelism. And I'm completely aware of the political connotations *evangelical* now carries—connotations that not every believer accepts. So yeah, the word's got some baggage.

I want to lose some of that baggage—let's say it accidentally got routed to Fiji—and look at what *evangelism* really means, from a purely spiritual perspective.

Author C. S. Lewis has a great statement about what it means to talk about your faith with another person. It's like one beggar telling another beggar where to get food, he wrote. Now, what's offensive about that? Not a thing.

In fact, it's helpful, encouraging, and friendly. And those, I think, are great words to describe exactly how it should be to talk about our faith with someone else.

Reluctant Reach-Out

How many of us jump at the chance to talk with someone else about last night's game or a favorite TV show, recording artist, or brand of peanut butter? Figuring out what's holding us back when it comes to having similar conversations about faith can help us move past our reluctance and actually help make a difference, in the world as well as in the strength of our own beliefs.

Is It Really Important?

Some of us simply aren't convinced that talking about faith is important. We have little awareness of what role we can possibly play in God's plan for the world. Even if we are aware, we dismiss it or ignore it. After all, we might reason, lots of people out there are better at communicating their beliefs than we are.

That was Moses' stance. In Exodus 3–4, God calls to Moses from a burning bush and tells him he is his chosen prophet to free the Israelites from their slavery. It was a great responsibility, yet Moses came up with excuse after excuse as to why he shouldn't do it: "What would I say?" he asks. "What if they don't believe me? Aren't there better public speakers out there?"

God knew what he was doing. To each of Moses' objections, God supplied an answer. Yes, he was saying, this is an important mission. And you're just the man for the job.

But I Don't Know the Script

Some of us believe that people who talk about their faith do so out of deep knowledge and a firm grasp of exactly what they're supposed to say—and when—as if there's a special script we have to follow if we're going to be successful in discussing our personal spiritual experience. Not true. It can help to have some Scripture memorized (or at least to know where to look for answers to people's questions), but don't forget C. S. Lewis's beggar example from earlier. Evangelism is really about one real person talking with another real person. So keep it real. Don't worry about scripts and canned responses. Be yourself.

What If ...?

Like Moses, we can imagine all kinds of reactions to what we have to say about trusting in God: *What if people aren't interested? What if they're offended? What if they think I'm some kind of "holier-than-thou" type?*

There are tons of "what ifs" that might occur when we start talking about our spiritual beliefs. But we can't let vague possibilities keep us from following God's clear commands. When it comes to talking about our faith, God's guidelines are pretty straightforward.

What Does God Expect?

When it comes to telling others about our faith, does God expect us to be like Moses leading a nation? Does he want everyone to move to some foreign country and be missionaries? Will we have to stand on a street corner in Times Square and preach at people? Or will we end up going door-to-door to hand out religious literature?

I don't know where God wants you to go or exactly what he wants you to be doing. The details are different for each of us. But for all believers, God does have two specific evangelistic guidelines: go and do.

Go

In Matthew 28:19, Jesus gave his disciples guideline #1: "Go and make disciples of all nations, baptizing them in the name of the Father and of the Son and of the Holy Spirit, and teaching them to obey everything I have commanded you."

Jesus' first command is to go. But go where? This is where some faithful folks get nervous, afraid of just where "going" might take them. But Jesus' command was simply to go into the world.

We live in very big world. The opportunities are endless. For example, "going" might mean ...

- ◆ Taking advantage of opportunities at work or school to discuss your faith.

- ◆ Serving God in a foreign country.

- ◆ Sharing your faith with shut-ins and those in hospitals and nursing homes.

- ◆ Participating in short-term mission trips to other areas of the United States or to nearby foreign locales, such as Mexico, the Dominican Republic, or Jamaica.

- ◆ Mentoring a younger believer or someone considering faith.

- ◆ Volunteering for outreach activities at your local church.

Beware!

Many of us might protest that we don't have the gift for outreach. To an extent, yes, some people are more extroverted, more comfortable in new social situations. At the same time, avoiding God's call to go by saying "I don't have the gift" overlooks something significant: God isn't *asking* us to go. He's *telling* us.

Now, I can hear some sincere protests that going anywhere farther than work or school is out of the question. And I realize that some of us can't literally go due to various limitations. And yet there is still a way we can go: we can "go" by having a heart for the world.

God may not give you a missionary assignment overseas, but one thing is for certain: he wants you to have a heart for the entire world and to be in a place where you are contributing to all that God is doing. You may not be able to do it all, but you can do something. Literally or figuratively, you can go.

Faith 101

In Isaiah 6, God has a mission in mind. He needs someone who will confront his people with their sinfulness and lead them back into fellowship with him. So God asks his prophet Isaiah, "Whom shall I send? And who will go for us?" And Isaiah responds, "Here am I. Send me!" Not every prophet has been so willing to heed God's call and volunteer for duty. But without such followers, the spiritual course of our world would have been markedly different. Eventually God's will is accomplished to the extent that we're willing to say "Yes!" to God.

Do

What do you do when you go? You are involved in the most thrilling adventure in which you can ever engage: making disciples for Jesus Christ.

A dozen years or so ago, I had that opportunity in Haiti. It was a rather intense time to be there. A coup was in the process of toppling the Duvalier regime. Innocent citizens were being shot in the streets. Late one night, we were forced to evacuate our motel by sneaking out a back door, boarding a small bus, and driving into the hill country, where we laid low for several days.

However, what made the experience so rewarding was the fact that we were there on a mission for God. We shared the good news of faith in Jesus.

When you have the opportunity to touch a life that is saturated by hopelessness, consumed by despair, and overcome by despondency and give a person something for which to live … there's nothing else like it. That's precisely what you do when you introduce people to God.

Going and doing are definitely challenges. They may not be easy to accomplish. You may not experience immediate rewards. In fact, you might never know what effect, if any, your words have had on another person.

Yet our being present in the world like this is just one more way God demonstrates his love for the people he has created. Our culture tends to be self-absorbed and self-centered. And in too many cases, we have allowed this misinformed and misguided thinking to creep into the church. Paul offers some powerful and poignant words in 1 Corinthians 10:24: "Nobody should seek his own good, but the good of others."

Paul, who was always more outward-looking than inward-looking, questioned the kind of thinking that led some early Christians to shut themselves off from unbelievers and hang out only with other believers. The church said, "We are here for us." And Paul said, "No, you're wrong. God has put us here for *them*, the world."

Behold!

I've heard a story about a lighthouse off one of the most treacherous areas of the Northeastern coast. As a result of the lighthouse's steady beacon and the community's dedicated rescue activities, hundreds of lives were saved every year. But eventually, the people who participated in rescue efforts began enjoying themselves too much. They decided they'd rather get together for parties and dinners than get all hot and wet overseeing ocean rescues. What happened? They quit looking outward. Since then, hundreds of people have been lost at sea off that coast.

Witness Is Also a Noun

Another word for evangelism is *witnessing*. The idea is that, like a witness testifying in court, believers are to be willing and able to explain what God has done in their lives and what their faith means to them.

We can get so involved with the idea of witnessing—the how, when, where, and why of it—that we sometimes forget that *witness* is a noun as much as it's a verb. Jesus said to his disciples shortly before leaving this planet, "You will be my witnesses." (Acts 1:8) It's not only what we say that counts; it's also what we do.

There's a movement unfolding in some Christian circles today called "random acts of kindness." A random act of kindness is simply some good deed you do, expecting nothing in return. It's a sacrificial act of giving that demonstrates God's love to others.

I know of a pastor whose entire church decided to practice random acts of kindness once a month. One Saturday, they loaded up their cars with toilet-bowl cleaner and brushes. Then they went into businesses in their town and asked business owners, "Can we clean your toilets?"

Can you imagine the response? "Is this some sort of a joke?" When the business owners realized it wasn't, they gladly accepted the offer.

Throughout the year, the church did all kinds of other creative things. They washed car windows. They raked leaves. They distributed bottled water at a Fourth of July parade. And they did it all for free.

You're Not Alone

Making disciples isn't a job any of us can do on our own. If you try, you'll likely end up like those graying "weekend warriors"—all-out sports enthusiasts who are just a tad older, out of shape, and out of practice. They think they can beat everyone else on the field their first time out. Then they inevitably end up with sprained ankles, sore muscles, and fractured egos.

Because you've made it this far in the book, it shouldn't come as a shock when I say that God can empower us to talk about our faith. When we commit ourselves to reaching out to those around us, Jesus assures us: "Surely I am with you always, to the very end of the age." (Matthew 28:20)

That was good news for the original disciples, too. They knew that as they went out and confronted a world that was like a flock of shepherd-less sheep, they could encounter resistance, rejection, and retaliation. They knew, like all missionaries do, that talking with others about our beliefs is not a continual joyride filled with laughter, fun, etc. While there certainly is the element of joy, fulfilling God's call can be difficult.

We don't do God's work on our own strength alone. We do it by the power of God's Spirit. He serves as a co-laborer with you, empowering and energizing you as you go about the task.

Jumping Over the Hurdles

Sometimes we can feel plagued by any number of hurdles as we seek to follow God's call:

♦ The hurdle of our fears, afraid to give up the old securities for the uncertainty of a new adventure.

◆ The hurdle of excuses: "I have a career … I have a family … I can't adjust … I'm just too shy."

◆ The hurdle of our own lethargic ways. We become careless, indifferent.

No matter what hurdles we may face as people of faith, we have the power of the Spirit to help us overcome them.

The need in our world is big. Perhaps at first glance it may appear too big, so overwhelming that you find yourself thinking, *I can't do a thing.* Don't believe it. When you rely on God's Spirit, you can become effective for the cause of Jesus Christ. You can pray. You can give. And some of you reading these words can even physically go—wherever "go" might eventually take you.

Reaching Out—and Building Up

As you seek opportunities to talk about your faith with others, consider any or all of the following suggestions:

◆ Ask one non-Christian neighbor if there is any need in his or her life that you can pray about. Pray for that need as soon as possible.

◆ Pray that God would grant you the courage to speak biblical truth.

◆ Remember those who have given their lives for the sake of the gospel.

◆ Offer a prayer for all the missionary families your church supports.

◆ Ask God to show you ways in which you might be a missionary to your own community.

◆ Imagine the greatest thing God could do in the lives of your unbelieving friends. Pray for it.

◆ Ask God to show you what role you can play in bringing that "greatest thing" to pass.

◆ Share one thing you've learned about God with at least one friend who does not attend church.

◆ Ask God to take away any fear you might have of reaching out to others in need.

◆ Pray that you would meet trials in such a way that others would actually ask, "How do you do it?"

◆ Ask God how you can bring a spirit of encouragement to another believer.

Take the opportunities in hand, no matter where you find them. Pray about them. And ask God to lead you as you take steps to reach out to those around you on his behalf.

The Least You Need to Know

◆ God calls all believers to share the message of his love.

◆ The opportunities for serving God are endless.

◆ Despite the hurdles, God empowers us to fulfill his call.

Chapter 24

The Journey That Never Ends

In This Chapter

- A mature faith
- The spirit-filled life
- Faith resources

Saying "yes" to God is the first step on a great adventure, a journey of faith that never ends—literally.

As our lives progress and change, so does our faith. As we discover more about God, grow closer to God, weather struggles with God, and see more of his hand at work in our lives, we mature in our faith. This is the last chapter of this book, but it's hardly the last word on the topic of faith. A huge world of faith sits before you, waiting to be experienced and enjoyed.

Maturing in Our Faith

Spiritual maturity simply refers to our ability to keep on going with God—to grow closer to him, to know him better. Maturing in our faith doesn't mean we ever become perfect. It doesn't mean we acquire all the answers to all the heavy theological issues. It means moving beyond the ABCs of faith, progressing from spiritual milk to solid spiritual food.

That may sound like strenuous work. But consider the payoff: you gain as you grow.

Deeper Discernment

Hebrews 5:14 summarizes the first benefit in the life of the person who is committed to spiritual growth: "Solid food is for the mature, who by constant use have trained themselves to distinguish good from evil."

That word *train* refers to the process of working out. It takes time and commitment to build muscle when you work out at the gym. It also takes time to develop spiritual maturity. When we say "yes" to God, we aren't suddenly, overnight, able to draw the distinction between right and wrong. We don't suddenly recognize God's voice in all things or acquire godly wisdom. It's a process, one that requires spiritual muscles given "constant use."

As you commit yourself to growing closer to God, your spiritual discernment and wisdom will increase.

Several years ago I was talking with a missionary, and I asked him how he did his job in cultures that permit polygamy. "Do you walk up to a tribal chief or the community leader and say to him, 'Today, you became a Christian. So now you have to get rid of some of these wives'? If so, how do you handle the fallout?"

Faith 101

Torn between two "rights"? If you feel as if you're lacking discernment about a particular choice in your life, commit the decision to prayer. Ask God to clearly show you the best solution. Then trust the answer and move ahead.

He explained to me that when a man comes to Christ through his missionary work, the man begins a very long discipline process. He is taken through an in-depth study of Scripture. He's taught how to pray and to be open to God's Spirit. At the outset, nothing is said about polygamy. But as a result if this spiritual development, there's the hope that he will recognize the dangers of polygamy and decide against marrying any more women.

It was an answer loaded with wisdom. This missionary knew one could come to Christ without being expected to have all the answers—or make all the appropriate changes—instantaneously.

Improved Insight

Maturing believers are increasingly sensitive to their own blind spots, their areas of vulnerability. In other words, they have a realistic view of themselves—where they're strong and where they're weak.

In Hebrews 6:4–6, we find some of the Bible's most provocative verses. I think they're worth considering as we look at what it means to mature in our faith:

> It is impossible for those who have once been enlightened, who have tasted the heavenly gift, who have shared in the Holy Spirit, who have tasted the goodness of the Word of God and the powers of the coming age, if they fall away, to be brought back to repentance, because to their loss they are crucifying the Son of God all over again and subjecting him to public disgrace.

At first glance, it may sound like the writer is saying, "If you abandon your relationship with Christ, you can't get it back." But he's not talking about the act of salvation. He isn't suggesting that if you walk away from Christ, you can't be "re-converted." Rather, he says, if you have tasted life with Christ and the Holy Spirit lives in you, but you deliberately choose to live in sin, it will be a struggle for you to repent and turn back to God. Why? Because you will have become hardened.

Christians who are growing in faith will be sensitive to the kinds of actions and attitudes that can begin to build walls around our hearts, walls that can limit God's work in our lives.

At this point in your faith journey, you might think that kind of "heart hardness" is impossible in your case. You may be right. But the maturing believer won't assume that nothing can go wrong in their relationship with God. With the improved insight that comes with spiritual maturity, though, we can take corrective steps to keep our relationship with God open and alive.

Richer Rewards

I love the image that appears in Hebrews 6:7: "Land that drinks in the rain often falling on it and that produces a crop useful to those for whom it is farmed receives the blessing of God."

As you mature in your walk with God, your life is like rich farmland that takes in every drop of water. Nourishment finds its way into the hidden crevices of your soul, and the crop of God's blessings is produced.

What are some of these blessings we can savor?

◆ Our ability to love those around us will increase.

◆ We'll become more willing to reach out to those in need—and more attuned to seeing need in the first place.

◆ Peace and joy will replace anxiety and unhappiness in our lives.

◆ Our positive impact on those around us will spread.

Suddenly, our lives become both more bountiful and more beautiful in the eyes of God and world.

God is inviting you to engage in the joyful adventure of moving from the fundamentals of faith to discovering a faith marked by all these characteristics. After all, this is the only chance we have to live for him.

One Life to Live

Sometimes I enjoy just taking a relaxing walk through a cemetery. Sound a bit bizarre? Well ... to be honest, I'd recommend we all do that about once every 6 months. There's a sense of holy urgency that builds when we're reminded that we only get one chance at living.

Most of us avoid thinking about that. We bristle at the thought of planning our funeral or drafting a will. But the great thing about walking through a cemetery is that, while it inevitably turns our minds toward our mortality, it also reminds us that "Hey! I'm not dead yet! I've still got a lot of life to live."

When I think of the fact that I'm now at the beginning of my life's "third quarter," some of the questions I ask myself are, *Today—right now, at this moment—am I really alive? Am I really enjoying life, celebrating my faith, living life to the fullest as Jesus intended? Am I making progress, or am I marching in place, going through the motions and playing the game?*

> **Faith 101**
>
> If we're really going to make the most of this life, we have to open ourselves up to living in the Spirit of Jesus.

In Luke 8 and 9, Jesus has been performing some miraculous acts. He has healed and even brought the dead back to life. After seeing this, the disciples were probably wide-eyed with amazement. Then Jesus calls them together and tells them they're going to be sent out into the world to do the very same kinds of things. "He gave them power and authority to drive out all demons and to cure diseases, and he sent them out to preach the kingdom of God and to heal the sick." (Luke 9:1–2)

This brings to mind the words Jesus would say to the disciples in John 14:12, that "anyone who has faith in me will do what I have been doing. He will do even greater things than these."

Wow. That's life in the Spirit. It's the experience of challenging and changing, impacting and influencing, transforming and teaching.

Here's how it happens: when you say "yes" to Jesus Christ, you are filled with a new Spirit. It's a Spirit that is holy, that brings you to life in a new way, making you a new creation. "Because of his great love for us, God, who is rich in mercy, made us alive with Christ." (Ephesians 2:4–5) When that happens, you can anticipate some incredible changes.

You've Got the Power

"When Jesus had called the Twelve together, he gave them power," reads Luke 9:1. The disciples were no different from you and me. They had their baggage, their unique personalities, their individual quirks. None of that, though, kept them from being empowered by God to take their faith and run with it.

You've got that same God-given power today. You don't have to do anything to do to acquire it. You don't have to jump through hoops before you can flip that power switch on.

You *do* have to set aside the doubts about yourself and your shortcomings. Accept what God wants to give you: power for the journey ahead.

Take Action

Here's a second thing that is going to happen when you live in the Spirit: you will live *pro*actively, not *re*actively.

One of the things that strikes me about Jesus' teaching in these verses in Luke is that he instructs the disciples to take action and not wait for step-by-step guidelines for what they should be doing. (Apparently, Jesus was no micromanager.) Jesus gives them a big-picture plan: preach and heal the sick. Then, in Luke 9:5, "If people do not welcome you, shake the dust off your feet when you leave their town, as a testimony against them."

Jesus is saying, "You've only got one life to live. Don't waste time. There are some things in life that you won't be able to control. Don't bother reacting to negativity and resistance. Move on, and create a new opportunity in the next town down the road."

I've known some remarkable young college students who have, nevertheless, demonstrated their lack of maturity through their unwillingness or inability to show much initiative. That's not a slam against them; they simply haven't yet gained the maturity to be proactive. So they wait for the phone call about that possible internship rather than follow up themselves. They depend on their advisers to chart their academic course rather than shape their own futures. Maybe they even graduate, expecting a job offer to come along without any outgoing effort on their own part.

 Faith 101

Looking for places to be proactive? Consider keeping a list of "need notes" on your refrigerator or bulletin board. When you see, hear, read about a specific need—among friends, families, acquaintances, whoever—write it down. Then make a separate list of the things you can do to help meet those needs. Review the notes periodically—and take action.

Proactivity is a hallmark of a maturing faith, just as it's a hallmark of maturity in general. As we grow, we gain confidence in our relationship with God, in our knowledge of what's expected of us, and in our assessment of our abilities. Out of that confidence, we can muster the initiative to act.

Take Responsibility

What did Jesus tell the disciples to do when they went into the towns? Preach and heal. He didn't say, "Ask permission." He commissioned them with divine authority.

In the same way, we don't need permission to do God's work. At the moment you opened your life to him, he commissioned you with power to represent his name.

I can recall, several years ago, cutting my lawn and then needing to go inside to take a phone call. After I hung up, I went back outside, got the broom, and went out to sweep the grass clippings from the driveway and sidewalk. To my surprise, the grass had already been swept.

"Who swept the driveway?" I asked my family.

One of my boys said, "I did it."

I was elated. (The fact that I remember this incident years later should tell you something about how infrequently this happened at my house.)

Now, was I ticked that my son didn't come to me and say, "Dad, may I please have your permission to sweep the driveway?" Of course not. My children have each arrived at a point in life where they now have a lot of rights and privileges. They don't have to ask, "May I have a piece of fruit from the refrigerator?" or "May I go over to my friend's house?"

You are a member of Jesus' family. You don't have to go through your faith journey wondering if it's okay to take responsibility. You don't have to look around at the needs of the church (and I mean "church" in the broadest sense) and say, "Why doesn't someone do something about that?"

Jesus says *you* do something about that. Go into the homes, the towns, the schools, the hospitals—the *world*—and make a difference.

Live Openly

When Jesus sent out the disciples, he told them, "Take nothing for the journey—no staff, no bag, no bread, no money, no extra tunic." (Luke 9:3) I don't believe Jesus wanted to make their journey harder than it had to be. But I do believe he wanted to convey two important messages about what it means to have a mature, growing faith.

The first is the idea of trust. I believe Jesus was saying, "Trust me for the essential things you need to make it through life. Don't rely on your own ability to plan and prepare."

In fact, I used to think trust was the *only* thing Jesus was wanting to teach with this command. But I've come to see something new in this passage. Clothing, food, money—they all have something in common. They can easily become excess baggage (literally!) that turns into distractions.

If we're distracted, we might overlook the next surprise from God, the serendipitous event, the new opportunity we never saw coming. Jesus is saying, "Don't weigh yourself down with things of this world that are beside the point. Don't get distracted."

Taking a walk through a cemetery every once in a while has a way of putting the things of this life in their proper perspective. We can get so stressed out about our jobs, our belongings, our bills, our plans. Instead, Jesus says, "Trust me. Don't get caught up in the things you see or the things you either have or don't have. Instead, get caught up in the things you *can't* see, the things above."

> **Behold!**
>
> Being open with God means being willing to trust his leading, obey his commands, and share with him the desires of your heart.

Just think of the kind of person you can be if you will embrace all that it means to grow in your spiritual life: an empowered, proactive, responsible, and open disciple.

Tools for the Trip

There are any number of helps for the journey ahead. But I'd like to touch on a half-dozen or so resources/tools that can help to deepen your understanding and build up your faith in the months and years ahead.

Bible Background

You're probably tired of hearing me say this by now, but I can't help it: everything comes back to the Word of God, the Bible.

If you haven't yet read the entire Bible, I'd encourage you to make that one of your goals—and the sooner the better. There's no getting around the fact that the better acquainted you are with Scripture, the stronger the foundation you'll have for growing your faith in the future.

I admit, though, that it can be hard going to start with Genesis and work your way straight through to Revelation. It can be done, but you might prefer to follow one of the many "read through the Bible in a year" plans available. For example, *The One-Year Bible* (available in several different translations from Tyndale House) offers daily readings from the Old Testament, the New Testament, and the book of Psalms. Stick with the book for a year, and you'll have completed the entire Bible.

> ### Behold!
>
> Currently, the most popular Bible translation is the New International Version (NIV). The NIV combines modern scholarship with a very easy-to-understand English translation that manages to be both conversational and authoritative. (The NIV is the translation I've used in this book, unless otherwise noted.)

A Community of Faith

If you've hung with me during the rest of the book, you already know I think it's important to plug in to a local church and get involved in a faith community. If you haven't already taken that step, please consider doing so soon.

If you *have* gotten involved in a local church, let me offer my congratulations. That's a great step—and one that's going to benefit you in many ways.

As you involve yourself with that church, consider taking the additional step of joining (or—*gasp!*—starting) a small group. Typically, such groups involve 6 to 12 people who meet weekly to discuss a Bible passage or a popular Christian book, share prayer

> **Faith 101**
>
> Dozens of study guides, tailor-made for small-group use, are available. (See Appendix B for a list of some popular study-guide series.)

concerns, and pray for one another. It's a time of fellowship and learning in a much more intimate setting than most of us will experience when worshipping with the church as a whole.

Another advantage of a small group: accountability. It can be possible to be fairly anonymous in a larger church congregation, but we build relationships in small groups that encourage us to be more open about the challenges we're facing, our missteps, our successes. Being able to share all these things about our lives—the good as well as the not-so-good—can soften our hearts and open us up more to the working of God's power.

Journal-ism

When my co-author Bob and his wife, Sylvia, traveled to Europe several years ago, they made a point of taking along a blank journal. Each night before they drifted off to sleep, they both took turns writing down where they'd gone and what they'd seen and done during the day. Now, when they want to relive some of those 2 weeks of their lives, all they have to do is look back in their travel diary. Inevitably, they're reminded of people and events they'd have otherwise forgotten.

You might find it beneficial to take a similar approach and keep a faith journal. It can offer snapshots of your spiritual journey that can help you track your progress and inspire you in the future.

Faith 101

Your faith journal can be anything that works for you, but consider this: pick up a "blank book" at the bookstore for your journal. On the left-hand pages, record notes about what's going on in your life, questions you've been asking God, answers you've been discovering, meaningful song lyrics, or inspirational quotes from Christian writers. On the right-hand pages, write down your prayer concerns. If there's room, allow space at the bottom of these prayer pages to note how God is answering your prayers—what you think his answer is, when it came, and how it was revealed to you.

Down the road, when you may be feeling spiritually dry or out of touch with God, look back at your faith journal. Seeing how God has been working in your life in the past can help you gain renewed assurance that he continues to work in your life today. Remembering how you trusted him in the past can help you trust him for your future.

Read and Hear

I'm not one of those Christians who believes Christians shouldn't listen to "secular" music or read "secular" books. However, there are times when we can truly be blessed and encouraged only by the work of Christian singers/songwriters and Christian authors.

I won't even attempt to suggest possible artists and authors to you; all our musical and literary tastes are going to be different. I'll just encourage you to seek out the material that suits your personal tastes and inspires and instructs you.

You can sample a lot of Christian music—from pop to hip-hop to easy-listening to heavy metal—thanks to the growing prevalence of Christian radio stations across the country. You can also hear Christian songs on Internet-based radio stations. And these days, you're as likely to find Christian artists at Best Buy as you are to find them at a Christian bookstore. And of course, a number of online retailers carry a complete line of Christian products.

If you're hungering to read something written from a Christian perspective, visit your local Christian bookstore or a larger chain bookstore that stocks Christian titles (such as Borders and Barnes & Noble). Again, don't forget to go online if you can't find what you want locally.

> **Faith 101**
>
> For some ideas of good books to read to help you mature in your faith, check out the suggestions in Appendix B.

Regardless of what you get and how you get it, don't expect to necessarily agree with everything presented by every artist or author. At the same time, don't dismiss something simply because it's unfamiliar. Weigh the words against the Bible. Ask God to help you be discerning. And be open to being changed and "matured" by what you hear and read.

Faith is the adventure of your life. Go at it with all of your heart, mind, body, and soul.

The Least You Need to Know

- ◆ Maturing in faith means moving from spiritual milk to solid spiritual food.

- ◆ God expects us to take charge of our spiritual growth.

- ◆ Mature faith is marked by empowerment, proactivity, responsibility, and openness.

- ◆ Numerous resources can aid your spiritual growth and enhance your faith journey.

Glossary

Apocrypha   The Apocrypha is a collection of books of pre-Christian and early Christian religious writings that were not universally deemed appropriate for inclusion in the traditional Bible. (A number of Bibles available today do include the books of the Apocrypha.) The decision of which writings to include and which books to leave out of the Bible was determined by church leaders during the first through fourth centuries.

canon   The 66 books of the Bible—39 in the Old Testament and 27 in the New Testament—that have been commonly agreed upon as being divinely inspired and authoritative for Christian faith.

communion   The celebration of Jesus' last meal with his disciples (also called the Lord's Supper or the Eucharist), which continues to be celebrated today as a way for believers to collectively reflect on Jesus' death and resurrection.

community of faith   Any gathering of believers who meet to expand their faith and deepen their relationship with God. Whether your community consists of a small group meeting for Bible study and prayer or a congregation of 2,000, God will meet you where you are and help you become the people he intends you to be.

covenant   A formal, binding agreement made by God with his people.

discernment   The God-given wisdom to recognize God's will and to choose wisely between good and evil—or even good and not-so-good choices.

evangelism   The act of communicating—through both actions and words—the message of God's love to those who do not yet believe.

Gospel   *Gospel* with a small *g* literally means the "good news" for the world regarding Jesus Christ's life, death, and resurrection. In the Bible, the four New Testament biographies about Jesus—Matthew, Mark, Luke, and John—are also known as "Gospels," with a capital *G*.

Holy Spirit   The indwelling embodiment of God, the one that fills the hearts and souls of believers.

immutable   The unchanging, unalterable nature of God's character.

intercessory prayer   Prayers prayed for the benefit of others, asking God to intervene on another's behalf to help or to heal.

omnipotent   The all-powerful nature of God's character.

omniscient   The all-knowing nature of God's character.

Pharisees   Members of the largest, most influential religious/political Jewish sect in New Testament times. The Pharisees were devoted to strict observance of the Law and strongly opposed to pagan practices and anything suspected of diluting or corrupting the Law.

stewardship   The human responsibility, entrusted to us by God, to care for his creation and what has been given to us.

tithe   Ten percent of our income, given over to God for his use.

transfiguration   When Jesus underwent a miraculous change of appearance in the presence of the disciples Peter, James, and John. The event confirmed that Jesus truly was God's son, come to fulfill the Old Testament prophecies.

Appendix B

Resources for the Journey

Books

Alexander, David, and Pat Alexander. *Zondervan Handbook to the Bible*. Grand Rapids: Zondervan, 2005.

Bates, Judy Woodward. *The Gospel Truth About Money Management*. New Hope, 2003.

Bittner, Robert. *Your Perfect Job: A Guide to Discovering Your Gifts, Following Your Passions, and Loving Your Work for the Rest of Your Life*. Colorado Springs: Shaw, 2003.

Blue, Ron. *The New Master Your Money*. Chicago: Moody Press, 2004.

Chapman, Gary. *The Five Love Languages*. Chicago: Moody Press, 1996.

Cymbala, Jim. *Breakthrough Prayer*. Grand Rapids: Zondervan, 2003.

Foster, Richard. *Celebration of Discipline*. HarperSanFrancisco, 1988.

———. *Prayer: Finding the Heart's True Home*. HarperSanFrancisco, 1992.

Fowler, James. *Stages of Faith*. HarperSanFrancisco, 1995.

Guernsey, Dennis. *Sometimes It's Hard to Love God*. Downers Grove: InterVarsity Press, 1989.

Hybels, Bill. *Too Busy Not to Pray*. Downers Grove: InterVarsity Press, 1998.

Lewis, C. S. *A Grief Observed*. HarperSanFrancisco, 2001.

———. *Mere Christianity*. HarperSanFrancisco, 2001.

Lucado, Max. *It's Not About Me*. Nashville: Integrity, 2004.

Maxwell, John. *Relationships 101*. Nashville: Nelson, 2004.

McDowell, Josh. *The New Evidence That Demands a Verdict*. Nashville: Nelson, 1999.

Ogilvie, Lloyd J. *Asking God Your Hardest Questions*. Colorado Springs: Shaw, 2000.

Ortberg, John. *God Is Closer Than You Think*. Grand Rapids: Zondervan, 2005.

Ramsey, Dave. *The Total Money Makeover*. Nashville: Nelson, 2003.

Strobel, Lee. *The Case for Christ*. Grand Rapids: Zondervan, 1998.

———. *The Case for Faith*. Grand Rapids: Zondervan, 2000.

Unger, Merrill F. *The New Unger Bible Handbook*. Chicago: Moody Press, 2005.

Warren, Rick. *The Purpose-Driven Life*. Grand Rapids: Zondervan, 2002.

Yancey, Philip. *Where Is God When It Hurts?* Grand Rapids: Zondervan, 1997.

Magazines

Biblical Archaeology Review

Christianity Today

Marriage Partnership

Study Guides

Life Application Bible Studies. Carol Stream: Tyndale House.

Lifechange Bible Studies. Colorado Springs: NavPress.

LifeGuide Bible Studies. Downers Grove: InterVarsity Press.

Index

T